3D PRINTING WILL ROCK THE WORLD

2015

3D PRINTING WILL
ROCK THE WORLD

John Hornick

ISBN: 1516946790
ISBN 13: 9781516946792
Library of Congress Control Number: 2015913412
CreateSpace Independent Publishing Platform
North Charleston, South Carolina

Dedicated

to Sarah,

my wife, best friend, and great love

and

to Phyllis,

who gave me life

Contents

Foreword

Human history has seen four major disruptive technologies. First there was fire, then the wheel. Then came the Industrial Revolution, followed by the digital revolution. When these technologies emerged, no one foresaw their full potential. For example, at the dawn of the digital revolution, IBM's chairman and CEO, Tom Watson, foresaw a world market for no more than five computers. Digital Equipment Corporation's founder, Ken Olsen, said there was no reason anyone would ever need a computer in the home.[1] And just as some people wonder today what they would do with a home 3D printer if they had one, even Steve Jobs didn't really know what to do with his computer in the early days. A 1977 Apple computer ad said you could "paint dazzling color displays" and invent your own pong games.[2] At the time, these were the best predictions of the potential uses of a home computer. How little they knew, and how fast we learned.

Then came the Internet, which has been in widespread public use since only around the mid-1990s. In those early days, few people saw its potential. Even today we are still discovering its power. Only a few years ago, many people wondered why they needed a smartphone. In a short time, smartphones have become indispensable to our daily lives.

Although 3D printers have been with us for about thirty years, they are still in their infancy and are just starting to cross into the mainstream. Both companies and consumers are wondering how to use them. The people who will figure it out are the innovators of tomorrow—most of whom are kids today—and they will figure it out fast.

This book is a thought experiment about what *could be*, not what *should be*. It is written with conviction because it is my vision of how 3D printing can change the world. But my crystal ball is not perfect. Of course I don't know with certainty how 3D printers will change the planet, but as Albert Einstein once said, "Imagination is more important than knowledge." It is less important to be right than to stimulate people to think about these issues in new ways.

As you read this book, think about the implications of 3D printing for your life, your job, your company, your country, and the world. Think about the things I have not thought of. Think outside the box.

Morphing Manufacturing

ONE MACHINE DOES IT ALL

3D printers are the most powerful machines humans have ever invented because they can make finished products, with all their parts, fully assembled. Driven by a digital blueprint, they build layer upon layer of plastic, metal, or other materials and then fuse them with heat, lasers, electron beams, chemicals, ultrasound, or glue.[3]

Most of the products we use every day are made of many parts. They result from many manufacturing steps performed by different machines, each with its own operator. Each machine and operator does a certain job, such as cutting, grinding, drilling, or milling, then passes the part to another machine and operator that perform another job, and on and on along an assembly line until the part is complete. Eventually, all of the parts are assembled into a final product, either by machine or by hand.

3D printing rocks manufacturing by replacing all of these steps with fundamentally different machines and materials that substantially simplify the manufacturing process, reducing its costs and carbon footprint and eliminating the need for economies of scale.

According to the Brookings Institution think tank, 3D printing "will no doubt revolutionize manufacturing and usher in a new wave of innovation."[4] Harvard economist Ricardo Hausmann calls 3D printing a paradigm shift in manufacturing.[5] One 3D printer makes an entire part or an entire product in one step. It can make different products at the same time or different products one after the other, without tooling, retooling, or changing the way the machine is set up.[6] 3D printers can make structures no other machine can make, and complexity and customization are free. As IBM said in its 2013 study, "For enterprises…3D printing isn't just a curiosity, it's a revolution. It frees companies from the need to build standardized parts and pursue economies of scale."[7] Combined with advanced materials, 3D printing is the Holy Grail of manufacturing.

Big companies are using 3D printing to revolutionize manufacturing: Airbus, Boeing, GE, Johnson Controls. Boeing says, "This is the ultimate manufacturing method for us,"[8] and GE says, "This is the future of manufacturing."[9] Han Hendriks, vice president of Advanced Product Development at Johnson Controls, said,[10]

> Take a [car] door panel with 11 different materials, 20 different components, produced in different parts of the country, being brought together and assembled in this one plant, with a lot of tools, with a lot of equipment, with a lot of process steps. Now turn this into a situation where you have one printer printing those 12 different materials, those 20 different components, assembled all at once.

3D printing does two seemingly inconsistent things at the same time: it simplifies and streamlines manufacturing while enabling the flexible manufacture of fully assembled, infinitely customizable products, without barriers to complexity, and reduces the economy of scale to a batch of one.

THE NAME GAME

3D printing is also called additive manufacturing, direct digital manufacturing, and a few other variations. For many years after its invention in the 1980s,[11] 3D printing was called rapid prototyping. Some people in the industry don't like the name "3D printing" and prefer one of the more formal names, but let's face it, "3D printing" is sexier. Which machine would you rather see, my cool new additive manufacturing machine or my cool new 3D printer? And which college course will fill faster: "3D Printing 101" or "Additive Manufacturing 101"?

"3D printing" is also easier to say. I recently sat in a roomful of experts in this field, who constructed the most torturous sentences with "additive manufacturing." After someone broke the ice by saying "3D printing," the discussion loosened up and was much more productive. Calling it "3D printing" will help drive adoption and spread the technology much faster than "additive manufacturing."

"3D printing" also captures the essence of this revolutionary technology more accurately than "additive manufacturing." Some people refer to traditional methods as "subtractive manufacturing," which makes a nice symmetry with additive manufacturing. Some people also use "subtractive" to refer to old methods and machines and "additive" to refer to new ones. But some traditional processes, such as metal casting, plastic injection molding, and textile weaving, are both additive and old. So the additive versus subtractive and old versus new distinctions are not accurate. In this book, I use "additive manufacturing" to refer only to 3D printing. Other processes I refer to as "traditional methods" and "traditional machines."

CUSTOMIZATION AND COMPLEXITY ARE FREE

The strength of traditional manufacturing methods is their ability to mass-produce a thousand or a million parts, all exactly the same. Traditional methods are more and more efficient as more and more identical parts are made. As tooling costs are spread over more and more parts, the cost of making each part is reduced. Traditional machines can be used to make customized products, but costs increase with the degree of customization because the cost of tooling for custom parts is spread over far fewer parts, and such tooling needs to be changed for the customized steps. Custom parts usually also require more human labor, and labor adds cost to the finished part. By contrast, 3D printing makes customization essentially free because only the blueprint needs to be changed to change the part. Making batches of one custom part or a thousand custom parts costs essentially the same per part. According to a Deloitte report, "Multiple studies show that as few as one product can be 3D printed economically."[12] Unlike at any other time in history, manufacturers now can obtain the same economies of scale producing either one-of-a-kind parts or mass-produced parts.

Similarly, with 3D printing, complexity is essentially free. The only cost difference between 3D printing a simple part and a complex part is the cost of the raw materials and maybe the postprinting processing. 3D printing dramatically lowers the cost of complexity.

LOWER ALL-IN COSTS

3D printing also uses raw materials efficiently because it does not involve machining away most of the material to yield a finished part. It starts with raw material, such as spools of plastic filament or plastic or metal powders, and uses only as much as is needed. No waste. Also, less labor is needed because an entire part can be printed by a single machine. In fact, a few skilled operators can run a roomful of 3D printers, and soon the operators will be running advanced robots that run the printers. Adding to these economies is 3D printing's greater energy efficiency; less energy is used because fewer manufacturing steps are involved.

Even where it costs more to 3D print a part, as compared to traditional methods, 3D printing may still be cheaper in the long run. For example, 3D printing a part might make it lighter. Where the weight of a part affects costs over the part's lifetime, 3D printing may prove to be cost effective. For example, if a 3D printed aircraft part is 15 percent lighter than a traditionally made part, the aircraft fuel savings over the life of the part justify paying more to 3D print it.[13]

The bottom line is that 3D printing reduces the all-in costs of production. Further reducing the bottom line, the prices of 3D printers dropped steadily from 2001 to 2010. Although prices started rising in 2011, the long-term price trend is expected to be downward. The average cost of an industrial 3D printer was about $87,000 in 2014, compared to $90,000 in 2013.[14] IBM says 3D printing costs should fall by 79 percent by 2018 and by 92 percent by 2023, "making it more cost-effective than all but the largest production runs."[15]

NO ASSEMBLY REQUIRED

Current 3D printing technology can make near-finished parts, but most finished products have more than one part. For most products, 3D printers don't care how many parts they have. They can make finished products with all of their parts fully assembled.

Other finished products require more than one 3D printer. For example, the Smart Wing drone shown below was the first fully integrated, 3D printed complex structure. But more than one 3D printer was used. Stratasys, of Eden Prairie, Minnesota and Rehovot, Israel, a 3D printing industry leader, 3D printed the Smart Wing's outer shell. Its internal circuitry—strain gauge, antenna, power circuit driving the propeller, and LED circuit—were 3D printed using various conductive and dielectric materials, by Optomec of Albuquerque, New Mexico.[16]

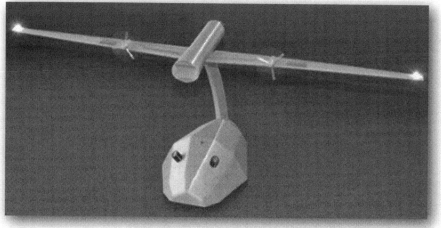

Photo courtesy of Optomec

In time, a single 3D printer will be able to print such products, fully assembled and ready to fly.

MAKING THINGS NO OTHER MACHINE CAN MAKE

Traditional manufacturing methods are stuck in the 2D world. For example, a drilling machine can turn a channel shown in a 2D drawing into a highly precise hole in a finished 3D part, but that hole remains two dimensional because it must be drilled in an x, y plane. If it is drilled, the hole can't turn a corner. Drilled holes also cannot be asymmetrical or wider in one area than in others. Although holes that turn corners *can be* made by casting, castings have limitations because parts must be removed from the mold.

3D printing has no such limitations. Because 3D printers build up parts in layers, there is never any mold to be removed. Holes can change direction, bend around corners or planes, or get wider or narrower as they twist and turn through the part in three dimensions, and several such holes can be interwoven into the same part.

3D printing also enables the manufacture of other structures that were previously difficult or impossible to make, such as honeycomb structures. Building honeycombs inside a part makes it strong and reduces weight. But they are difficult to make with any process other than 3D printing, especially for the interiors of parts with complex shapes, or where the honeycomb is thicker or thinner in different places. Only one source other than 3D printing can manufacture complex honeycomb support structures: bees. But bees can't build them with metal or carbon fiber. 3D printers can.

3D printers can also make parts with complex geometries, such as the bridge strut shown below.[17]

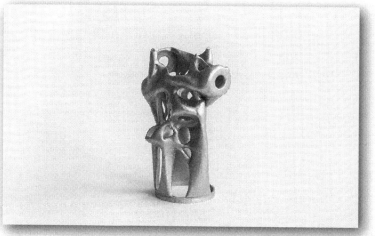

Photo courtesy of Davidfotografie/Arup

3D printers can make parts that are partially porous and partially solid. Such characteristics are important for parts like human hip implants. In the acetabular cup shown below, the recipient's tissue can grow into the pores, making a better marriage between the body and the implant.

Photo courtesy of Arcam

3D PRINTING IS NOT JUST ONE PROCESS

"3D printing" and "additive manufacturing" are umbrella terms for many different technologies and processes. The most common are described below. Others vary somewhat from these methods or result from a combination of their elements. But each type of 3D printer builds parts or products layer upon layer, usually from the bottom up, sometimes from the top down.

Each different type of 3D printer is suited to certain applications. Many print plastics and other nonmetal materials, with varying degrees of fit and finish. An increasing number of machines prints metals. According to Terry Wohlers, author of the well-known annual Wohlers Report on the state of the 3D printing industry, "[i]ndustrial AM [additive manufacturing] systems are producing high-grade metal parts with properties that match or exceed the properties of cast metal parts."[18]

Today's 3D printers do have limitations. Each type of machine has its strengths and weaknesses, and no single machine can make all types of products—at least not yet. Most machines print either only plastic or only metal. Faced with an alphabet soup of acronyms for various 3D printing processes, as well as the names that machine manufacturers use to market their machines, ASTM International (formerly the American Society for Testing and Materials) developed the following standard additive manufacturing categories:[19]

Binder Jetting
Directed Energy Deposition
Material Extrusion
Material Jetting
Powder Bed Fusion
Sheet Lamination
Vat Photopolymerization

Each process is summarized below.

Binder Jetting

Also called digital part materialization (DPM), this is an inkjet method, somewhat like a 2D inkjet printer. Binder Jetting employs one or more jets to dispense chemical binders layer-by-layer into a bed of powdered polymer, stainless steel, bronze, tungsten, or soda lime glass powder, or sand for making molds. These machines make excellent molds and can also make finished, full-color parts, after additional heat-treating. 3D Systems (United States) and ExOne (United States) make industrial grade Binder Jet printers. Voxeljet (Germany) makes Binder Jet printers with a very large build platform. A Voxeljet machine 3D printed replicas of James Bond's Aston Martin DB5 for the movie *Skyfall*.[20]

Directed Energy Deposition

"Laser Engineered Netshaping" or laser cladding

Directed Energy Deposition (DED) is also known as laser cladding. Perhaps the best examples of DED systems are the Laser Engineered Netshaping (LENS) machines made by Optomec of Albuquerque, New Mexico. LENS machines employ deposition heads, which are similar to inkjet heads, to supply metal powder to the focus of a laser beam, which melts the powder into the desired shape. Using multiple metal inputs, these machines can 3D print metal alloys on the fly. LENS machines make structural finished parts. Trumpf (Germany) has a similar DED process, and both DMG Mori Seiki (Germany/Japan) and Yamazaki Mazak (Japan) make a hybrid DED machine and multiaxis computer numerical control (CNC) mill. Efesto makes a laser cladding machine that builds up layers of metal on existing parts.[21] NASA and Penn State University are using the Efesto machine for a process they call Radiant Deposition, which builds up layers of metal powder radially on a rotating rod. The metal powders can be changed while a part is being built, also creating metal alloys on the fly.[22]

Electron beam freeform fabrication

Electron beam freeform fabrication (EBFF) focuses an electron beam on metal alloy feedstock in wire form, which is fed into the beam in a vacuum, creating a molten metal pool that solidifies immediately. NASA plans to use EBFF machines to build parts in zero gravity. Sciaky (United States) calls its version of this process electron beam additive manufacturing (EBAM) and makes a giant version (9 by 4 by 5 feet) that welds wire feedstock with an electron beam.[23]

Material Extrusion

Fused deposition modeling (aka fused filament fabrication)

Fused deposition modeling (FDM) machines extrude a thermoplastic filament, usually acrylonitrile butadiene styrene (ABS) or polylactic acid (PLA), through a tiny heated nozzle onto a build platform, building the part from the platform up. A second nozzle may extrude material to create supports that are removed after the part is built. Most consumer-level 3D printers are FDM machines, which flooded the market after early FDM patents started to expire in 2009.[24] Currently, hundreds of companies, most of them start-ups, manufacturer consumer-grade FDM machines worldwide. In the prosumer and industrial arenas, FDM machines are used mostly for prototyping but may be used for finished plastic parts. Stratasys, an industry leader, pioneered FDM machines. Stratasys's subsidiary, MakerBot, makes consumer- and prosumer-level FDM machines, as do 3D Systems and many small companies.

Plastic freeforming

A proprietary process of Germany's Arburg, plastic freeforming (PFF) machines combine a carrier that moves along three or five axes with a stationery nozzle similar to an FDM extruder. However, rather than the continuous bead of FDM machines, PFF machines extrude droplets of build material. The high speed at which it deposits the droplets makes PFF somewhat like Material Jetting (see below).

Material Jetting

Aerosol Jet

Aerosol Jet machines, also called direct-write machines, use a mist gener-ator to atomize a wide range of metal or nonmetal build materials to print circuitry or parts on a variety of substrates, including onto existing parts. In this process, printhead nozzles deposit inks, such as silver nanopar-ticles, with extreme precision onto various substrates to make micro- and macroscale structures, such as electronic circuitry.[25] The aerosol stream of build-material particles is refined on the fly and aerodynamically focused as it is deposited. After being deposited on the substrate, the materials may be thermally or chemically treated. Optomec (United States) is the leader in this technology. Its machines can 3D print circuitry on any sub-strate.[26] Camtek's printed circuit board printer (Israel) and Neotech's light beam sintering (Germany),[27] as well as Nanodimension (Israel), nScrypt (United States), and XJet (Israel), seem to be using similar technology. The Lawrence Livermore National Laboratory is also working in this area.[28]

Ballistic particle manufacturing

Ballistic particle manufacturing (BPM) machines use an inkjet-like meth-od to fire particles of thermal plastic material, which solidify into the de-sired shape as they cool. A defunct South Carolina company of the same name pioneered this technology, which was best suited for prototyping. Another company, Incremental Fabrication Technologies, had a similar process that fired metal particles. The Arburg Freeformer seems to be a variation of this technology, using plastic. There are no known BPM ma-chines to examine today, but the metal cold spray machines made by CSIRO (Australia), Flexible Robotic Environments (United States), and Trinity College (Ireland) may also be variations of this technology.

PolyJet

Like Binder Jet machines, PolyJet machines are also multijet inkjet-like machines. The difference is that while Binder Jet machines jet binders onto powdered build material layer by layer, PolyJet machines jet actual build material layer by layer. Most use UV light to cure the layers of photopolymers. PolyJet machines can print multiple materials simultaneously (including support materials that are removed from the final product) and are suitable for making finished parts. PolyJet machines are made by 3D Systems, Stratasys, and Solidscape.

Powder Bed Fusion

Laser melting

Laser melting (LM) machines (aka direct metal printing, direct metal laser sintering, metal laser melting, selective laser melting, selective laser sintering, and laserCUSING) are powder-bed machines that use a laser to melt layers of plastic, ceramic, or metal powders. Because the part is fused from the surrounding bed of powder, sometimes no support structures are needed; the surrounding powder provides support, then simply falls away when the part is removed from the bed. These machines can make finished parts with complex internal and external geometries. EOS (Germany) machines use this process to make tooling and medical implants, and GE uses it to make aircraft parts, such as fuel injectors for the leading edge aircraft propulsion (LEAP) engine. Using Powder Bed Fusion, GE 3D printed, as a single piece, a cobalt-chrome fuel nozzle that formerly had been assembled by welding together twenty different parts.[29]

3D Systems/Phenix, which calls its process direct metal printing; Concept Laser (Germany), which calls its process laserCUSING; EOS, which calls its process direct metal laser sintering; Renishaw (United Kingdom); and SLM Solutions (Germany), which calls its process selective laser melting, all make laser melting machines. Matsurra (Japan) makes a hybrid machine that combines laser melting and a CNC mill. Laser maker Fonon (United States) also makes a laser sintering machine for metal powders.[30]

Electron beam melting

In electron beam melting (EBM) machines, an electron beam builds up parts from a powder bed in a vacuum. Similar to laser melting machines, EBM machines make finished structural parts. Sweden's Arcam is the leader here.

High speed sintering

High Speed Sintering (HSS) is a powder bed method that fuses polymer powders with infrared heat and infrared-absorbing inks. Developed by Neil Hopkinson at the United Kingdom's Sheffield University and Loughborough University, HSS works as quickly as injection molding, and can build parts as large as a washing machine.[31]

Sheet Lamination

Laminated object manufacturing

Laminated object manufacturing (LOM) machines laminate sheets of paper, plastic, or other materials, which are then cut into the desired shape with a laser or knife. LOM machines are well suited to making models, which feel somewhat like paper-mache. MCOR (Ireland) makes LOM machines that print full-color models using standard photocopying paper. A particularly freaky example is a full-color model of an MCOR employee's disembodied head.

Ultrasonic lamination

Another Sheet Lamination company, Fabrisonic (United States), uses a 3D printing process called ultrasonic additive manufacturing (UAM), in which sound waves fuse layers of metal foil.[32]

Vat Photopolymerization

Digital light processing

In digital light processing (DLP), mirrors project the image of each layer of an object onto the surface of a vat of photopolymer. The light source cures the image, building up the product layer by layer. Germany's EnvisionTec and several smaller companies make DLP machines.

Stereolithography

Stereolithography (SLA) is the granddaddy of them all, the original form of 3D printing commercialized in the 1980s by Chuck Hall, who went on to form 3D Systems, an industry leader.[33] SLA machines use a UV light source to cure a vat of liquid photopolymer resin, layer by layer. SLA-printed parts have a smooth, close-to-finished surface and are well suited for making jewelry molds. SLA can also be used for prototyping and making simple finished parts. Most SLA machines are prosumer or industrial, but consumer-level SLA machines include the Formlabs, Autodesk EMBER, and B9 SLA printers. Industrial-grade SLA machines are made by 3D Systems. The Lawrence Livermore National Laboratory is developing a high-speed variation called microstereolithography to create ultrastiff but lightweight parts.[34]

CLASS BY ITSELF: MULTI JET FUSION

On October 29, 2014, HP rocked the 3D printing industry by announcing what could be a game changer among game changers. HP said its long-awaited 3D printer will be at least ten times faster than the competition because it fuses an entire layer at the same time and will make stronger and more durable parts, at substantially lower cost. According to HP, 3D printing one thousand gears with its proprietary Multi Jet Fusion process takes only three hours, compared to eighty-three hours with Material Extrusion machines. Expected to hit the market in 2016, HP's machines, built on its Thermal Inkjet 2D printer technology, do not fit squarely into any of the ASTM International's seven categories of 3D printing processes. HP seems to combine as many as four types of 3D printing processes: Binder Jetting, Material Jetting, Powder Bed Fusion, and possibly Directed Energy Deposition (DED). But Multi Jet Fusion also seems to do something more. According to HP's white paper, one x-axis carriage of the machine seems to jet materials to form a bed, after which a y-axis carriage with an array of thousands of tiny nozzles jets "chemical agents" onto the layer—at a rate of thirty million drops per second—followed by a shot of energy from the first carriage that fuses the layer while more material is deposited. Because the system is modular and the order of these steps can be varied for particular applications, it is possible that the machine could do DED too.[35]

The proprietary chemical agents are more than the binders of Binder Jet machines. In fact, they may not be binders at all. Instead, they are for fusing, detailing, coloring, and transforming the build material on the voxel level. As HP says, its machines have the "discretion of drops," thirty million of them per second. Unfused material in the bed serves as support, as in Powder Bed Fusion. Parts do not appear to need postbuild steps, such as heat treatment or infiltration to increase part density. HP says its machines are modular and scalable and will deliver fully functional, final parts with sharp edges, smooth surfaces, and accuracy, detail, color, and material characteristics (including texture, strength, translucency, elasticity, and electrical and thermal properties that are continuously variable through the part) not seen before in 3D printing.

MOVE OVER, HP?

Northbrook, Illinois, start-up Impossible Objects (IO) developed a process that it calls Composite-Based Additive Manufacturing (CBAM) for 3D printing high-performance end-use parts and tooling. Like Multi Jet Fusion, CBAM uses standard thermal inkjet technology, but the similarity ends there. Combining elements of Sheet Lamination, Binder Jetting, Material Jetting, and Powder Bed Fusion, the CBAM inkjets deposit a layer of the part onto a sheet of fiber, such as carbon fiber, aramid fiber (aka Kevlar), or fiberglass, using a proprietary fluid. The machine then jets polymer powder onto the fluid, sweeps away dry powder, and repeats the process for the next layer. The fiber sheets provide inherent support as the structure is built. After the part has been built, the layers are heated and compressed to fuse the polymer with the fiber sheet. Simple abrasive blasting is used to remove the selvage fiber sheets and clean up the surface.

According to IO, CBAM makes parts with high strength-to-weight ratios from a wide variety of materials. Build speed is up to ten times faster than other 3D printing processes and could eventually rival the speed of injection molding. Parts are up to ten times stronger than those made with other polymer-based 3D printing processes.[36]

CUTTING-EDGE PROCESSES

While 3D printers are on the cutting edge of technology, some seem to border on science fiction.

Bioprinters

Bioprinters are a specialized form of 3D printer used to print tissue and organs. Much like desktop inkjet printers jet ink, these machines jet living cells, along with support material called scaffolding. So many companies and academic institutions are developing bioprinters that it is hard to keep up, but notable developers include 3D Bioprinting Solutions (Russia), Advanced Solutions/BioAssemblyBot (United States), Aspect Biosystems/ University of British Columbia (Canada), Bio3D Technologies (Singapore), Cyfuse (Japan), EnvisionTec (Germany), N3D Biosciences (United States), Organovo (United States), OxSyBio (United Kingdom), Regenovo (China), and Unique Technology (China). Universities include Harvard University, Wake Forest University, University of Louisville, University of Tokyo, and the Utrecht Life Sciences network of universities, hospitals, and government (Netherlands).[37] These institutions intend to print tissue and eventually replacement human organs for their own research or for sale to others. For example, Organovo has printed veins and beating human heart cells,[38] as well as human liver tissue for drug testing. The Wake Forest Center for Regenerative Medicine has bioprinted organ prototypes.[39] The University of Toronto has bioprinted skin to treat burn victims.[40] Princeton University has 3D printed a human bionic ear.[41] Sabanci University in Turkey has bioprinted aorta cells.[42] Washington and St. Louis Universities and the University of Illinois are developing a membrane to fit around the heart like a glove, sense heart troubles, and electrically stimulate the heart when needed.[43] Not to be outdone, the University of Louisville plans to 3D print a human heart by 2023.[44]

Collomated UV light curing

In this process, collomated UV light is directed through a layer of quartz and a mask with thousands of small holes onto a photosensitive resin to form self-propagating photopolymer waveguides, which in turn quickly form microlattice structures. The research in this area is mostly secret and conducted by HRL Laboratories, believed to be owned by Boeing and General Motors.[45]

Electrophoretic deposition

Developed at Lawrence Livermore National Laboratory, electrophoretic deposition applies an electrical field in a 2D pattern to a liquid medium containing suspended colloidal nanoparticles. The particles travel parallel to the electrical field and collect along the pattern on the substrate electrode. The pattern is then altered to build additional layers and complex 3D components. Multiple materials can be built into one structure, resulting in highly precise parts.[46]

STAR TREK REPLICATORS MAY BE JUST AROUND THE CORNER

As amazing as these machines and processes are, they are still fairly primitive, just as personal computers and cell phones were in the 1980s. For example, no single machine can print an entire complex product like a smartphone, yet. Also, parts that emerge from today's 3D printers need improved edge sharpness and surface smoothness, to reduce or eliminate postprocessing steps.

The Massachusetts Institute of Technology's Center for Bits and Atoms hopes to solve these problems and take the technology in a fundamentally different direction with what it calls "3D assemblers." Unlike 3D printers, which use materials such as plastics and metals to build parts, the MIT machines will assemble complete, functional products—including fixed and moving internal and external structures and internal electronics—from atoms and molecules,[47] nanomaterials, or programmable matter.[48]

NASA and the Ames Research Center in Silicon Valley are engaged in a project called "Biomaterials Out of Thin Air: In Situ, On-Demand Printing of Advanced Biocomposites." The project's goal is to use molecules in the surrounding environment to 3D print useable material, essentially making something from nothing.[49]

The US Army, the University of Pittsburgh, the Harvard School of Engineering, and the University of Illinois are working on a project to make materials that modify their own structures at the macro level:[50]

> Rather than construct a static material or one that simply changes its shape, we're proposing the development of adaptive, biomimetic composites that re-program their shape, properties or functionality on demand, based upon external stimuli.

Products resulting from this project will shape-shift, such as metals that adapt to their environment, uniforms that automatically morph from desert to jungle camouflage, or helicopter landing gear that can transform from wheels to skids to floats, depending on where the chopper wants to land.

Though impressive, these efforts have not yet been commercialized. A Boston-based start-up called Voxel8 took the first commercial step toward building machines that create fully functional products, such as its first product, a quadcopter. Voxel8's machine used Material Extrusion to print the body of the drone with a polymer while simultaneously printing the internal circuitry with conductive silver ink. The machine paused at preprogrammed points during the build process to allow the operator to insert electronic components, such as the motors. When the printing was finished, the 'copter flew out of the printer.

Eventually, Voxel8's machines will build complex products from multiple materials and will not require an operator to pick and place electronic components during the build process. The company's founder, Jennifer Lewis, envisions bringing together existing technologies capable of automatically fabricating fully functional electronic devices: [51]

> With our desktop printer, we're already embedding these kinds of functional objects. We're doing it by manual pick and place, but it's very easy to conceive that, on our road map, transitioning to automated pick and place is the future.

Lewis believes Voxel8's machines will be able to make fully functional devices, without human intervention, within a few years.

OLD PROCESSES HAVE A PLACE

It is not quite accurate to say that 3D printers can produce ready-to-use parts—at least not yet. "Near finished" would be more accurate. After the part is printed, it may require some postproduction work, such as removing support structures needed in the printing process, heat-treating or sintering, sanding, polishing, painting, plating, or powder coating. Vat polymerization parts made with photopolymers may need an extra shot of UV light. Excess powder must be removed from parts made by Binder Jetting and Powder Bed Fusion. Such extra powder may be removed, or the surface finish of raw parts may be refined with blasts of shot, beads, or the build powder, or by milling or polishing. Metal parts made with Binder Jet machines must be heat-treated, then infiltrated with another material, such as bronze or cyanoacrylate (the main ingredient of Krazy Glue). Some metal parts are heat-tempered to remove internal stresses, then hot isostatically pressed (HIP) to seal any pores or fissures and increase density, then treated with hardening agents.[52]

3D PRINTERS AND TRADITIONAL MACHINES CAN BE FRIENDS

In some cases, especially at the current state of 3D printing technology, a product can be made more efficiently with a combination of 3D printers and traditional manufacturing methods. To address this need, companies like Japan's Matsuura and the German-Japanese joint venture DMG Mori Seiki combine a 3D printer and a milling machine into one big box. What 3D printing giveth, the mill taketh away.[53] The FABtotum machine is a consumer example of such a hybrid.[54] Another consumer machine, the Luinar TriBOT, combines a 3D printer with a CNC router and injection-molding machine.[55] 3D Systems' Continuous, High-Speed Fab Grade Printer, which it developed for Project ARA, its joint venture with Google to 3D print smartphones, combines 3D printing and traditional manufacturing in a high-speed assembly line.[56] Voxel8 plans to combine 3D printing with automatic pick-and-place machines.[57] Professors Ryan Wicker and Eric MacDonald of the University of Texas at El Paso's Keck Center want to integrate 3D printing and copper-embedding systems to make 3D printed electronics in the factory of the future.[58]

3D printing can also make traditional methods work better or faster. 3D printing is great for rapid prototyping, which can help bring a product to market in a fraction of the time that was required before 3D printing. A product designer can design a product and all of its parts, 3D print prototypes, see how they look, work, and fit together, tweak them until they are just right, then send them to be made by traditional machines or by 3D printers. By using 3D printers in the product design process, the designer can create ten prototypes in the time it formerly took to make one, which gets products to market much faster than with traditional methods. Many companies are dipping their toes into 3D printing by using consumer-grade machines (selling for $5,000 or less) for prototyping.[59] By using 3D printers for rapid prototyping, Unilever cut product development times by 40 percent.[60] Tag Heuer, the French watchmaker, turns digital blueprints for new watches into 3D printed prototypes overnight.[61]

Molds used for castings, jigs used for cutting, drilling, and milling, fixtures used for holding and moving parts from machine to machine, and tools used for special operations are important cogs in the machinery of traditional manufacturing. 3D printing is ideal for making all of these things, and for streamlining processes. For example, without 3D printing, mold designs are sent directly to the mold maker. Weeks later, the mold arrives. If it is defective or the design needs tweaking, more weeks pass as the mold is remade. Tri-Coastal Design experienced this very problem until it started using 3D printers to develop molds. "Now, if we have to make changes," says creative director Ross Danis, "the changes are occurring to 3D printed prototypes rather than the actual mold of the [part]; in that sense, we save a lot of time and money if we have to make changes."[62]

Volvo is using industrial Material Extrusion machines to make specialty tools used on its truck production lines. By 3D printing the tools with thermoplastic instead of making them in metal by traditional methods, Volvo cut the time to design and produce tools from thirty-six days to two, substantially improving production workflow.[63]

Many parts today are made by a cheap and efficient method called injection molding, in which liquid plastic is injected into a mold, which quickly forms the part. Injection molding can make parts extremely well but requires making molds for each part and set-up times that take the machine down while it is being converted to make a different part. Time is money. Errors can also creep in at each step along the way. The McKinsey consulting firm, which tracks disruptive technologies with a big picture view, wrote in a 2013 report that: [64]

3D printing...has the potential to create significant value by shortening setup times, eliminating tooling errors, and producing molds that can actually increase the productivity of the injection molding process. For example, 3D printed molds can more easily include "conformal" cooling channels, which allow for more rapid cooling, significantly reducing cycle times and improving part quality. We estimate that 3D printing of tools and molds could generate $30 billion to $50 billion in economic impact per year by 2025, based on an estimated $360 billion cost base for production of injection molded plastics in 2025 and assuming that about 30 to 50 percent of these plastics could be produced with 3D printed molds at around 30 percent less cost.

Companies are starting to integrate 3D printers into the manufacture of products assembled from injection-molded parts. For example, FLIR, the thermal imaging company, used a 3D printed model of the final product "to figure out an optimal way to assemble the unit."[65]

Although 3D printing may eventually replace many types of traditional machines, for now they can work hand in hand.

3D PRINTERS + MATERIALS = THE HOLY GRAIL OF MANUFACTURING

The ability of 3D printers to make almost anything depends partly on how they operate and partly on the materials they can print. A machine capable of 3D printing virtually anything will require materials that don't yet exist—or that are just starting to exist—for instance, materials that enable a product currently composed of twenty to twenty-five materials to be 3D printed from only three or four materials. 3D printing is driving the development of such materials.

The materials used by most 3D printers include the usual suspects: plastic filaments, resins, metal wire, powdered plastics and metals, ceramics, composites, and even food. If you work at Google's headquarters, you can 3D print your choice of pasta shapes for lunch.[66] Most 3D printing today, especially on the consumer level, is done in plastics, mostly ABS and PLA. But a growing range of conventional materials can be 3D printed. On the industrial level, metals are being printed,[67] as are ceramics[68] and glass.[69] Wood-like materials are also available for both industry and consumers.[70] Less conventional materials are in development. For example, "shrilk" is made from shrimp shells and silkworms. Lightweight and durable, it may be suitable for food-safe and biocompatible applications.[71]

Many 3D printers use only a single feedstock or material. Others print with multiple materials or materials with variable qualities. For example, the Stratasys Connex machines simultaneously print multiple materials to yield parts that can be either rigid or flexible in different areas, with areas of varying degrees of flexibility in between.[72] Other materials can conduct electricity in some areas of a part and not in others.

Advanced materials are also advancing 3D printing. MIT developed a bone-like material.[73] The University of Glasgow is developing organic compounds for 3D printing medicines.[74] Cambridge University and PARC (the Palo Alto Research Center) are 3D printing thin-film transistors on flexible material.[75] MIT's Self-Assembly Lab is developing wood-like and carbon fiber materials that are 3D printable into programmable shapes that change when exposed to heat or water.[76]

The North Carolina State University developed a flexible, stretchable metal that is liquid at room temperature. The material is also self-healing both structurally and electrically, which means that if it breaks, it fixes itself and maintains its electrical connection.[77] China's Tsinghua University and the Chinese Academy of Sciences developed self-forming metal.[78] To get an image of this material, picture the evil cyborg in *Terminator II*, which could regenerate and reform itself no matter what Arnold Schwarzenegger did to it.

Beyond *The Terminator*, the University of Warwick in the United Kingdom has developed a Star Trek–worthy material called Carbomorph, which is an inexpensive conductive plastic that can be used to create conductive tracks and sensors—such as touch sensors—in 3D printed objects.

To demonstrate Carbomorph's qualities, researchers 3D printed a fully functioning game controller and did so with a low-cost, consumer-grade 3D printer.[79]

An even more amazing material is graphene, which is a one-atom-thick layer of mineralized graphite. Three millions layers of graphene are a single millimeter thick. It is two hundred times stronger than steel, harder than diamond, and more conductive than copper. A sheet of graphene the thickness of a layer of kitchen plastic wrap can support the weight of an elephant. If that weren't amazing enough, graphene is conductive and can be transparent.[80] In *Star Trek IV: The Voyage Home*, the *Enterprise* travels back to the twentieth century, where Scottie—tasked with building a tank to transport humpback whales through a time warp—complains that transparent aluminum has not yet been invented. Why didn't he just use graphene!

The worldwide interest in developing graphene for 3D printing and other uses is exploding. In 2013, the European Commission spearheaded a €1 billion initiative called the Graphene Flagship, comprised of seventy-six companies and universities from seventeen countries, to develop and commercialize graphene in ten years.[81] Graphene 3D Lab of Calverton, New York, is dedicated to developing graphene for 3D printing.[82] Down Under, the mining company Kibaran Resources has teamed with Australian 3D printer maker 3D Group to form /3D Graphtech Industries for the same purpose.[83]

In a different class of materials are chiplets, being developed by PARC. Think of chiplets as smart microbuilding blocks that contain transistors, photovoltaics, microvalves, sensors, and actuators. They can be assembled like tiny, smart Legos. Someday, their functionality will be 3D printed as needed to build complex, integrated structures.[84]

We are witnessing a golden age for materials science, which together with 3D printing will fundamentally change the way we make things. Terry

Wohlers says, "Materials are key to the future success of 3D printing."[85] I couldn't agree more.

3D PRINTING OUR WAY TO A GREENER WORLD

Simply combining the revolutionary manufacturing methods of 3D printing with materials like Carbomorph, graphene, liquid and self-forming metals, and chiplets will shake manufacturing at its core. But in addition to enabling the manufacture of fundamentally different products in fundamentally different ways, 3D printing has other advantages. Unlike traditional machines, which cut or mill or grind or drill away as much as 90 percent of the feedstock, 3D printers generate less waste because products are made from little more than the amount of material that ends up in the finished part.

3D printers also have a smaller carbon footprint than traditional machines. Some people have argued that operating a 3D printer uses more energy to create a part than traditional machines. For example, they say that the lasers of direct metal laser sintering or the electron beams of electron beam melting use far more energy than milling and drilling machines. They may be right if you look only at the energy used by the 3D printer, but the all-in energy footprint of 3D printing is usually less than that of traditional machines. Such all-in costs include the costs of making the manufacturing machines. Making a part with traditional methods requires multiple machines, all of which must be manufactured, and all of which have their own carbon footprint. All of those machines also gobble energy while they make parts, and final products must be assembled. All of these steps leave carbon footprints. By comparison, a product can be 3D printed using far fewer machines, and no assembly is required, resulting in less energy usage. The all-in costs also include the price of the materials, including the quantity wasted by traditional machines. Even where 3D printing a part uses more energy than traditional methods, its carbon footprint can be lower over the life of the part, as is true of lightweight aircraft parts.[86]

Traditional manufacturing is also usually done far from where the products are needed and used. The reason for this is that traditional manufacturing requires a lot of labor, so things are made where labor is cheap. But this requires shipping and warehousing. Labor, shipping, and warehousing all have carbon footprints. Because far fewer machines and less labor are required to 3D print parts and products, they need not be made in far-off lands, so the carbon footprints are reduced if the parts are 3D printed near the point of need.

STATE OF THE ART

The poster children for 3D printing today are the aerospace, automotive, and health-care industries. The companies using 3D printing for aerospace and automotive are among the largest and most influential in the world, and they are using 3D printing to streamline manufacturing and reduce costs. But people will probably notice the effects of 3D printing on health care sooner than they notice the effects in any other area. The adoption of 3D printing by these industries is giving the technology visibility and credibility, and helping to drive the industry forward. Gartner predicts full industry adoption of 3D printing by 2019.[87]

Aerospace

Boeing is a big user of 3D printing. It has been 3D printing for many years, flies tens of thousands of 3D printed parts,[88] and is very proud of its 3D printed air duct, which formerly was comprised of about twenty parts and now is printed as one. Printing air ducts as a single part reduces inventory, makes them easier to install and inspect, eliminates certain manufacturing problems like tolerance stacking, and makes the ducts lighter. Lighter components mean less fuel, and less fuel means lower airfares.[89] Boeing calls 3D printing "the ultimate manufacturing method for us."[90]

NASA 3D printed a rocket injector that not only reduced 160 parts to 2, but can withstand temperatures in excess of 6,000 degrees Fahrenheit and more than twenty thousand pounds of thrust.[91] Not to be outdone, the European Space Agency and Airbus successfully test-fired a 3D printed spacecraft engine combustion chamber and thruster nozzle. During the thirty-two-minute test, the parts withstood a temperature of 1,253 degrees Celsius (2,287 degrees Fahrenheit).[92]

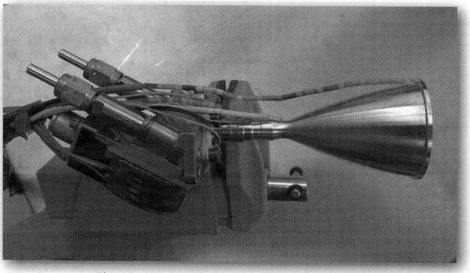

Photo courtesy of Airbus Defense and Space

Elon Musk, of SpaceX (and Tesla), said "Through 3D printing, robust and high-performance [rocket] engine parts can be created at a fraction of the cost and time of traditional manufacturing methods."[93]

Airbus expects to be 3D printing thirty tons of metal airplane parts by 2018. One of its first 3D printed achievements was a wing bracket, traditionally manufactured with many steps. With 3D printing, it was made in one step.[94] The bracket in the background was made by traditional methods. The bracket in the foreground was 3D printed. Notice its more open, organic design.

Photo courtesy of Airbus Group

Airbus's 3D printing has moved far beyond the wing bracket. Its A350 XWB aircraft contains over a thousand 3D printed parts. According to Peter Sander, Airbus's head of emerging technologies and concepts:[95]

> We are on the cusp of a step-change in weight reduction and efficiency—producing aircraft parts which weigh 30 to 55 percent less, while reducing raw material used by 90 percent. This game-changing technology also decreases total energy used in production by up to 90 percent compared to traditional methods.

Northwestern Polytechnical University in China 3D printed a titanium aircraft wing spar.[96] 3D printing is well suited to manufacturing with titanium because it eliminates the need to weld the metal, a difficult process with titanium.[97]

GE acquired two additive-manufacturing companies[98] and believes that 3D printing "is the future of manufacturing," that "additive manufacturing [is] a game-changing technology," and that "by 2020, well over 100,000 end-use parts in GE/CFM engines will be produced through additive manufacturing."[99] But because such high demands for 3D printing will exceed current worldwide 3D printing manufacturing capacity,[100] GE opened a factory in Alabama to 3D print parts for thousands of leading edge aircraft propulsion (LEAP) engines with Powder Bed Fusion. The first part will be a fuel nozzle.*

By 3D printing this nozzle, twenty parts are reduced to one, which weighs 25 percent less than the traditionally manufactured nozzle but is much more durable.[101] GE expects to use 3D printing to make many more parts for the LEAP engine. By 3D printing them instead of using traditional methods, the company expects to save one thousand pounds on a six-thousand-pound engine.[102] An Alaska Air study showed that removing five in-flight magazines from a commercial jet could save $10,000 per year in fuel.[103] Just imagine how much shaving a thousand pounds off the weight of each engine could save.

Although GE's LEAP engine fuel nozzle is probably the most famous 3D printed part, GE's 3D printed, cobalt-chrome engine sensor housing for the GE90 turbofan engine deserves as much attention because it is GE's first flying, FAA-approved 3D printed part. Powder Bed Fusion

---

* My colleague Rachel Gordon, of the IDTechEX market-research firm, says that no discussion of 3D printing is complete without showing the GE LEAP engine fuel nozzle. Every 3D printing speaker shows a photo of it. I am not including it here because the nozzle that shows up everywhere, including in the article at this link (http://www.gereports.com/post/116402870270/the-faa-cleared-the-first-3D printed-part-to-fly), may not be the real nozzle. According to Steven Taub, Senior Director of Advanced Manufacturing for GE Ventures, who spoke at the Infocast Additive Manufacturing Summit in Santa Clara, California, in April 2015, the design of the real nozzle is a secret.

enabled GE to design and manufacture the part in far less time than traditional methods required.[104]

Other aerospace companies are starting to reap the benefits of 3D printing. In 2015, France's Turbomeca opened a 3D printing facility to make 3D printed production parts for helicopters. Its first 3D printed part was a fuel injector nozzle for helicopter engines, made with Powder Bed Fusion.[105] Britain's BAE Systems plans to take it even further. Matt Stevens, who heads BAE's 3D printing division, says, "It's long term, but it's certainly our end goal to manufacture an aerial vehicle in its entirety using 3D printing technology."[106]

To prove what 3D printers can do, Australia's CSIRO (which is like the US national labs), along with Monash University and Deakin University, used Powder Bed Fusion to 3D print a replica of an entire Microturbo gas turbine jet engine.

Photo courtesy of Monash University, Deakin University, CSIRO, Microturbo, and SIEF (Science and Industrial Endowment Funding), which sponsored this project

Monash University plans to commercialize the technology through its commercial arm, Amaero Engineering.[107]

Not to be outdone, New Zealand's Rocket Lab 3D printed its Rutherford rocket engine, named after native son Ernest Rutherford, a Nobel Prize–winning physicist. Using Arcam's electron-beam-melting Powder Bed Fusion process, Rocket Lab printed the engine's thrust chamber, injector, turbopumps, and main propellant valves, using titanium alloys. Some of these parts could not be made by traditional methods and were 3D printed in days rather than months.[108]

Photo courtesy of Rocket Lab

Automotive

All major automakers use 3D printing, mostly for rapid prototyping and for making jigs and fixtures used on production lines. BMW also uses 3D printing to make ergonomically efficient tools that reduce worker fatigue and improve efficiency.[109] Bentley used 3D printers for prototyping for many years before 3D printing high-precision metal parts for its EXP 10 Speed 6 luxury coupe. Bentley's Wolfgang Durheimer said:[110]

> 3D metal printing has allowed the grille mesh, exhausts, door handles and side vents to be delivered with micro-scale design detail precision. The iconic Bentley mesh grille, for example, is no longer a flat plane of latticework but includes varying depth with a complex 3D geometry only visible when viewed at an angle. Bentley's renowned quilted leather has inspired three dimensional texture to the precision glass of the headlamps.

The Oakridge National Lab and the University of Tennessee 3D printed a beautiful Shelby Cobra body.

Photo courtesy of Oak Ridge National Laboratory

Students at the Nanyang Technological University in Singapore 3D designed and built a solar-powered car with 150 3D printed parts.[111]

Photo courtesy of Nanyang Technological University, Singapore

To show what 3D printing can do, electronics manufacturer TE Connectivity used Material Extrusion to make most of the parts for an entire functioning motorcycle, including the polymer frame, wheel bearings, and rims; its bronze headlights were made with Powder Bed Fusion.[112] The rear hub and drive sprocket was 3D printed as one piece. A photo of the motorcycle can be seen at http://www.gizmag.com/te-3D printed-motorcycle/37729/.

Health care

Health care has a broad range of 3D printing developments that seems amazing today but that will probably seem commonplace in a few years, as even more impressive advances eclipse them. Walter Reed Army Medical Center has 3D printed titanium cranial implants[113] and replaced a woman's jaw with a 3D printed prosthetic.[114] In 2013 doctors replaced 75 percent of a man's skull with a 3D printed implant made by a company called Oxford Performance Materials.[115] In the United Kingdom, doctors replaced half of the pelvis in a man with a rare type of cancer.[116] Tens of thousands of replacement hip cups have been printed and implanted into patients.[117]

Other 3D printing developments in health care include noses,[118] skin,[119] customized coverings for artificial limbs,[120] cosmetic ears,[121] and bionic ears.[122] About 95 percent of all hearing aid shells are 3D printed.[123] The molds for about seventeen million teeth aligners are 3D printed every year.[124] 3D printed tracheas and tracheal splints are almost routinely saving newborns with serious breathing problems.[125] The 3D printers used for this work are not always expensive, high-end machines. Consumer-grade 3D printers and materials have been used for tracheal implants. Doctors at the Feinstein Institute for Medical Research used a MakerBot machine (about $2,000) and ordinary PLA filament to 3D print custom scaffolding on which living cells were cultured for a tracheal implant.[126] MakerBot machines have also been used to 3D print patient-specific, biodegradable, medicinal implants for treating bone infections and cancers.[127]

The human heart is the subject of considerable 3D printing efforts. Aorta cells have been 3D printed at Sabanci University in Turkey.[128] The University of Louisville expects to 3D print a human heart by 2023.[129] Kentucky-based Advanced Solutions intends to use its BioAssemblyBot printer to accomplish the feat.[130] In 2013, a California high schooler 3D printed a proof of concept customizable artificial heart.[131] And, to save existing hearts, Washington University in St. Louis is developing an elastic, 3D printed membrane that wraps around the heart like a glove. Its embedded sensors detect impending problems, and embedded electrodes deliver a life-saving shock when serious arrhythmias are detected.[132]

Organovo, of San Diego, California, is 3D printing tissue used for drug testing and is working on a 3D printed human liver, which could eliminate animal testing of new drugs and enable safe and effective drugs to be brought to market much faster and at lower cost than they are today.[133] Others are working on 3D printable drugs, to be printed at home or where they are needed.[134]

Low-cost 3D printers are being used in war-torn developing countries, such as the Sudan and Uganda, to make prosthetics for amputees, of which there are fifty thousand in the Sudan alone.[135] The US Army also wants to use 3D printing to counter some of the horrors of war. In a joint project with the University of Nevada, the army plans to 3D scan soldiers, from head to toe, and store the data in case the soldier loses a limb in combat. As Dr. James Ma said:[136]

> The idea is to image someone when they are in a healthy state so that the data is available if it's needed at a later point....We have soldiers who get injured. They lose limbs and other tissues and it's a challenge to reconstruct them in the field. But if they are imaged beforehand, you can send that over the Internet and have a 3D printer in the field to produce the bone.

The Oak Ridge National Lab's award-winning, lightweight, low-cost 3D printed hand may be used in robotics, prosthetics, surgery, and hazardous materials handling.[137] A hydraulic pump powered by an electric motor located in the palm of the hand provides pressurized fluid to the finger joints, which cause gripping motion. An electric motor turns a cam that drives two master pistons each connected to five slave pistons, which cause the fingers to open or close. Since the fingers are hydraulically coupled, the digits will naturally conform to any device they grasp.

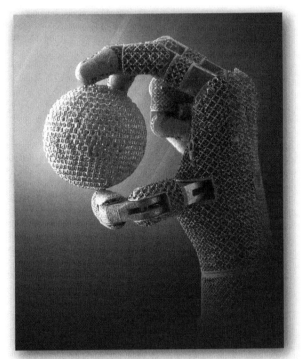

Photo courtesy of Oak Ridge National Laboratory

3D printers have also been used to aid facial reconstructive surgery, with impressive results, including a full-face replacement in Belgium.[138] Researchers at Michigan Tech are using graphene and 3D printed scaffolds to rebuild damaged nerve tissue.[139]

Italy's Del Bene Orthopedic Laboratory switched from traditional manufacturing to 3D printing for its human prosthetics and cut its production times by 75 percent. Biomedical engineer Marco Avaro says, "For a tibial prosthesis, I used to need eight hours. Now, I only need two." They have found that 3D printing prosthetics has other advantages. According to Avaro, "If we take the case of degenerative diseases, the geometries can become particularly difficult, very asymmetric, and the 3D printer can reproduce exactly what we need."[140]

A great medical application for 3D printing is surgical models and guides. Models of patient organs are being 3D printed and studied by surgeons before the first incision. Better to find anatomical anomalies and formulate strategy while studying models than while a patient lies on the operating table.[141] Surgeons at Miami Children's Hospital 3D printed a replica of a four-year-old girl's heart to plan her complicated surgery.[142] Doctors at Boston's Children's Hospital practiced on a 3D printed model of a teenager's brain before operating on the real thing.[143] Texas Children's Hospital 3D printed the hearts, lungs, stomachs, and kidneys of twins conjoined at the chest and abdomen so that surgeons could plan and practice their separation, which was a success.[144] Similarly, Chinese surgeons used a life-sized 3D printed model to practice separating conjoined twins who shared a single digestive tract. The model included many of the anatomical features they would encounter during surgery, such as bone joints and skin connections, which the surgeons practiced cutting to determine how best to separate the infants.[145] 3D printed models are also being used to train tomorrow's brain surgeons.[146] 3D printed surgical guides, such as guides customized for a patient's knee, enable surgeons to locate cuts precisely.[147] The printing of such guides is aided by software that turns 2D x-rays into 3D models.[148] Some hospitals are 3D printing surgical models and guides in-house. For example, Belgian 3D printing company Materialise opened a 3D printing center in Fuwai Hospital, China's largest cardio facility. According to the hospital, this collaboration will enable Fuwai to "become China's leading center for 3D printed heart model education, spreading knowledge of the technology and how it can be used by surgeons to the benefit of the Chinese public."[149]

3D printing is also being used for cosmetic surgery. A New York start-up, MirrorMe3D, 3D prints models showing what you will look like after cosmetic surgery.[150] Many Hollywood stars probably wish this company had existed before they went under the knife.

2

Reinventing Design

DESIGN FOR MANUFACTURE VERSUS MANUFACTURE FOR DESIGN

Products have always been slaves to how they can be made. If a design cannot be made with traditional machines, it remains trapped on paper or in a computer. Thus, product designers have been forced to design for manufacture. 3D printing changes that. In a 3D printed world, designers no longer need to design for the limitations of existing machines because 3D printers can build almost any design, regardless of complexity. With virtually no limitations on manufacturing, 3D printers will rock how we create because they can manufacture for design, which turns the creative process on its head. Product designs no longer need to be broken into multiple parts, according to manufacturing constraints. Designers can immerse themselves in the creative process because they can 3D print prototypes immediately. The mediocrity and monotony of mass-produced designs can be replaced with mass-customized and mass-personalized designs. Because almost any product can be 3D printed, the design can follow the designer's vision and is limited only by the imagination.

GE Oil & Gas uses hybrid machines that combine Powder Bed Fusion with precision milling to make energy control valve parts at a plant in Japan. By 3D printing the parts, designers are free to give them complex shapes that are difficult or impossible to make with traditional methods, such as hollow structures, complex curves, and meshes. 3D printing also reduces the part delivery times from three months with traditional methods, to two weeks. Alvin Jeffers, a senior executive for GE Oil & Gas's global supply chain, said:[151]

> A completely new form of product manufacturing has been realized through the advanced technology of the metal 3D printer and the full utilization of that technology through the outstanding creativity of Japanese designers. Advanced manufacturing has changed the conventional definitions and mechanisms of manufacturing, namely design and production, while offering an abundance of merits to customers, such as faster manufacturing times and greatly reduced costs. I am confident that it will become a new standard in the manufacturing industry in the near future.

REINVENTING DESIGN

Harvard Business School marketing professor Theodore Levitt once said, "People don't want to buy a quarter-inch *drill*. They want a quarter-inch *hole*."[152] Traditional manufacturing makes us use quarter-inch drills to bore quarter-inch holes, and designers and engineers design products accordingly. In a 3D printing-enabled world, however, such constraints no longer exist. Designers simply specify a hole's location; no tool is needed to drill it.

Take for example a part with built-in cooling channels. An important goal of the part's design is to dissipate heat as the part is used. The layout of cooling channels in parts made by traditional methods is limited by those methods, such as cutting, milling, or casting. The ability to 3D print the part allows the designer to embed nonlinear cooling channels that conform to the part's shape and are optimally arranged to dissipate heat.

The beauty of 3D printed parts is that the complexity of their design has no bearing on their cost of production. Complexity is free. Gone are the days when management kills a new product because it is too expensive to build. With 3D printing, complex features like optimal cooling channels add nothing to manufacturing costs. To make such channels by traditional machines—if they could be made at all—would increase costs astronomically. 3D printing saves the manufacturer money and produces a superior part.

The importance of free complexity cannot be overstated. Because product designers need not be concerned with whether or not a complex part can be made, or with how much it will cost, a once impregnable barrier to design has been broken. Also, because 3D printing involves far less waste, designers are free to use materials that would have been too expensive to use with traditional machines.

3D printing also frees designers from the tyranny of multipart designs. In a product composed of multiple parts, each part has its own geometry, design limitations, manufacturing requirements, documentation, approval process, and design and manufacturing costs. The more parts in a product, the greater the final cost. Traditional methods incapable of fashioning complex finished products in a single piece force designers to create multipart designs.[153] Multipart products also require assembly, resulting in added costs, while introducing opportunities for mistakes. Because 3D printing can create complex products whole, the design process can focus on the forest, not the trees. The designer can design the product to optimize its functionality, even its beauty, without worrying about how each part will be made and whether all will work together properly, and without incurring all of the related costs.

DESIGN IMMERSION WITH RAPID PROTOTYPING
During its first thirty years, 3D printing was used mostly for rapid prototyping. The ability to take a design from the drawing board to a 3D printed prototype enabled product designers to make better designs. Very shortly after designing a part, the designer could hold it in his hands. He could then quickly tweak or redesign the functionality of the part, shave off

weight, and make it look better. Another prototype could then be printed, followed by more tweaking. This rapid iterative process refined designs, improved fit and finish, and brought products to market faster. Perhaps more importantly, rapid prototyping with 3D printers kept the designer immersed in the design process. Rather than designing a part, waiting days or weeks for a traditionally made prototype, and tweaking the design over several more weeks or months, the designer of a 3D printed proto-type remained focused on the design. Focusing on a task always yields better results.

3D PRINTING AND THE DESTRUCTION OF MONOTONY

3D printing also frees designers from the bonds of sameness. Before 3D printers could make production-quality parts, designers were forced to design for mass production. Each design for each product was destined to remain essentially unchanged in thousands or millions of exact copies. Because 3D printing enables parts to be easily customized, the designer can design for mass customization, rather than mass production. Rather than making a single design that results in zillions of identical copies, the designer's creativity can result in thousands or millions of mass-custom-ized products.

Customization can happen on any scale. Joel Piaskowski, Ford's director of design, foresees car designs customized for individuals or specific needs.[154] Daihatsu, the Japanese carmaker, is taking a step in this direction with its Effect Skins project. Using the Daihatsu Copen roadster as the basic design, the project allows owners to apply any one of twelve types of "effect skins" in ten colors to areas of the body panels. According to Osamu Fujishita, Daihatsu's chief engineer, "With this single project, we are combining automotive car, manufacturing [sic] and 3D printing to bring a new personalized automotive experi-ence to our customers."[155]

Toyota is also using 3D printing to mass-customize the i-Road Personal Mobility Device, its one-person car. Owners will be able to customize many parts, by color, surface texture, and possibly shape.[156]

On the human scale, the MadLab TACTUM project is developing a system for designing customized 3D printable and wearable objects directly on the body. Early results include an ergonomic smartwatch wristband and a wrist brace. TACTUM's leader, Madeline Gannon, wants to use the system to develop custom prosthetics and orthopedics.[157]

To realize the full potential of 3D printing, designers may have to break old habits and start to think in different ways. As leading 3D printing industry consultant Todd Grimm said, "The designer or engineer needs to forget everything he has previously learned and design something radically different."[158] But this will not be easy. According to Carolyn Seepersad of the University of Texas at Austin, "Researchers in cognitive psychology and engineering have demonstrated that designers experience a powerful tendency to adhere to designs they have encountered previously."[159] 3D printing allows designers to break old design habits. As 3D printers become more and more powerful and more commonly used, as designers start to realize their capabilities, and as schools start to teach design for additive manufacturing, new habits will replace the old.

Bernat Cuni, founder of cunicode, made this point more powerfully when he said that 3D printers "technologically empower designers."[160] Bernat hit the nail on the head: 3D printers are incredibly powerful and flexible tools that empower designers to make things they could not make before, and to make them in different ways. According to Lynn Gambill, chief engineer for manufacturing engineering at aerospace manufacturer Pratt & Whitney, 3D printing is[161] allowing designers to think about production without any of the prior manufacturing restrictions. You can make thin walls without having to worry about shape complexity. It gives designers a chance to imagine what the part might look like instead of what it historically has looked like. What you'll start to see more and more—and not just in aerospace—is that the shapes of parts could look very different.

3D PRINTING AS A CATALYST FOR CUSTOM DESIGNS

Obviously, the designer can't make thousands of custom designs. Also, the average person may lack the skills or interest to design, customize, or personalize products. Instead, 3D printing is driving the creation of new design tools, many of which will enable constrained customization. For example, rather than designing a single product, a designer can create a platform on which a basic design can be customized—within limits—by the customer, and the design can then be 3D printed. This is exactly what Isaac Katz, the Mexican artist and jewelry designer, has done. He displays his basic jewelry designs on his website (www.isaac-katz.com) along with online design tools that allow the customer to customize the design. After selecting size and choice of metal, the customer moves sliders on the screen, transforming the design to his or her liking, creating personalized bling that may bear only a passing resemblance to the original design. When the customer is satisfied with the design, Isaac 3D prints and ships it.

Image courtesy of Isaac Katz

London start-up OwnFone created a line of simple, inexpensive, highly customizable 3D printed cell phones for children, seniors, and the blind. Visitors to the OwnFone website can choose the look, shape, and color of the phone, or even draw a full-color design that is printed on the phone's face.[162] A child's phone might be customized with buttons that look like anything from tigers to Lego bricks, printed with family members' names—Mom and Dad, Grandma and Grandpa. For the blind, buttons can be customized in Braille.[163]

By providing customization tools, designers and companies can leverage basic designs into mass-customized products. Such interactive design processes also have a multiplying effect: they turn customers into co-designers who create more designs. 3D printers turn such designs into reality.

FROM DESIGN TO PRINT

Designers have three sources of 3D printable digital blueprints: creation, modification, and scanning. Using 3D design software, the designer can create a design from scratch, modify an existing digital blueprint, or reverse engineer an existing product. The designer can also use a 3D scanner, which captures objects' precise shapes and physical dimensions and turns them into digital blueprints that can be 3D printed.

The 3D scanner is an important tool in the designer's toolbox. Some people believe 3D scanners may be just as revolutionary as 3D printers. In combination with 3D printers, 3D scanners have done amazing things. Most 3D scanners scan the exterior surface of an object. But CT scanners, like the scanners used by hospitals to scan the human brain, can be used to scan the *interior* of objects, resulting in digital files that, when 3D printed, exactly reproduce the original object, inside and out.

Archeologists working with ancient cuneiform medallions in the Middle East developed a method of CT scanning that enables otherwise impossible studies of priceless artifacts. The scans created designs that were exact digital copies both outside and in. When archeologists later 3D printed the designs, they broke open the 3D printed copies and found ancient writing on the inside![164]

Used to their utmost, these tools will transform the world of design. Chris Anderson summed up the potential of combining a 3D scanner with a 3D printer in *Makers: The New Industrial Revolution:*[165]

> someday if you want to duplicate an object, you need only point your phone at it, following the phone's directions to move around the object and zoom in on sections, and press "print." A duplicate, perhaps even in color, will appear in your desktop 3D-printer.

With such power, the average person need not surf the Internet for 3D printable blueprints. She can simply scan any item, anywhere, tweak its digital design if she wants, and send it to her printer. The product will be waiting for her when she gets home.

USING 3D PRINTING AS PART OF THE DESIGN PROCESS

Designers can also make 3D printers part of the design process. For example, designers can 3D print tools directly into products, to aid the design process or to make better products. A designer might design a product that contains sensors that measure stress and fatigue, then 3D print actual sensors in the product.[166] Such sensors provide feedback to the designer, who can modify the design accordingly. Sensors could also be 3D printed into production parts. Imagine structural brackets for bridges whose built-in sensors continuously monitor structural integrity and wirelessly alert authorities to danger. A company called Fabrisonic is using a Sheet Lamination process called ultrasonic additive manufacturing (UAM) to embed sensors in layers of metal.[167]

The importance of incorporating the capabilities of 3D printers into the design process cannot be overstated. If parts and products are designed without 3D printers in mind, they may not take full advantage of this technology. Similarly, if they are used only to print parts and products conceived and designed for traditional manufacturing, the full benefits of the technology are squandered. Only by designing for 3D printing will makers use these machines to their fullest potential.

DESIGN CROWDSOURCING

One of the many effects of the Internet is the phenomenon of crowdsourcing design. Designers have probably always collaborated, but the Internet takes crowdsourcing to a new level. Various platforms available on the Internet allow designers to collaborate on projects. Local Motors, headquartered in Phoenix, Arizona, is a great example (see https://localmotors.com/#).

Local Motors is a low-volume custom vehicle manufacturer, building open, crowdsourced designs in microfactories. Independent designers collaborate on every aspect of a vehicle's design and are rewarded for their efforts. In 2011, Local Motors' network of independent designers collaborated to win the US Defense Advanced Research Project Agency's (DARPA) combat support vehicle design challenge.

Photo courtesy of Local Motors

The Local Motors crowdsourced design was designed and built in less than four months, which is about one-fifth of the time it takes a big car maker to do the same thing.[168]

OPEN INNOVATION

Many designers make their designs available to the world. Some designers do so under Creative Commons licenses, and others publish their designs without restrictions of any kind. Under a Creative Commons license, designers use simple, standardized copyright license agreements to give others permission to use, share, and build upon their designs, or specify restrictions applicable to different types of users.[169]

3D printing is driving the availability of many open-source designs. For example, the Thingiverse website (http://www.thingiverse.com/), which was created by MakerBot, a manufacturer of consumer and prosumer 3D printers, is a free library of thousands of designs that anyone can 3D print.

Many 3D printers are also based on open-source designs. In 2004, Adrian Bowyer invented the RepRap 3D printer, which is designed to reproduce itself (think *Terminator 3, Rise of the Machines*), although it cannot yet print all of its own parts. All of the RepRap's design specifications are freely available on the Internet. As Bowyer said, "Just as the clover does not charge the bee for its pollen, I gave all the RepRap designs and software away for free." Tens of thousands of RepRap printers are believed to have been made.[170]

3D printing is especially suited to open collaboration. Design collaborators can quickly convert their ideas to products, then collaborate on improvements, and so on until the finished product emerges from the printer's build chamber.

Open-source designs are also well suited to 3D printing. Eventually, consumer-grade 3D printers will be able to make almost any product.

Many products, such as common household and kitchen tools, toys and dolls, decorative items, and sports and gardening equipment, will probably be available as open-source designs. Designers who open such designs essentially donate them to the public for the collective good of humanity. According to IBM, "Where just a few years ago consumers were sharing just 20 to 50 new open source product designs every month, today we count more than 30,000 new designs every month."[171] This is also happening in industry, where, IBM says, "just 20 percent of products were open source five years ago and in 2013 that percentage had climbed to 33 percent."[172]

DESIGN REMIX AND MASH-UPS

A natural result of crowdsourcing, open innovation, and making designs available on the Internet is "design remix," in which product and part designs are tweaked, combined, and transformed. Design remix can be a continuous and iterative process among multiple designers, or it can involve independent designers working alone, remixing other designers' work. A design that enters one end of a remix process may emerge from the other end looking nothing like the original. For example, Argentinian designer Agustin Flowalistick remixes Pokemon Bulbasaurs and posts them on the Internet under a Creative Commons license for others to download and 3D print. Other designers then remix Flowalistick's designs. Some of the remixes resemble Flowalistick's designs, and some have been remixed to the point that they are unrecognizable as derivatives of the original remixes.[173]

Designer Matthew Plummer-Fernandez starts with objects like watering cans, action figures, and spray bottles, scans them, and then morphs the designs into unrecognizable 3D printable blueprints for inspired sculptures.[174]

Photos courtesy of Matthew Plummer-Fernandez

Mash-ups are a similar design concept, in which unrelated products or parts are mashed into a single design, such as Netherland's designer Alan Nguyen's shoe-phone, which is a shoe and smartphone 3D printed as one piece.[175]

Design remixes and mash-ups are not new, but they may have been difficult or impossible to turn into 3D objects before 3D printing. The ability to turn remixed and mashed-up designs into real objects is a great example of 3D printing's power to free designers of the constraints of traditional manufacturing methods.

BUSTING ROADBLOCKS TO INVENTION

The limitations of traditional manufacturing have not only hindered designers from creating and improving designs for existing products. They have also stymied invention. For example, titanium is highly desirable as a structural metal because it is very strong and very lightweight. But it is difficult to weld pieces of titanium together, and that difficulty limited innovative uses of titanium.[176] Enter 3D printing. Titanium powder can be fused into production-quality parts using Powder Bed Fusion, which makes an end run around the difficulty of welding the stuff. This frees up researchers to innovate with titanium.

Other researchers hope to use 3D printing to advance nuclear fusion.[177] For example, one goal of the European Space Agency's AMAZE project (a loose acronym for "Additive Manufacturing Aiming Towards Zero Waste and Efficient Production of High-Tech Metal Products") is to 3D print tungsten alloy parts that can withstand the heat of a nuclear fusion reactor—about three thousand degrees Celsius—without breaking a sweat.[178]

Bioprinters are a special type of 3D printer that open up a brave new world of invention previously thought impossible. Researchers at a handful of bioprinting companies, such as Organovo in San Diego, California,

Nano3D Biosciences in Houston, Texas, Bio3D of Singapore, OxSyBio and 3Dynamic of the United Kingdom, and China's Regenovo, are using bioprinters to develop human skin, liver tissue, and organs.[179] Bioprinted liver tissue—and eventually entire livers made of human cells—offer the possibility of identifying safe and effective pharmaceuticals and bringing them to market sooner, at lower cost. Inventing such tissue structures may also speed drug inventions. Researchers at Harvard, MIT, Stanford, and Sydney Universities; the Fraunhofer Institute for Interfacial Engineering and Biotechnology; Brigham and Women's Hospital; and Japan's Saga University together with start-up Cyfuse Biomedical are developing vascular networks for such organs.[180]

Thus, 3D printing reinvents the process of invention itself, giving researchers a tool with which to invent what was once uninventable.

3

Making Us Makers Again

WE ARE MAKERS AT HEART

We are all makers at heart. For all of human history, except the last hundred years or so, when people needed something they made it. Manufacturing was democratized. All sorts of people made all sorts of things, for themselves and for each other, in villages, towns, and cities all over the world. At first they worked on a small scale, making what each person or family needed to survive: spears, bows, and arrows for hunting; food, wine, and beer to eat and enjoy; vessels to hold the things they made. As societies formed, they specialized: a single artisan made a particular product for a village. Blacksmiths made tools and shod horses, weavers made fabric, shoemakers made shoes, farmers grew crops. Then along came the Industrial Revolution, which made an amazing variety of products of a consistent quality widely and easily available at reasonable prices. Makers became buyers.

3D printing will rock who we are, taking us back to our maker roots and redemocratizing manufacturing. As personal 3D printers become better and better, faster and faster, and capable of making more and more sophisticated products, the human drive to make will be rekindled.

President Barack Obama made this point at the 2014 White House Maker Faire:[181]

Our parents and our grandparents created the world's largest economy and strongest middle class not by buying stuff, but by

53

building stuff—by making stuff, by tinkering and inventing and building; by making and selling things first in a growing national market and then in an international market—stuff Made in America.

3D printers will make us makers again.

MAKERS AND MAKERS

The Maker movement is a loosely organized effort to return us to our making roots. Makers are self-reliant do-it-yourselfers who love to tinker, invent, and build things. They are mostly an open-design, open-manufacturing community and believe in collaborative innovation.[182] Many follow a loosely defined philosophy laid out by Mark Hatch, former Green Beret and CEO of TechShop, in his book *The Maker Movement Manifesto*. His philosophy has nine pillars: making, sharing, giving, learning, using tools, being playful, collaborating, supporting the Maker movement, and embracing change.[183]

A hallmark of the Maker movement is collaboration, the sharing of ideas and skills. Collaboration is infectious and self-perpetuating and speeds innovation. Makers who benefit from collaboration share their knowledge and skills to encourage others to make things and collaborate, and so it goes in a grand cycle that benefits civilization. As Chris Anderson wrote in his book *Makers: The New Industrial Revolution*:[184]

[I]deas, shared, turn into bigger ideas. Projects, shared, become group projects and more ambitious than any one person would attempt alone. And those projects can become the seeds of products, movements, even industries.

Maker collaboration also gets results faster. The independent designers who collaborated to win the DARPA combat support vehicle design challenge designed a functioning vehicle in one-fifth the time Detroit takes to do the same thing.

Makers don't always require perfection. They are often willing to accept parts and products that are "good enough."[185] Good-enough technology is how advanced technologies get their start. Innovators create new products with rudimentary functionality, then they tinker with them, gradually or even rapidly improving them. Consider the first personal computers. Readers of a certain age will remember how heavy, clunky, and slow PCs and laptops were in their early days. Primitive by today's standards, these machines nonetheless were good enough to merit the dedication of their inventors, who turned them into sophisticated products in a relatively short time.

3D printing has been around for about thirty years. At its start, both the printers and their products were good enough to encourage the inventors and early adopters to keep going. Scott Crump, the founder of Stratasys, famously created his first FDM printer in his garage. That first printer and Crump's first product—a toy frog for his daughter—were good enough to spur him to start what is now a multibillion-dollar company.[186] Today's printers and their products have a long way to go. They are still relatively primitive, particularly in terms of speed and the breadth of products that a single machine can make. But today's printers and products are getting better all the time, and they are good enough to drive the development of this technology to the point that the machines can make almost anything.

According to Bre Pettis, founder of MakerBot, 57 percent of American adults identify themselves as makers.[187] This may sound like a lot, but the Maker movement is only a small fraction of the world's makers. The Western world is full of makers, as is Asia. And developing countries have even more makers than industrial and postindustrial societies. The human need to make and work with our hands is strong. Makers and tinkerers are everywhere: architects, artists, bakers, blacksmiths (they still exist) and other iron workers, brewers, carpenters, cigar rollers, clock- and watchmakers, cooks, crafters and craftspeople of all kinds, distillers, electricians, factory workers, farmers, filmmakers, fine artists, floral arrangers, framers, furniture makers, gardeners, gearheads, graphic artists and cartoonists, interior designers, inventors, installation artists, jewelry makers, knitters, masons, mechanics, metal workers, musicians, origamists, painters, photographers, plumbers, publishers, repair people, scrapbookers, seamstresses, sculptors, sheet-metal workers, software programmers, tailors, weavers, welders, winemakers, writers, and woodworkers. Making is deeply engrained in human nature.

But making has become more difficult in recent years. We have been seduced into buying rather than making, and big companies produce most of the things we use. For start-ups, the barriers to entering a manufacturing business are high. But the roadblocks are falling, and our maker nature is reemerging. In 2012, 86 percent of voters in Massachusetts passed a Right to Repair law that requires automakers to give car owners access to diagnostic and repair information, so they can fix their own cars.[188] 3D printers are a tool for unblocking the road to becoming makers, again.

FROM WOODSHOP TO TECHSHOP

Talking heads who believe the cost of consumer-grade 3D printers (about $400 to $5,000) will deter their widespread adoption underestimate the human drive to make. There are about six million woodworkers in the United States, both professional and amateur.[189] Amateur woodworking is a multibillion-dollar industry. About half a million table saws are sold every year, ranging in price from about $300 to well over $3,000, and a table saw is only one of many machines and tools needed to outfit a woodshop.[190] There is no reason why people will not spend the same for a machine that can make whatever they want. Other people buy lawnmowers and TVs and computers ranging in price from about $500 to $20,000, and they buy them in droves. They will buy 3D printers, too, especially if their neighbor has one.

Amateur woodworkers and other makers work mostly in basement and garage shops. Many choose to make things from wood because wood and the tools and machines to work it are readily available and reasonably priced. Soon after the turn of the twenty-first century, other means of making became more widely available.

Started as an outreach by MIT's Center for Bits and Atoms, fab labs are places where makers can use industrial-grade tools and machines in the company of other makers. All fab labs are open to the public and use common tools and processes so that labs can share information and designs. They are outfitted with traditional machines, digital-design tools (mostly open source), electronics workbenches (mostly based on the open Arduino platform), and, increasingly, consumer-grade 3D printers. One of the largest fab labs, if not *the* largest, opened in 2015 in Haifa, Israel, in the Madatech National Museum of Science, Technology, and Space.[191] FabCafes, a similar concept, have popped up in Barcelona, Taipei, and Tokyo.[192] In 2011, the Idea 2 Product lab was launched in South Africa, where makers can use 3D printers for learning, experimenting, and developing products. The labs have now spread to New Zealand, Singapore, the United Kingdom, and the United States.[193]

Cities are also fostering makerspaces to generate start-ups and rejuvenate their cores. St. Louis launched eight makerspaces, accelerators, and coworking spaces between 2011 and 2013. Oakland, California, opened the airplane-hangar-sized Nimby and the Crucible. Portland, Maine, gave makers a home in the Open Bench Project, which is outfitted for 3D printing and design, as well as wood- and metalworking. Holyoke, Massachusetts, opened Brick Coworkshop in an unloved paper mill. Reno, Nevada, has the immense Generator makerspace.[194]

Hacker spaces are similar places. They are community-operated workspaces where makers and hackers can meet, work, and collaborate. They are less formalized than fab labs and may not be as well outfitted. As of 2012, there were an estimated seven hundred to a thousand hackerspaces worldwide. Their members tend to be fiercely independent and freethinking, and to distrust authority. But they trust each other and collaborate and perpetuate and grow the Maker movement.[195]

Men's Sheds are a bit more formalized than hackerspaces and have a broader mandate (pun intended). They started in Australia as places for men to go for their personal well-being. They are organized into five categories, depending on their members' interests: clinical, communal, educational, recreational, and work focused. The work-focused Men's Sheds are for makers. There are about one thousand Men's Sheds in Australia and others in England, Ireland, Finland, Greece, and Scotland.[196]

All of these makerspaces are nonprofits. A recent for-profit makerspace, TechShop, offers polished, well-outfitted machine shops for makers of all kinds. They are outfitted with consumer-grade 3D printers, woodshops, electronics workbenches, textile shops, digital-design tools, and industrial-grade machine and welding shops. TechShop offers machine time, classes, and community for its maker members.[197] TechShop is banking on humans' instinctive drive to make things and to do so in a community of other makers.

A start-up called Betaversity is taking makerspaces on the road with its BetaBox Mobile Prototyping Labs. BetaBoxes are shipping containers outfitted with 3D printers, CNC routers, and other machines. Betaversity rents out BetaBoxes to start-ups who can't afford fancier digs.[198]

There are hundreds of makerspaces in the United States and thousands throughout the world.[199] You can search for a space to express your inner maker at www.100kgarages.com, www.hackerspace.org, and http://makerspace.com/makerspace-directory.

MAKERS ARE 3D PRINTING NEW START-UPS

The recent flood of consumer-grade Material Extrusion 3D printers was started by makers. Beginning around 2009, several of the pioneering patents for Material Extrusion 3D printers expired.[200] Material Extrusion machines are the simplest kind of 3D printer and can be made from readily available, inexpensive parts. Although some do-it-yourselfers had been making their own 3D printers for years, the expiration of the patents meant that anyone could produce and sell basic Material Extrusion machines, and a boom in consumer-grade 3D printers followed. Early efforts included the RepRap open-source, self-replicating printer and Fab@Home, a printer produced by a group of students at Cornell University.[201] By 2014, more than 250 start-ups worldwide were selling their own Material Extrusion machines.[202]

One such start-up, MakerBot, is a great example of the classic American success story. Born from the RepRap project, MakerBot was started by Adam Mayer, Zach Smith, and the charismatic Bre Pettis in 2009 in Brooklyn, New York, where they made the first MakerBot printers in the Bot Cave. Stratasys bought MakerBot in 2013 for $403 million.[203] The MakerBot 3D printers not only enable makers to make, but are made in America.

3D PRINTERS MAY RETURN US TO OUR MAKER ROOTS

3D printers will rekindle the human drive to be makers. Of course the hurdles are high. As a culture we have lost many of our maker skills and know-how. Some people say we have become lazy, preferring to order products on the Internet rather than leaving our homes to buy them. With such an attitude, they say, how can we expect people to start making things again?

To make us makers again, 3D printers must be very easy to use and must make high-quality and fully functional products very quickly. The

printers must be safe, odor-free, economical to operate, and good looking. They must be as easy to use as a bread machine. I know what you're
thinking: "How many people use bread machines?" True, many people
own bread machines but don't use them, but that is a mark of our buying
culture. My point is that before the bread machine, baking bread was such
a chore that most people had stopped making bread. The bread machine
made it extremely easy to make bread. Insert the ingredients, and the
machine does the rest, producing a loaf of bread with virtually no effort.
When 3D printers are as easy to use as a bread machine and produce
products of greatly diverse functionality with little effort, and when selecting and making a product is as easy as using an app on your smartphone,
people will make things again.

3D printers can also boost self-satisfaction and pride. To design a
product and then turn the blueprint into a real thing is incredibly empowering. Imagine the thrill of pointing to a product admired by your friends
and saying, "I designed that, and I made it."

REDEMOCRATIZATION OF MANUFACTURING

3D printers can also make us feel that we are not tiny gears in a very big
machine. As the effects of the Industrial Revolution trickled down into everyday life, it became more and more difficult for small businesses to bring
complex products to market. In the early days of the automobile and the
airplane, many small companies made cars and planes, partly by hand and
partly with small-scale production techniques. In those days, manufacturing was still democratized. Almost anyone could be a manufacturer. Two
brothers made the first practical airplane in a bicycle repair shop.[204] Then
increasing scale and complexity required megabucks to build increasingly
sophisticated aircraft, which led to mass production, which killed the little
guy.[205] By the time the Great Depression ended, virtually all of those independent makers had disappeared, either forced to close their doors or
swallowed up by a big company. And today, for a start-up to introduce

an independently produced car is a gargantuan task. Witness Brickland, DeLorean, Fisker, and Tesla.

3D printers can empower small businesses to make big things, to re-democratize manufacturing, which according to the Brookings Institution is an inevitable effect of 3D printing.[206] Because it costs less to 3D print a finished product, small businesses can make sophisticated products that compete with the big guys. The return of the entrepreneur to products like planes and cars is envisioned by people like Professor Andy Keane of the University of Southampton in the United Kingdom:[207]

> What's interesting to us is the way 3D printing can enable small companies to work. Three guys in a garage can suddenly have the manufacturing capability to produce things of immense complexity, which, once upon a time, they couldn't have dreamed of. You don't have to be McDonnell Douglas to do it anymore. I kind of hope that 3D printing will democratize the whole aerospace business back to where it was a hundred years ago, when there were lots of small companies doing interesting things.

This type of making is what humans are good at. It feeds our souls and turns our eyes to the stars. It fosters design competition and technical innovation, the creation of products we only dreamed of. 3D printing can make us makers, again.

4

Shrinking the World and Bringing Jobs Home

REVERSING THE TREND

America has been bleeding factory jobs since World War II, as have other countries with high intellectual capital and high standards of living. The UK is in a similar pickle. As its empire slowly faded, so did factory jobs. While delivering a speech in Australia, I heard the same laments we have heard in the United States for years: jobs are being lost to countries with substantially lower wages. And factory job shrinkage is not confined to the English-speaking world. In the 1980s, Japan was America's manufacturing nemesis and seemed economically unstoppable. But it now shares our boat. With a stagnant economy and high manufacturing costs, Japan is offshoring some manufacturing to China, which replaced it as the number two economy. 3D printing will reverse these trends, rocking *where* we make things by bringing manufacturing back to the countries that are losing it.

3D printing will fuel a manufacturing renaissance in countries with high intellectual capital and high manufacturing costs, such as the United States, the United Kingdom, Japan, and Australia. When companies can make things, profitably, at the point of need, without concern for economies of scale, we will eliminate boom-and-bust economies. Large companies will be replaced by thousands or tens of thousands of small companies, and regional manufacturing will repatriate jobs, putting most countries on a sustainable path. A global shift from centralized to distributed manufacturing could lead to short-term conflicts between nations. However, countries that currently dominate global manufacturing will, in the long term, make products mostly for their own people.

MORE OUTPUT, FEWER JOBS

The United States has lost millions of manufacturing jobs, which have been moving offshore for decades. In 2014, America's trade deficit in physical goods was $738 billion.[208] More disturbingly, US manufacturing output has been increasing as employment declines. In fact, while manufacturing output has steadily increased since the end of World War II, US manufacturing jobs peaked around 1975 and have been steadily declining ever since.[209]

This probably means that US manufacturers are becoming increasingly efficient because they can make more things with fewer people. But as we lose more and more jobs to faraway places, a big question arises: What are Americans to do for work? 3D printing may be a big part of the answer to that question.

BRINGING JOBS HOME

3D printing enables products to be made where they are needed, not in remote places from which they are shipped to the point of need. Because 3D printers can make entire parts or products with fewer machines, fewer steps, and therefore fewer people, they can eliminate the benefits of making things where labor is cheap. Right now, China is a manufacturing powerhouse because factory wages are low. As China's costs of skilled labor rise, it may find itself in the same position as the United States, United Kingdom, Australia, Japan, and most of Western Europe. According to the Boston Consulting Group, the net cost of manufacturing in China will soon match that of the United States.[210]

China also has other problems that may cause it to slip from its manufacturing high horse. But there are plenty of other countries waiting in line to become the next, or the next, or the next low-cost place to make things: Thailand, Vietnam, the Philippines, all of Africa, much of South America, and Eastern Europe. 3D printing can break the boom-and-bust cycle of chasing the next cheap labor force.

The same product made by ten or twelve traditional machines, in ten or twelve steps, by ten or twelve or more operators, can be made with one 3D printer. Currently, 3D printed parts and products need substantial postproduction work to make them ready to use. In time, however, that problem will mostly disappear. Fully formed, ready-to-use products will emerge from 3D printers, much as Athena sprang full-blown from the head of Zeus, although those products may be very different from the products we know today.

For some products, labor cost is not the only factor determining where they are made. And 3D printers are not the only machines that increase factory efficiency and reduce labor costs. The use of robotics also reduces manufacturing and labor costs. According to a report from the McKinsey consulting firm:[211]

> For industries with high-value goods, in which rapid innovation is more important than absolute cost, the combination of 3D printing of products and advanced robotics…could make proximity to end markets and access to highly skilled talent more important than hourly labor rates in determining where production is located. This could lead some advanced economy companies to produce more goods domestically, boosting local economies. However, this may not create many manufacturing jobs, as the 3D printing process is highly automated.

Even for lower-value goods, the combination of 3D printing and advanced robotics may make it economically feasible to make them in expensive places. But the implications are obvious: more manufacturing in America and our fellow-traveler countries, but not many jobs running the machines. Ten manufacturing jobs lost in low-wage countries may create only one job in a 3D printing economy, but let's be careful to compare apples to apples. If it takes ten people to operate the traditional machines needed to make a single part, it may take only one person to operate the 3D printer that makes that part in America. To the optimist, that is one more manufacturing job than we had without 3D printing. To the pessimist, we still need nine more jobs. But the pessimist is missing an important point: if the part is made in America (or Australia or Japan) by a local worker operating the 3D printer, most if not all of the supply and distribution chain will be there, too, or at least it can be.

DISTRIBUTED MANUFACTURING

Beginning in the latter third of the twentieth century, manufacturing became highly centralized in Asia, first in Japan and then in China and, to a lesser degree, in Taiwan and South Korea. In the early twenty-first century, we became accustomed to thinking of products being centrally made *en masse*, in huge factories staffed by thousands of people in white uniforms, in whatever Asian country could do it most efficiently.

Before China became the manufacturing flavor of the day, Japan was cranking out huge numbers of products from central locations (and still does). Before Japan, it was America. In America's manufacturing heyday, which declined after World War II, most cars came from giant factories in Detroit. Most steel came from gargantuan US steel mills. America had huge factories with lots of workers.

Before about 1970, things were different. Manufacturing was not centralized in one country or a few countries. Certainly the United States was the world's greatest manufacturer, but many countries had manufacturing might. The Brits had a manufacturing empire until after World War I. In the 1930s and early 1940s, Germany and Japan certainly demonstrated their ability to make things. Up to World War II, manufacturing was more evenly distributed across the planet. Some places had more factories than others, but countries and companies were generally able to compete in the world manufacturing arena.

After World War II, workers in many Western countries began to enjoy a substantially higher standard of living than their parents or grandparents. But this came at a price: as wages rose, companies found it harder and harder to make things profitably in the places where they would be bought and used. Factories began to move offshore. Factory workers lost jobs. Remaining US factories employed fewer people.

Moving offshore cost many US manufacturing jobs. As time marched on, US companies found that they simply couldn't compete with highly centralized foreign manufacturers. One by one, products stopped being made in America, or by American companies: TVs, cameras, clothes. Products that could still be made in America, such as cars, now faced stiff competition from Asia. The same happened in many other countries. Instead of globally distributed manufacturing, more and more products were made in only a few Asian countries. Distributed manufacturing gave way to centralized manufacturing.

Because chasing cheap labor is unnecessary in a 3D printed world, this technology can break the grip of centralized manufacturing. But don't assume that huge factories will simply replace their traditional machines with 3D printers, and life will go on as before. As 3D printers become more and more capable of making almost any finished product, centralized mass production may no longer be needed and, as a business model, may become as antiquated as the dinosaur. Like a superstrong magnet, 3D printing will pull manufacturing away from the manufacturing hubs and redistribute it, product by product, among thousands or tens of thousands of smaller factories across the globe. China and Japan will remain manufacturing giants but will serve mostly their own people. Things will again be made throughout the world and even in places where few things have ever been made, such as Africa, large parts of Asia, and South America. As the Atlantic Council said:[212]

> If production is decentralized, then mass production of hundreds of thousands of a given product may be done by producing thousands on one hundred printers that are near the source of demand around the world rather than at one factory producing hundreds of thousands of the same item.

The rising tide of 3D printing can float all boats. Distributed and regional manufacturing could also grow the economies of developing countries, helping to relieve hunger and homelessness.[213] According to a report by Allied Market Research, the 3D printing market in emerging economies should reach $4.5 billion by 2020, which is a compound annual growth rate (CAGR) of 37.4 percent.[214] As Columbia professor Hod Lipson and industry analyst Melba Kurman wrote in their book *Fabricated: The New World of 3D Printing,* "The upside of democratizing the power of production is that disenfranchised people gain personal empowerment."[215]

Compared to the way it used to be, distributed manufacturing will be very different in a 3D printed world.

REGIONAL MANUFACTURING

During the twentieth century, manufacturing became more and more centralized. It wasn't always that way. Before the Industrial Revolution, products were made near where they were needed. This was partly because shipping and communication weren't as easy as today, so economies were more localized, and mass production had not been invented. 3D printing can take us back to the days when most things were made where they were needed, or nearby. As Banning Garrett said in the Atlantic Council report "Could 3D Printing Change the World?," "The Internet first eliminated distance as a factor in moving information and now AM [additive manufacturing] eliminates it for the material world."[216] Reversing the globalization trend of the last fifty years, 3D printing will make the world smaller.

As the 3D printing magnet pulls factories back to the United States, the United Kingdom, Australia, and Japan, don't expect them to look like the massive factories of yesteryear. And don't expect manufacturing to be confined to a few major hubs. Instead, think small and think many. 3D printers don't need huge factories. Because one machine will be able to make a finished product, thousands of such machines can distribute manufacturing over thousands of places, via thousands of small companies. No single machine will be called on to mass-produce a product. Instead, it will make the quantity of the product needed locally and customize it, too.

Some experts speculate that 3D printing will replace mass production, while other experts say it will never happen. As a general rule of thumb, critics should probably never say never, but these experts may not be addressing the right question, which is whether mass production is needed in a 3D printed world, which I discuss later in the book. Here I'll say that it makes no sense to 3D print huge numbers of products in faraway places, then ship them all over the world. 3D printers soon will be able make entire products, fully assembled and ready to use. They will do so with minimal labor, making things on an as-needed, when-needed, and where-needed basis. Supply chains will be shorter and more localized, and distribution chains also will be shorter, with little physical distance between the maker and the user.

3D printing also eliminates or reduces the need for warehousing. Products can be made just in time and delivered immediately. Even where products need to be kept in inventory, 3D printing can be used to print multiple parts as one, reducing the variety of parts that need to be warehoused.

IBM expects that 3D printing and smart robotics will result in "a radical relocalization of global manufacturing." According to its report,[217]

> 3D printing and robotic assembly will significantly reduce the need for large supplier networks or vast extended supply chains. The reduced requirement for scale will also have a big impact on the location of production: the optimal manufacturing location by 2022 is regional or local rather than global.
>
> The result of this is a supply chain that is no longer big, complex, and global. Rather, it will be comparatively small, simple, and local.

Andrew Sissons and Spencer Thompson reached the same conclusion in their white paper "Three Dimensional Policy: Why Britain Needs a Policy Framework for 3D Printing,"[218] as did the Atlantic Council in its strategic foresight report "Could 3D Printing Change the World?"[219] So did Hod Lipson and Melba Kurman in *Fabricated: The New World of 3D Printing.*[220] The Wohlers Report made a similar observation:[221]

> When a single AM [additive manufacturing] machine can build complex parts, the economies of scale associated with large centralized factories with assembly lines are reduced. The distribution of all or part of the manufacturing on a more regional or even local basis becomes economically feasible.

HP said it simply when it announced its own 3D printer: "3D printing will revolutionize part manufacturing and the part distribution supply chain by offering local, on-demand production."[222]

Instead of Goliath factories making millions of identical products in centralized locations, 3D printing and robotics can bring manufacturing to small towns all over the world, where thousands (or tens of thousands) of small companies will make things in smaller quantities where they are needed and used. Just as making was once highly localized, 3D printing can make it so again.

Whether by accident or plan, America seems to be embracing regional additive manufacturing. During his 2013 State of the Union address, President Obama said, "Last year, we created our first manufacturing innovation institute in Youngstown, Ohio. A once-shuttered warehouse is now a state-of-the art lab where new workers are mastering 3D printing."[223] He was referring to America Makes, the National Additive Manufacturing Innovation Institute, a joint public/private partnership underwritten by the government, businesses, and universities in Youngstown, Ohio.[224] Youngstown State University also opened a Center for Innovation in Additive Manufacturing.[225] The plan is not just to open 3D printing factories but also to focus the entire city on generating manufacturing jobs. As Walter Wessel wrote, "On all fronts, from elementary schools, to public libraries, to local manufacturers, and local Makerspaces, the same energy that once made Youngstown a thriving industrial focal point during its steel-making heyday is now being focused to turn the city into a 3D printing powerhouse."[226]

President Obama also said, "There's no reason this can't happen in other towns. So tonight, I'm announcing the launch of three more of these manufacturing hubs, where businesses will partner with the Departments of Defense and Energy to turn regions left behind by globalization into global centers of high-tech jobs." Joining the flagship institute in Youngstown are innovation institutes and manufacturing hubs in Detroit, Chicago, and Raleigh-Durham, North Carolina.

The Chicago hub, called the Digital Manufacturing and Design Innovation Institute, will establish a state-of-the art proving ground for digital manufacturing and design, including an open-source online platform called the Digital Manufacturing Commons that "allows users to share real-time designing and manufacturing data during the design-make process and across the product life cycle." [227] The purpose of the Detroit hub, called the Lightweight and Modern Metals Manufacturing Innovation Institute (also known as LM31), is self-explanatory. The North Carolina hub is a consortium of businesses and universities led by North Carolina State University, charged with developing advanced power electronics.[228] If all goes as planned, these regional hubs will be joined by eleven more, all focused on emerging technologies. "Now's the time," the President said, "to reach a new level of research and development not seen since the height of the Space Race."[229]

Such regional hubs are just the beginning. There may always be regions that are bigger and richer than others, or that make some things better than others, or where it makes sense to make them because that is where their raw materials are. But as additive manufacturing progressively becomes the method of choice, there is no reason why products cannot be made almost anywhere, by thousands or tens of thousands of small companies. In fact, this is already happening. The number of independent 3D printing companies is growing all over the world. These "service bureaus," "fabricators," or "fabs" are small factories 3D printing prototypes, parts, and products for big and small companies, and even for consumers. Some have only one type of 3D printer and specialize in making certain types of parts. Others have banks of different kinds of 3D printers and are capable of making things that push the envelope of the technology.

Of course thousands of small, local businesses may not 3D print every product. Surely specialists will emerge. One company may 3D print only fuel injectors for jet engines, another may make bespoke hip or knee replacements, both using metal Powder Bed Fusion to print them in one piece. Another may 3D print airplane seats, in one piece, from materials that can be stiff or cushiony, as needed and on demand. Some 3D printing companies will have better customization choices, such as for silverware or eyeglasses or shoes. Others will make one product, or even one part, very well and sell it to a neighboring business to complete the product that it 3D prints. For example, two companies together might collaborate to produce custom blenders, with one company 3D printing the blender base—motor, switches, and outer shell—while the company next door 3D prints the pitcher from glass or a glass-like composite. Other companies will make products only needed locally, such as replacement parts for farm machinery. The face of distributed, regional manufacturing will be as varied as entrepreneurs can conceive and local markets will support.

CAN'T CHINA STILL DO IT CHEAPER?

Cynics might say that low-cost countries will always be the manufacturing powerhouses. If ten Chinese (or Vietnamese or Colombian) workers can now make a product cheaper than ten US (or UK or Japanese) workers, it will still cost less for one Chinese worker to 3D print the same product than it will cost one US worker to do so. This argument assumes that 3D printing will not change the world in other ways. In fact, it will change everything.

Today, many products are made in low-cost labor markets mainly because they cannot be made profitably in high-cost markets, not because companies prefer to make their products outside their borders or import them from foreign makers. When companies in far-off lands start making products of comparable quality to US-made products, at a substantially lower cost, companies are forced to move manufacturing operations to such countries. But if those companies could build their products at home, and still compete, they would do so. Why make a product in Asia and ship it to America if it can be made competitively at home? Why buy it from a foreign company if it can be made in America?

The cost of one US worker versus one Chinese worker is also only part of the equation. Although the labor costs of one skilled worker in the developing world may always be lower than the cost of one worker in the United States (or Japan), the product still needs to be individually packaged, bundled with more of its kind, handled by at least one or two shippers, loaded onto a ship, sailed across the world, unloaded, then handled by at least one or two more shippers before it reaches its final destination. It may also pass through several more layers of customs agents, warehousing, distribution, and retail before it ends up in your living room. By comparison, your local 3D fabricator can print your customized product, and you can pick it up on your way home from work. It may not even need a box. Thus, to compare the cost of making products in low-cost countries to high-cost countries, you need to look at total costs, or all-in costs, and figure out which costs can be avoided by making products close to where they are needed.

Mass customization is another reason why distributed and regional 3D printing can beat centralized manufacturing. One hallmark of the Industrial Revolution was uniformity: products could be mass-produced economically, with uniform appearance, quality, and features. 3D printers can make a one-of-a-kind product as cheaply as a million, so there is no need to mass-produce to obtain economies of scale. Or to be more accurate, economies of scale can be achieved for one-off products. More importantly, there is no reason to have mass uniformity in appearance and features. Customizing a product's appearance to the user's needs or whims is as easy as tweaking the digital blueprint, which will become easier and easier with time, with no reduction in quality. Although millions of products *could* be mass-customized in faceless factories in low-cost lands, customization is the currency of the little guy, not monolithic manufacturers.

Anyone over the age of forty can probably remember a time in America when service was king. Small businesses thrived because merchants knew their customers' names, cheerfully ordered special products for them, held the last of something aside just for them, delivered the product to their door, and extended personal credit. Personal service was the rule, not the exception, even when fueling your car, where the attendant would fill your tank, check your oil, and clean your windshield. Maybe those days and that type of personal service are long gone (at least in America; it is still common in Asia), but the ability to make customized 3D printed products is an incredible opportunity for new service-oriented small businesses.

Combining the one-of-a-kind economies of scale of 3D printing with customization yields a powerful paradigm shift to personalized product manufacturing. This style of making is best done locally, by small businesses. There may always be a place for certain mass-produced products of huge companies, but many products that are mass-produced now could be 3D printed and customized in smaller quantities by many smaller companies that serve mainly local markets.

Moreover, although mass-customizing or mass-personalizing products in a central factory is possible, shipping them may not be. Today, large factories make massive quantities of the same item, pack them in boxes, and ship various quantities of the same product to different places. But shipping is much more complicated for mass-customized products. Seven copies of a customized product would need to be shipped to one place, five hundred copies of another customized product would need to be shipped to another place, and one copy of ten thousand other customized products would need to be shipped to ten thousand different places. In a large centralized factory, the logistics of shipping such items as they come out of the 3D printers would be a nightmare. Because the total output of regional manufacturers will be much smaller, logistics and shipping will be easier.

China is building immense 3D printing factories at great expense. If they plan to use them to make things for their own people, it may be money well spent. There are certainly enough Chinese people to buy and use the goods that such megafactories can make. Because the cost-effectiveness of 3D printing does not depend on economies of scale, China would better use its money to build regional manufacturing hubs around which local economies could grow and flourish. More bang for the buck, more people served.

If products can be 3D printed at home at competitive costs, manufacturing will return for another reason: national pride. Consumers would feel better knowing a product came from a homegrown business or a local manufacturer, rather than from a foreign factory that was only able to make the product because the offshore worker displaced a local worker. Thus, if faced with a choice of 3D printing a product in a low-cost economy or making it at home at a competitive cost, most companies will do the right thing and bring jobs home.

Of course it would be easy to screw it up. Governments could easily destroy the home-court advantages of 3D printing with laws and regulations relating to intellectual property rights, taxes, insurance, product safety, import and export control, and what 3D printers are and are not allowed to print. Bowing to political correctness, the popular scare of the day, and a few squeaky wheels, governments are skilled at regulating innovation into the rubbish heap. Instead, they should provide tax incentives to foster regional additive manufacturing and ask of every proposed law and regulation whether it is more likely to bring jobs home or destroy them.

It is important that governments not screw this up. 3D printing may be the last best chance for countries like the United States to secure their manufacturing future. In fact, failing to develop regional additive manufacturing would jeopardize the national security of any country that has lost or is losing its factories. America and its fellow travelers cannot afford to be in the position of not being able to make anything and everything they need in times of crisis.

SIZE MAY NOT MATTER

Since the dawn of the Industrial Revolution, manufacturing has been based on economies of scale. It was not cost effective to make the tooling and dies to manufacture only one car. After investing thousands of dollars back then—or millions today—to build a single car, the sale price would have been out of reach for all but the rich. Historically, mass production has been the only way to cover the ramp-up costs of making products.

It is very difficult to think any other way. Although custom coach builders made custom cars for the wealthy in the early days of the automobile, such luxuries were eventually replaced by homogenized Hudsons, Fords, and Chevys. Even today, custom products are mostly toys of the wealthy, offered by small companies run by a few artisans. Big manufacturing companies don't think in terms of making one-of-a-kind products. Even people who think and write about 3D printing are stuck on questions like: Will 3D printing ever be capable of mass production? If so, when? When will it be fast enough to compete with mass production techniques like injection molding?

Maybe these are valid questions. Maybe not. I'll explore this topic later. But one of the great strengths of 3D printing is that it can achieve economies of scale with a single product. Because of this, customization adds nothing to the product's cost; the ability to customize is gravy. The real benefit is that after mastering 3D printing, small companies can make the product in small quantities on small production lines. With 3D printing, size no longer matters.

IBM grasped this concept and flipped it on its head: "Compared to traditional manufacturing, significantly lower production volumes will be necessary to operate efficiently. Capital expense requirements will decrease."[230] IBM's point is that 3D printing not only makes it economical to make high-quality, finished products without mass production, but it is also most efficient when making smaller quantities. And what company wouldn't want to design its factory so that less capital was needed to build it? This is exactly the opposite of how companies have thought for more than a century. Instead of assuming that efficiency demands large production numbers and that economies of scale require huge capital investments, 3D printing makes small-scale fabrication not only financially feasible but also optimally efficient at such a scale.

At least one big consumer goods company, which sells products by the millions, is starting to think small. Seeing the future of 3D printing and smart robotics, it is "preparing for an era when volumes for individual products will be measured in the hundreds or thousands, not millions. It is actively looking at swapping out plastic injection molding systems for 3D printers and determining how product design must change to use the full power of 3D printers."[231] Unfortunately, IBM, who reported the news, was not at liberty to reveal the name of this forward-thinking company.

Thinking small with 3D printing will not be a radical change for many US companies. Although US manufacturing usually calls to mind huge companies like Ford, GE, Boeing, and Pfizer, roughly half of US manufacturing companies are small businesses with fewer than ten employees. A quarter of US manufacturing companies employ fewer than five people.[232] For US manufacturing, small has become increasingly more beautiful since the turn of the twenty-first century. The number of US companies with more than fifty employees shrank for the first ten years of this century, while the number of companies employing fewer than fifty people has steadily grown (except for an adjustment during the economic crisis in 2008–2009). Really big companies (employing more than five hundred people) did the worst, losing numbers faster than smaller companies. Sixty percent of new jobs generated from 2009 to 2013 were created by small businesses.[233]

Thus, the scale at which 3D printing works best is already business as usual for half of US factories. Although grasping many of the benefits of 3D printing requires an epiphany and a radical commitment to update old ways of thinking, American businesses already understand that small is beautiful.

ECONOMIC IMPACT
For more than half a century, the United States and Great Britain have been bleeding jobs. The bleeding started more recently Down Under and in the Land of the Rising Sun, and Australia's and Japan's wounds are getting worse, not healing. 3D printing holds the promise not only to staunch the hemorrhaging of jobs to low-cost markets but also to reverse the flow.

This will happen on both the industrial and consumer levels. The use of 3D printers on the industrial level will continue to grow, redefining how products are made, how they look, and even what they are. 3D printing will change who makes products, who sells them, and who buys them. New businesses will be created to serve and exploit industrial 3D printing. According to a McKinsey 3D printing study:[234]

> 3D printing could become an increasingly common approach for highly complex, low-volume, highly customizable parts. If used in this way, we estimate that 3D printing could generate $100 billion to $200 billion in economic impact per year by 2025 from direct manufacturing of parts. The market for complex, low-volume, highly customizable parts, such as medical implants and engine components, could be $770 billion annually by 2025, and it is

possible that some 30 to 50 percent of these products could be 3D printed. These products could cost 40 to 55 percent less due to the elimination of tooling costs, reduction in wasted material, and reduced handling costs.

On the consumer level, there is already an explosion of companies making low-cost, consumer-grade 3D printers. Although these machines are primitive and incapable of making much more than Yoda heads and smartphone cases, they serve a crucial role: introducing more and more people, especially kids, to the potentials of the technology. Among those people will be a very special few who will recognize the potential of consumer-level 3D printing and help to transform its future. The very fact that such early adopters will be frustrated by the current limitations of consumer 3D printers will spur some of them to improve the current technology and guarantee its rapid improvement. According to the McKinsey study:[235]

> 3D printing could generate economic impact of $230 billion to $550 billion per year by 2025 in [certain markets]. The largest source of potential impact...would be from consumer uses, followed by direct manufacturing and the use of 3D printing to create tools and molds.

But because the 3D printing-related jobs are likely to be distributed and regional, 3D printing will put more US and Australian dollars, pounds sterling, and yen into more local pockets, rather than into a few centralized corporate coffers. The average business in a 3D printed world is likely to be small, and there may be tens of thousands of them, serving local or regional markets or very specific product niches. Don't get me wrong. I am an unapologetic capitalist and don't begrudge any company any amount of profit. But 3D printing has the potential to redefine the corporate world, replacing the S&P 500 with the S&P 50,000.

WHEN WILL THE JOBS COME?

IBM examined whether it would be feasible to make a hearing aid, a mobile phone, an industrial LCD display, and a washing machine using 3D printing, smart robotics, and open-source technology. They dissected each product, piece by piece:[236]

> For each component, we assessed whether or not it could be 3D printed or have an embedded electronics component replaced with an open source alternative. We assessed each assembly step in the same way, determining if sophisticated skilled labor was required or if it could be assembled with the newest generation of robots.

IBM's conclusion surprised even me. Within only a few years, "a significant portion" of these products could be 3D printed by robots, they said, using open-source components, at reduced cost.[237] Of course, this is a double-edged sword. The reason washing machines and smartphones may be able to be 3D printed at reduced cost is that robots will replace some people on the factory floor. Reduced costs may bring the manufacturing of such products back to our shores, but the jobs for humans in these factories may be few and highly skilled. But they are still net-gain manufacturing jobs because a product that was not and could not be made in the United States may once again be made here, and its supply and distribution chains come along with it.

But I haven't really answered the "when" question. IBM does not say the entire product can be 3D printed in five years, or when such manufacturing will return to the United States. But the process has already begun. And as the machines get better and better, faster and faster, and more and more sophisticated, the jobs will come as more and more of this kind of manufacturing is done in countries with high labor costs. Bill Gates said that we tend to overestimate the things that can happen in two years and underestimate the things that can happen in ten.[238] The *New York Times* predicts that 3D printers will "become a part of our daily lives...much sooner than anyone anticipated."[239] 3D Systems' CEO, Avi Reichental, echoes the *New York Times* when he says, "We live in exponential times."[240] My prediction is that by 2025, 3D printing will be fully integrated into a vibrant US manufacturing economy.

ROCKING GEOPOLITICS

Some countries may not like the 3D printed world that lies ahead. As manufacturing is gradually but inexorably repatriated to countries that are currently losing the ability to make things, the countries who are today's low-cost manufacturing powerhouses may experience death by a thousand cuts. The same could be true of corporate conglomerates, as small becomes ever more beautiful.

In a 3D printed world, distributed and regional manufacturing means no more centralized manufacturing centers, no more huge factories employing thousands of people, no more global supply and distribution chains, but also no more boom-and-bust economies.

As Briar Thompson wrote in her insightful Pacific Security Scholars policy brief on 3D printing, "This could have flow on effects for international relations, particularly changing relationships with low-cost, low-wage countries currently manufacturing many goods for export."[241] As global manufacturing shifts from centralized mass production to regional and distributed manufacturing, geopolitical tensions could rise. Those who stand the most to lose will not go gently into that good night. Trade wars or real wars may be fought over where and how products will be made, but such wars are usually a losing game, a last-ditch effort to preserve a way of doing things that no longer works. For long-term geopolitical stability, the world really needs a manufacturing system that avoids boom-and-bust cycles. Booms are great while they last, but they can be hell when they end. Regional and distributed manufacturing driven by 3D printing holds the promise of flourishing economies, worldwide.

5

Rocking Business as Usual and Creating Jobs You Never Heard Of

EVERY NOOK AND CRANNY

During his 2013 State of the Union address, President Obama rocketed 3D printing to the national consciousness when he said, "A once-shuttered warehouse is now a state-of-the art lab where new workers are mastering 3D printing; that has the potential to revolutionize the way we make almost everything."[242] The president's words heralded the first days of the 3D printing manufacturing renaissance. But the jobs created by 3D printing won't be your grandfather's factory jobs.

3D printing democratizes manufacturing. Lower costs mean lower barriers to entry, and the effect on industry will be profound. Business as usual will be rocked on a global scale as 3D printing reaches into every nook and cranny of almost every economy; eliminating assembly lines and reducing the number of jobs for unskilled workers, while creating new jobs for skilled workers; simplifying supply and distribution chains; shaking the foundations on which companies, markets, and economies are built; blurring the lines between manufacturers and customers; encouraging some companies to sell designs, not products; and forcing others to do so (especially companies that depend on selling replacement and spare parts). Traditional manufacturing, distribution, shipping, warehousing, and retail will experience earthshaking disruptions.

On the consumer level, most homes will have a 3D printer. Everything will change when consumers can make almost any product they need or want *away from control* (meaning that no one knows about it and no one can control it). When consumers start making rather than buying on a large scale, the need for mass production will diminish. Markets once dominated by a few huge players will be transformed as existing companies, start-ups, former customers, and end users start making, selling, and using products and services that never existed before.

END OF THE LINE

Harvard economist Ricardo Hausmann said in an interview about 3D printing:[243]

> Historically you think of manufacturing as an assembly line with thousands of workers, the UAW [United Auto Workers union], and benefits. But here we are talking about very small batches, made close to consumers, and customized. It will still be manufacturing, but a different kind of job in a different kind of company whose organization we don't yet know.

The days of thousands of unskilled American factory workers performing highly repetitive, mindless tasks along an assembly line are gone for good. Bob Appleton, who consults for the US Marine Corps, wrote that 3D printing "is the most disruptive technology since the assembly line."[244] This is because 3D printing will essentially eliminate it. An additive manufacturing factory will employ few, if any, unskilled workers and not many skilled workers. The factory of the future in the United States, the United Kingdom, Australia, and Japan will be inhabited mostly by 3D printers, robots, and other advanced machines, all driven by software. Some people will be needed on the factory floor to make sure everything is humming along, but the jobs they will do then may not exist today. The systems they will run also may not exist today or exist only in rudimentary form. Some of the companies they will work for do not exist today, or may be very different in ten years from what they are today. Anyone who doubts this should look at the thirty companies that make up the Dow Jones Industrial Average. Only four of the companies on the Dow in 1956 are on it today, only sixteen from 1991.[245] Even without the paradigm-shifting potential of 3D printing, big companies come and go. Kodak is a great example.

As technology advances, there will be little place on the factory floor for unskilled workers. In fact, even today there are fewer and fewer jobs for workers without skills or a college education. Between October 2008, when the world economic crisis began, and mid-2014, the US unemployment rate hovered in the 6–10 percent range.[246] But during that same time period, the unemployment rate for college-educated workers (bachelor's degree or higher) was only about 3–5 percent.[247]

In a 3D printed world, the demand for skilled workers will increase,[248] but as Ricardo Hausmann said, we don't know yet exactly what their jobs will be like. Some of those jobs are easy to guess. People will be needed to run the 3D printers, robots, and other machines. People will be needed at every step of the now-localized supply and distribution chain, even though their jobs will be radically different than they are today. People will be needed to build the factories, the 3D printers and other machines, and the robots, and to make the materials the printers will use. People will be needed to write the software for the machines. People will be needed to service the machines.

These jobs were easy to guess because they originate in old business models, old paradigms. In the sections that follow, I explore the types of jobs that may emerge from the havoc that 3D printing will wreak as it replaces—or even if it only supplements—traditional manufacturing.

WHAT DOES DEMOCRATIZED MANUFACTURING LOOK LIKE?

Distributed and regional manufacturing are the result of democratized manufacturing, and are possible only when the barriers to entry are low enough that new companies can start making things that economics made impossible before. Bringing jobs home, making the world smaller, making small beautiful, and rocking geopolitics are all effects of the democratization of manufacturing and cannot happen without it.

Enabling companies to make things and generating jobs sounds great. But the democratization of manufacturing cannot be viewed through a business-as-usual lens. Big companies cannot assume that simply installing 3D printers will make everything right and that homegrown profits will just start rolling in. The effect of lowering entry barriers is that all manufacturers will be forced to evolve, and competition may become fierce. The company that enters one end of a 3D printing factory will look very different when it comes out the other.

The democratization of manufacturing has a natural spreading effect, redistributing the ability to make things. For example, if two companies supply all of the products in a particular market, such as hammers, the democratization of manufacturing that product could bring forty-eight new companies into the market. Assuming the hammer market does not grow, the original two companies' markets shares could drop from 50 percent each to 2 percent each. The effects of worldwide distributed and regional manufacturing could be much greater. Thousands or tens of thousands of fabricators will be able to 3D print hammers, on demand, for their local customers. Or anyone may be able to print one with a personal machine at home. In a world without barriers to entry, where any company or any person can make almost anything, big companies may find it harder to stay big.

There will probably always be big companies because democratization of manufacturing is not a guarantee of success. Product design, innovation, quality, price, efficiency, value-added, and service ultimately will separate the winners from the losers. Big companies also may stay big, or get bigger, by acquiring upstart competitors. But the industries, companies big and small, and products that result from 3D printing–driven democratization of manufacturing will look very different than they do today.

BREAKING CHAINS

According to IBM, "[d]espite having yielded so much success, the era of big, complex and global supply chains is drawing to a close."[249] To illustrate 3D printing's disruptive potential, let's look at the steps necessary to get a Sears Kenmore washing machine from the factory to you.† Sears management orders, say, one thousand washing machines from its Chinese manufacturer, who orders from its Chinese suppliers the parts and supplies that it doesn't make, such as steel, circuit boards, and paint. Those parts and supplies are transported to the factory and arrive exactly when they are needed, as the washing machine makes its way down the assembly line, passing from worker to worker, robot to robot. The machines are then boxed up, warehoused until they are ready to ship, and transported to the shipyard. They are then loaded into shipping containers and lowered into the hold of the ship. The ship then sails for the United States, dodging pirates along the way. When the ship arrives, probably in California, longshoremen unload the containers. The washing machines are then warehoused until they clear US customs. They are then transferred to trucks or trains, or both, and shipped to distribution centers, where they are warehoused. Some of the machines are then loaded into trucks or trains, or both, and shipped to stores, where they are warehoused until you buy one. Your washing machine is then loaded onto a truck and driven to your house, where it is unloaded and installed. This is a simplification. I probably missed many steps.

---

† I chose Sears because it was the Amazon of the late nineteenth century and most of the twentieth. With its slogan, "Sears Has Everything," it shipped any product from its extensive catalog to anyone, anywhere. Sears would benefit from returning to its roots.

In a manufacturing world dominated by 3D printing, most of those steps would be eliminated. A floor sample of the machine sits in a show-room or is described online. After you order it, it is 3D printed by a fabricator in your area, on demand, and delivered to your door, with minimal protective packaging. No inventory, no cargo ships, one truck, no foreign workers, and a much smaller carbon footprint. Remember, IBM says that "a significant portion" of your washing machine can be 3D printed by robots, using open-source components, at reduced cost, in a few years,[250] and it will probably look radically different from the machine you know today. After that, it will not be long before the whole machine can be 3D printed by authorized fabricators all over the country.

To make and deliver your washing machine this way, Sears will substantially simplify its supply chain and save a lot of money. It also eliminates risks, such as the risk that the ship will sink, pirates will attack, trucks will crash, warehouses will catch fire, or that the machines won't sell, forcing Sears to sell remaining inventory at fire-sale prices. Of course, there are also far fewer people responsible for making and delivering your 3D printed washing machine.

Breaking and simplifying supply and distribution chains is good for the planet, Sears, and you. But not everyone everywhere will be happy. Not only will many unskilled jobs be lost, but businesses, economies, and countries where the chains are broken will be completely disrupted. Because manufacturing countries have a lot invested in the existing system, the social and economic effects will be devastating unless they plan for the day when the chains are broken. If these countries fail to plan, geopolitical instability, if not war, could result. As 3D printing industry analyst Alex Chausovsky observed, "Economies that rely on cheap factory labor…may find themselves in deep trouble—with all the security consequences that go with that."[251] Although distributed and regional manufacturing may eliminate boom-and-bust economies, failure to plan for the last bust could have serious results that ripple across the face of the planet.

But there need not be a last bust. Let's remember that the countries that stand to lose the most from such disruption have their own people with their own product needs. The supply and distribution chains that now stretch across the oceans can be shortened to accommodate distributed and regional manufacturing needs in disrupted countries. Jobs for un-skilled workers will surely be lost, but 3D printing will cause a radical re-distribution of jobs in countries that relied on worldwide supply chains, as businesses adapt, fail, or are newly invented.

BLURRING LINES AND SHAKING FOUNDATIONS: A PARABLE

Things are pretty simple today. Companies know where they stand in the competitive landscapes of their industries. They know what a supplier is, and they know who their customers are. But in a world where virtually any-one can manufacture, the lines will blur between manufacturers, design-ers, retailers, and customers.

Parts industries are great examples. Many industrial manufacturing companies sell big machines with lots of parts. Some make little profit sell-ing the machine but make big money selling replacement parts. Selling parts is how big companies become really profitable. Take Ford, for ex-ample. It loves to sell cars, but it really loves to sell parts. "An estimated $72.7 billion worth of car parts were sold in 2010, ranging from engine parts to door handles."[252] Melba Kurman, the noted 3D printing com-mentator, believes that 3D printing puts the auto-parts industry at risk.[253] Retail auto-parts supply stores will soon be able to print replacement parts on demand, and to customize them too. Some parts may be printed from digital blueprints provided by Ford for a fee. Others will be printed from blueprints provided by generic parts companies for a fee. Others will be printed from open-source blueprints, or from pirated blueprints, for no fee. Aside from Ford's obvious lost parts sales, its former customer, the au-to-parts store, can become a manufacturer and designer of custom parts, and a competitor.

An example of things to come is the set of open-source 3D printable blueprints for a Toyota engine posted on Thingiverse, along with detailed assembly drawings. The blueprints include everything needed to 3D print a working model of the Toyota 22RE engine, used in cars and pickup trucks in the 1980s and 1990s. Although the average car owner may only be able to print parts for this engine in plastic today, independent fabs or auto-parts stores could print the parts in metal, and in the not-too-distant future consumers may be printing in metal, too.[254] Also, for some parts, plastic replacements may be OK, and advanced 3D printable composites may make it possible for consumers, fabs, and auto-parts stores to replace metal parts with composite parts.

Photo courtesy of Eric Harrell

Any company that sells parts is at risk. Here's why. Zefram Warp Drives, a fictional company founded by Zefram Cochrane after his invention of the warp drive in 2063, makes warp drives that customers, such as the

Federation of Planets, put to heavy use. Parts such as the gravimetric field displacement manifold (also known as the warp core)[255] break and wear out, so ZeframWD sells replacement warp drives and cores to the Federation. It sells them for a tidy profit because it has made the replacements for decades, fixed costs are low, and it faces little competition.

Somewhere on Earth, however, an enterprising company, Scan Depot, reverse engineers and scans the warp core and other warp-drive parts inside and out. Scan Depot then sells the parts' digital blueprints through its website and offers to 3D print them on demand for ZeframWD customers. Scan Depot prices the blueprints at one-tenth of ZeframWD's price for a new part and 3D prints parts for one-third of ZeframWD's best discounted price. For a little more money, Scan Depot customizes the warp core or other parts to the customer's specs.

The Federation, however, decides to buy only the digital blueprints. Federation engineers like to tweak their warp drives, so standard warp cores rarely fit. So the Federation outfits its starships with 3D printers. With onboard printers, engineers customize warp-core blueprints and print parts as needed, no matter what the stardate or where in the galaxy they might be. The Federation thereby eliminates warehousing and shipping and saves lots of money. ZeframWD, of course, loses sales and watches the Federation, a major customer, become a major competitor.

The picture for manufacturers could change even more. The Federation does not always need a new warp core. It may be possible to repair or rebuild an old one, which was impossible before 3D printing.

This is already happening today. RMIT University in Australia used Directed Energy Deposition to repair the leading edge of hundreds of turbine blades used in power generation.[256] RMIT repaired the blades onsite, using portable 3D printing equipment. Without this process, the turbine manufacturer would have sold hundreds of new replacement blades—at a pretty penny per blade—but it looks like it will be selling far fewer new blades as time, and blades, wear on.

Refurbishing expensive parts is a perfect job for some types of 3D printing. For example, Laser Engineered Netshaping (LENS) from Optomec of Albuquerque, New Mexico, can be used to add new metal to any existing metal object. The LENS printhead can easily be integrated with traditional machines, such as a CNC router, to finish the refurbished part. The refurbished parts are as good as or better than the originals, and the process costs far less than buying a new part. This is great news for the part owner and terrifying to the company that made the part in the first place.[257]

Companies are starting to worry about these scenarios today, and the scenarios are moving from theory to reality. Companies that rely on parts sales for a large percentage of their profits are starting to see that this could happen to them, soon. The farm- and construction-equipment company John Deere is thinking about transitioning some of its spare parts from physical inventory to digital blueprints. I'll talk later about options for companies like Deere.[258] According to the IBM 3D printing study:[259]

> The competitive advantage from both proprietary design and parts production is expected to erode as basic design blueprints become widely available via open source…And the service parts business will lead the digital transformation, leaving companies unable to generate profits from selling spares.

Melba Kurman contends that 3D printing eliminates artificial scarcity.[260] Until 3D printers came along, ZeframWD was the only source for replacement warp cores for its warp drives. It was not cost effective for other companies to make replacement warp cores because they could not achieve the economies of scale that ZeframWD reached long ago. The ability of 3D printers owned by customers or independent fabricators to print warp cores and other parts eliminated such scarcity. In an article by Kurman and Hod Lipson, they maintain that after 3D printed parts become easily available, it will be difficult for "companies to convince customers to pay their steeply marked-up prices. Why spend $100 for a floor matt [or much more for a warp core] when you could download the design file and print out the object on [your own] machine, or pay a professional 3D printing service to do it for you for a fraction of the price."[261]

The use of 3D printers to make parts is snowballing. In 2013, the parts segment of the 3D printing industry grew 65.4 percent to $1.65 billion, up from 56.5 percent growth and a market value of $643.8 million in 2012.[262] Industry commentator Robert G. Bugge predicts that government organizations will start making their own spare parts, like the Federation of Planets did, and shake corporate foundations by doing so:[263]

> With AM [additive manufacturing], Government departments and agencies (with their own AM printers) will now want to...make all of their own spares. They will no longer want to buy many of their spares from a contractor. By making some or most of their own spares they not only eliminate the contractor from the equation, but also many aspects of their own logistics systems that previously had to obtain, store and distribute the spares into the field. This will have an enormously disruptive effect on...the economic models used by contractors that compete for government contracts.

The *National Journal* makes the same prediction, saying, "DOD [Department of Defense] is using these 3D printing machines across the military services. An item can be printed from an electronic blueprint or scanning an existing part."[264] New America Foundation warfare expert Peter Singer foresees major 3D printing–driven shakeups in the defense supply chain: "Defense contractors want to sell you an item but also want to own the supply chain for 50 years. But now you'll have soldiers in an austere outpost somewhere like Afghanistan who can pull down the software for a spare part, tweak the design and print it out." As *Space Daily* commented, "This could lead militaries to cut out private defense companies altogether."[265] Imagine the political fallout. The bright side is that soldiers would leave the military with highly marketable skills.

Obsolete parts will be a major driver of governments and companies making their own replacement parts. For example, Dr. Khershed Cooper of the US Office of Naval Research wrote that[266]

> the benefits of AM [additive manufacturing] to the Navy are plenty. The Navy and DoD are dealing with aging systems. Legacy systems are increasing in number and facing obsolescence. If a part breaks, we are faced with nonexistent suppliers, unreliable foreign sources and unavailable drawings. In such a scenario it is possible to reverse engineer the damaged part and have a replacement produced by AM.

Organizations like the US Navy may initially adopt 3D printing to make replacement parts that are obsolete or unavailable from the original manufacturer. This will give them experience with the technology, show them what it can do, save them money, and eliminate the need to stockpile huge numbers of parts that may or may not be needed someday. From there, it will be a small step to making any part whenever and wherever it is needed, and customizing it, too, rather than buying it from the manufacturer.

Just as 3D printing is blurring the lines between industrial manufacturer and customer, the lines are also starting to blur on the consumer side. As 3D printing industry observer Michael Molitch-Hou said, "In terms of the sale of digital designs…this technology presents the first instance in which the lines between consumers and producers are really beginning to vanish."[267] Anyone can open a virtual retail shop on www.shapeways.com by posting 3D printable designs. Companies like Shapeways allow anyone to be a designer, manufacturer, and retailer. When a customer orders a print of a design, Shapeways prints and ships it to the customer.

WHY SELL PRODUCTS?

These examples suggest that future sales may be of designs, not products.[268] As the Wohlers Report observed:[269]

> In the world of AM [additive manufacturing], the central embodiment of an artifact—the thing that we buy and sell and improve—will be the information used to manufacture the object, not the object itself.

Using such designs, future products may be printed where they are needed, just in time,[270] by a company, a service bureau, or by you and me.[271] This raises important questions: Why would a company want to manufacture a product when it could sell the design instead? Why wouldn't it want to shift the manufacturing burden to its customers or to independent fabs?

Shapeways, for example, empowers individual designers and inventors to put finished products in customers' hands by doing nothing more than designing the product and posting it in a virtual retail store. The designer or inventor need not trouble herself with any aspect of the manufacturing, supply, warehousing, or shipping process and need not buy any equipment. She simply gets revenue after paying Shapeways' cut. If she sells five thousand units of her product, she gets the revenue without the hassle. So why would she even consider making the product herself?

Big companies have begun to ask the same questions. Let's visit ZeframWD again. It takes a lot of capital to build and run a warp-drive factory and pay all of the workers their wages and benefits. Still, ZeframWD made warp drives and parts for many years and was profitable because few other companies could achieve its economies of scale. It seemed like the Federation of Planters had an insatiable appetite for replacement parts, which kept ZeframWD's production lines rolling 24/7, 365 days a year. When Scan Depot started selling digital blueprints for the warp core and other parts, ZeframWD began to wonder why it needed factories; it could simply sell its digital blueprints instead. It also saw the handwriting on the wall: its biggest customer wanted to start making its own spares. So ZeframWD decided to beat Scan Depot at its own game and began to sell its own encrypted digital blueprints. If warp cores are printed from the official blueprints by customers or approved regional fabricators according to ZeframWD's strict specifications, ZeframWD will stand behind them just as if it made them in its own factories. ZeframWD's blueprints also come with its own secret sauce for how to 3D print a flawless warp core.

ZeframWD was surprised by the benefits of selling designs instead of actual warp drives. Its revenue from the sale of blueprints was much, much lower than from the sale of actual parts, but its profits increased because it decided to close most of its factories. Although its revenue per part is now lower than when it mass-produced them, its profits per part are higher because its overhead was eliminated after the parts were designed and translated into encrypted files. ZeframWD also stopped carrying huge inventories of spare parts, closed its expensive regional warehouses, and eliminated the costs of transporting parts across the galaxy.

It cost ZeframWD a lot of money to run its business the old way. It needed to maintain huge factories full of expensive, high-maintenance machinery. It had huge energy bills to operate those machines, which were exceeded by labor and materials costs. It transported parts to far-flung warehouses, each with a large inventory, so that customers could buy warp-drive parts whenever and wherever they needed them. By shifting the manufacturing burden to its customers and approved regional 3D printing fabricators, ZeframWD was able to eliminate the entire capital-intensive infrastructure needed to give customers that convenience. For example, by eliminating inventory in warehouses, ZeframWD increased its return on invested capital by 60 percent.[272]

Robert Bugge foresaw ZeframWD's predicament, its revamped business model, and the benefits to its largest customer:[273]

> If the Government wants to...use its own AM to make its own spares, then the contractor will need to change its pricing models because it can no longer count on the lucrative spares production that kept its production lines open. Certainly ownership of all [digital blueprints]...will command a higher initial product price, but that higher price may be paid for by the Government by the massive savings it will achieve as a result of reduced logistics cost and infrastructure.

ZeframWD now employs a staff of warp-drive engineers and product designers who design and test next-generation warp drives and customize them to customer specifications, rapid-prototyping specialists who 3D print new and customized warp drives to work out their kinks, digital-blueprint specialists who create 3D printable blueprints and specifications, quality-control specialists who monitor approved fabricators and assure that they 3D print warp cores and other parts according to ZeframWD's high standards, and customer-service specialists who honor ZeframWD's "Any Galaxy" warranty by working with a network of warp-drive repair specialists and approved fabricators who fix or replace defective warp drives. ZeframWD maintains a few regional in-house fabricators staffed by 3D printer specialists, who make custom-designed warp drives, cores, and other parts. Although ZeframWD employs far fewer factory workers than it once did, many of its former employees opened their own regional 3D fabrication shops or went to work for customers, running their in-house 3D printing operations. All of the specialists ZeframWD employs now are highly skilled workers who work in regional offices to serve local customers.

WILL COMPANIES BE READY?

ZeframWD was a much more efficient and profitable business after it stopped mass-producing warp cores and started selling only digital blueprints and bespoke warp cores and parts. But getting there could not have been more wrenching. As ZeframWD started to see the 3D printed handwriting on the wall, its first thought was "That can't happen to us. We are immune to third parties printing our warp cores because they are so mission critical." Then a ZeframWD board member saw a demonstration of a warp core that was CT-scanned, turned into a digital blueprint, then printed on a high-end 3D fabricator. The next board meeting was not a pretty sight. Fear ran deep.

The board then directed management to beef up the company's intellectual-property protections and put out feelers in Washington about changing the laws to outlaw scanning parts. The legal department drew up a hit list of companies that ZeframWD could sue. As the company's CEO, Zefram Cochrane, said, "We need to show our customers that we are on top of this problem, protect them from counterfeit warp cores, and send a message to the industry that anyone who sells digital blueprints for ZeframWD warp cores will face us in court." ZeframWD then realized that digital blueprints were being made from its own customers' CT scans of their own warp cores, designs that ZeframWD's customers fabricated on their own 3D printers. Suing its own customers didn't make sense.

ZeframWD then began the long and painful process of redesigning its business from the ground up. At first, pockets of the board and management fought it. People resigned. Others were fired. Egos were damaged. But slowly everyone started to see that ZeframWD needed to enter the twenty-fourth century, abandon its old ways, embrace change, and convert itself from a mass-production behemoth into a leaner, meaner engineering and digital-information company with a bespoke manufacturing boutique and a galaxy-wide network of regional authorized warp-core fabricators.

ZeframWD must have read IBM's 3D printing study, which said, "For leading global companies to prosper in this new environment, radical change is essential."[274] ZeframWD was lucky. It managed to make the painful leap from a company stuck in the mass-production paradigms of the Industrial Revolution to a company that took full advantage of the implications of 3D printing. Other companies will not be so lucky, and many are sleeping at the wheel, while their competitors, old and new, zip down the fast lane to integrate 3D printing, with all of its implications, into their businesses. Existing companies will be transformed along the way. In the manufacturing climate of 3D printing, they must adapt or die. For example, Samsung announced in the fall of 2014 that it would not enter the 3D printer business until at least 2024.[275] Perhaps sensing that it had made a Kodak decision, Samsung backtracked only a few months later, announcing that its Samsung X innovation team would explore 3D printing.[276]

One company making the right moves today is Roccat Studios, which makes peripherals for the PC gaming industry. Roccat makes a gaming mouse with button layouts customizable by the user. Roccat will also sell you the blueprints so you can 3D print your own mouse and button layout, choosing from a library of button layouts stocked by Roccat and other users.[277] Roccat seems to be anticipating ZeframWD's footsteps.

The Wohlers Report announced that another anonymous company is proactively planning to transform its parts business:[278]

A large manufacturer of industrial equipment expects to produce spare parts on demand using AM [additive manufacturing]. Currently, the company warehouses tens of thousands of parts for its customers.

Alex Chausovsky of IHS Technology says, "3D printing is like a train. You're either on the train or you're under it."[279] Most companies today do not even see this freight train barreling down the tracks, aiming straight at them. According to an IBM survey, only 17 percent of the companies interviewed said that the impact of 3D printing on the future of manufacturing would be significant "to a very large extent," 33 percent called 3D printing "not significant," and 70 percent "admitted to having little or no preparation for a software-defined supply chain."[280]

According to IBM, this "indicates that a substantial portion of manufacturers may be caught off-guard by the rapid changes underway."[281] A McKinsey survey got similar results, finding that 40 percent of the respondents were unfamiliar with 3D printing beyond what the media reports. McKinsey concluded, "Many leading companies seem surprisingly unaware of [3D printing's] potential—and poorly organized to reap the benefits." But on the bright side, 33 percent of the respondents believe 3D printing is not highly relevant to their businesses today but will become important within a few years.[282]

My take on these surveys: most companies have little or no idea what is happening in the world of industrial 3D printing.

THINK ABOUT THE HORSE

We saw that when ZeframWD reinvented itself, many of its factory workers lost their jobs, though some of them became approved regional fabricators. Still, people lost jobs. So how is it that 3D printing will spark a new industrial revolution, a manufacturing renaissance, and bring jobs home?

To understand the answer to this question, think about the horse. When the horse was the major form of transportation, there were saddle makers, whip makers, blacksmiths, wagon and carriage makers, wagon-wheel makers, stable owners, feed suppliers, and people to care for the horses. When the automobile came along, most of those jobs were lost. But think of how many new jobs were created by the invention of the automobile. 3D printing has the same potential.

To adapt to a 3D printed world, you must think about things in an entirely different way. This is extraordinarily difficult to do. As an example of how difficult this is, remember that the dawn of the automobile was thought of in horse terms. Early cars were "horseless carriages," and they looked like motorized versions of slightly modernized horse-drawn vehicles of the day. Carmakers like Daimler Benz and Rolls Royce made car chassis and carriage makers made the cars' upper bodies. The automobile was fitted into a horse-dominated world. The days of the horse linger even today, as a car's muscle is still measured in horsepower.

Just as the nascent automobile industry looked nothing like the horse industry but was thought of in horse terms, the 3D printed manufacturing renaissance will look nothing like the Industrial Revolution of the nineteenth and early twentieth centuries, yet it is natural and somewhat unavoidable to think of it in nineteenth-and twentieth-century terms. So, when President Obama in his 2013 State of the Union address said,"A once-shuttered warehouse is now a state-of-the art lab where new workers are mastering 3D printing," the images that naturally danced in everyone's mind were big factory smokestacks once again belching smoke, while thousands of workers 3D printed things on massive assembly lines.

But it won't be like that. For one thing, a 3D printing industrial revolution will be much cleaner and safer. For all of its might, the American factory of the nineteenth century was a dirty and dangerous place. Factories of the 3D printing renaissance will be cleaner, safer, and employ far fewer people. They will also be smaller, regional, and distributed all over the world. As ZeframWD learned, centralized mass production should not try to compete with customer-driven, 3D scan–based, customized regional additive manufacturing. ZeframWD survived because it stopped thinking in horse terms and started thinking in 3D printing terms.

President Obama also said that 3D printing "has the potential to revolutionize the way we make almost everything." The keywords here are "revolutionize the way." The ways of the 3D printing revolution will be as different from the ways of the past 150 years of manufacturing as the auto industry was from the horse industry. So whenever you question whether 3D printing can spark a manufacturing renaissance and bring jobs home, ask if you are thinking in horse terms.

WHICH INDUSTRIES WILL BE DISRUPTED FIRST?

We have already seen that, in the industrial space, companies reliant on parts revenue are at high risk. From warp drives to cars, to airplanes, to tractor parts, to medical devices, the category comprises most manufacturers in most industries. In fact, the business model of these industries is known as the "razor and blades" model. Companies' profits per unit from selling cars, airplanes, or razors are nothing compared to the recurring, high-profit revenues of selling replacement parts.

But many products are consumer products. This presents companies with another set of problems because, as time marches on, individual consumers will be more and more able to make such products themselves, or to have them made locally.

The McKinsey consulting firm predicts a major shakeup in consumer products industries:[283]

3D printing could have meaningful impact on certain consumer product categories, including toys, accessories, jewelry, footwear, ceramics, and simple apparel. These products are relatively easy to make using 3D printing technology and could have high customization value for consumers.

Global sales of products in these categories could grow to $4 trillion a year (at retail prices) by 2025. It is possible that most, if not all, consumers of these products could have access to 3D printing by 2025, whether by owning a 3D printer, using a 3D printer in a local store, or ordering 3D printed products online. We estimate that consumers might 3D print 5 to 10 percent of these products by 2025, based on the products' material composition, complexity, cost, and the potential convenience and enjoyment of printing compared with buying for consumers. A potential 35 to 60 percent cost savings is possible for consumers self-printing these goods despite higher material costs (the materials required for the products we focus on here, primarily plastics, are relatively inexpensive and getting cheaper). The savings over retail come not only from eliminating the costs of wholesale and retail distribution, but also from reducing the costs of design and advertising embedded in the price of products. It is possible that consumers will pay for 3D printing designs, but it is also possible that many free designs will be available online. Finally, customization might be worth 10 percent or even more of the value for some 3D printed consumer products.

Companies that plan for such disruption of their industries and stop thinking in horse terms may safely dodge the 3D printing freight train and hop aboard. Other companies will fail, either because they are stuck in horse thinking or because their business models are as unsustainable in a 3D printed world as camera stores and record stores (now there's a horse term) are in the digital world.

WINNERS AND LOSERS

3D printing will spawn businesses, products, services, and jobs that are as unimaginable today as the auto industry was to the world population at the dawn of the twentieth century. Hod Lipson observed that because 3D printing substantially reduces the cost of making complex things, it paves the way to products and industries that do not exist today. He believes this major cost reduction will lead to "a cascade of new innovation across many fields."[284]

I will try to give some sense of such things, but my crystal ball is not perfect. I will probably be as accurate as a similar writer may have been in 1910, trying to predict the auto industry in the year 2000.

Customization

Customization is one of 3D printing's strongest points. It is hard to imagine today how deeply customization will work its way into our everyday lives, but I suspect that in 2025 using customized 3D printed products will be as common as using mass-produced ones today. But those may be products that don't exist today or that are very different versions of today's products.

Customization may take many forms: industrial, personal, age or gender based, ethnic based, geography based, climate based, feature based, and design based. New businesses will try to capture the demand, with designers and engineers creating basic but highly customizable products. 3D printer companies will build machines to make such products. Software engineers will write programs to run and network such printers, balance workloads, optimize use of the build chamber, control the printing process, interface with the user, enable customization, encrypt digital blueprints, monitor quality, and perform product finishing. Materials companies will supply feedstock for the printers. These jobs are just beginning to exist today.

Printer networks

As more and more 3D printers are sold, they will probably be networked, whether in professional networks or what I call "Friends Networks." As industry writer Ivan Pope observed, 3D printer "networks are starting to spring up around the industry."[285]

Not all 3D printers do the same thing. This will always be true. Processes will differ and have their strengths and weaknesses. You may own a local 3D printing shop but lack the machine to print a customer's part. Enter distributed networks: tens of thousands of networked local printers. There are already start-ups in this space: 3DPrinterOS, 3D Hubs, Makexyz, Kraftworx, and Printr.[286] Until recently, such companies, and the jobs they created, never existed, nor did jobs for software engineers with the know-how to network such printers. More companies will emerge that somehow network 3D printers to make their combined strength far greater than their individual capacity.

Makerspaces

Although many makerspaces are nonprofit operations, many others are new businesses. In addition to for-profit TechShop and Idea 2 Product labs, other well-outfitted makerspace businesses are emerging. For example, the Las Vegas Tech Fund invested $100 million in Factorli, a one-stop, go-to place for start-ups to prototype and make small runs of new products.[287] Makerspaces are not only creating jobs for the people who staff them, but they are also incubators of small businesses based on members' ideas.

Marketplaces and libraries

The number of 3D printable blueprints available on the Internet is growing exponentially. They are being offered for use by a variety of companies, big and small. Some of these companies are providing libraries of existing product and part designs. Others provide software tools that enable users to create and customize designs. Some will print objects from the blueprints. Others leave printing to the end user. Some offer open-source designs, like Thingiverse (www.thingiverse.com), which is owned by MakerBot, which is owned by Stratasys, one of the largest 3D printer makers. Its chief competitor, 3D Systems, offers blueprints for printing at www.cubify.com, which 3D Systems will print for you or allow you to print for yourself, for a fee.

There are also many independent start-ups in this space, including:

3Discovered: www.3discovered.com
3D Share: http://3dsha.re/
CGTrader: www.cgtrader.com

Fabster: www.fabster.com
Kazzata: www.kazata.com
Myminifactory: www.myminifactory.com
Pinshape: www.pinshape.com
Ponoko: www.ponoko.com
Threeding: www.threeding.com

3Discovered and Kazzata deserve a special mention. 3Discovered's goal is to become the iTunes of 3D printed spare parts for major manufacturers, so that manufacturers can get out of the spare parts business and eliminate costly parts inventories. It plans to offer an IP-secure, searchable library of designs, which could be verified by an independent third party, such as Underwriters Laboratories, then printed by trusted fabs. Kazzata's goal is to be a marketplace for 3D printed spare parts.

The Yeggi search engine crawls the Internet for blueprints of 3D printable objects.[288] Yobi3D does the same thing.[289] Their business models may differ somewhat, but they are all making a go of it and creating jobs that never existed before.

Blueprint-based businesses
Fictional ZeframWD decided that it could eliminate overhead, increase profits, and keep its customers happy by morphing from Goliath-sized manufacturer into a blueprint library and David-sized custom factory. It now offers all of its parts designs for 3D printing by customers or regional fabricators. The jobs it provides today are very different from the old days.

Real companies like Hasbro are now dipping their toes in these waters. Hasbro announced deals to make some of its toy designs available for customization and 3D printing by 3D Systems or Shapeways. Imagine being able to 3D print your own Mr. Potato Head that looks remarkably like a selfie. These business models are all job generators.

Amazon is trying to find its place in the digital blueprint space, having filed a patent application for a business that provides blueprints to fabricators for customer-selected products. The fabs 3D print the product—either in a factory or in a roving 3D printing truck—and the customer picks up the product or receives it by home delivery. Amazon may also provide the blueprint to the customer to 3D print on her own machine. For instance, a customer with a broken water-faucet handle selects a replacement handle on a smartphone app, clicks to order, and selects either "pick up nearby," "deliver to me," or "print at home." If she selects "pick up nearby," Amazon sends the blueprint to an approved fabricator near the customer's home, and the handle is printed while she drives over to pick it up.[290]

Security

ZeframWD's and Hasbro's parts and products blueprints are their crown jewels. If they lose control of them, their businesses could be destroyed. On the consumer level, 3D printable blueprints are being created by designers, inventors, artists, jewelers, and many other types of makers. They have the same fear. They are happy to let customers and fabricators print their designs, but they want their fair share. Enter the security entrepreneurs. Several start-ups have their sights set on this problem and have created data-management, encryption, and blueprint-security companies.

Fabulous fabs

Regional manufacturing means most players will be independent fabricators, often called service bureaus. Some of the larger current players are iMaterialise, Sculpteo, Shapeways, and Solid Concepts. They are well equipped with the major types of 3D printers and ready to print parts and products at multiple locations, to the full limit of the state of the art. iMaterialise, Sculpteo, and Shapeways also offer designs that can be printed.

A growing number of independent 3D printing service bureaus can be found throughout the world. Some have been 3D printing for a long time, operating as rapid-prototyping shops. Some are start-ups. Others are old-school machine shops, like James Tool, which added 3D printers to its array of traditional machines.[291] Daniel Cohen observed that "numerous printing service bureaus—the modern-day equivalent of a small machine shop—continue to sprout up across the United States and offer their customers ample manufacturing capacity with almost no upfront capital costs."[292]

The importance of 3D printing fabricators cannot be overemphasized. They are the regional and distributed manufacturers of the 3D printing age. They are the employers of the factory workers of the 3D printing–fueled manufacturing renaissance. Individually, they may not employ a large number of people, but together they will be a major source of factory jobs.

Software developers' candy shop
Software engineers in the 3D printing job market will be like kids in a candy shop. They will be in high demand to write, update, and manage software to meet 3D printing–related software needs for anticounterfeiting; authenticating parts and products; authorizing, certifying, controlling, and managing service providers; converting designs and scans to 3D printable data; customization; design; digital rights management (DRM); encryption; file authentication; file management; manufacturing, machine-control, and optimizing use of the build chamber; networking; workload balancing; process monitoring and management; quality control; specification creation, control, and management; remote control; scanning; security; streaming; and many other needs yet to be discovered.

Entrepreneurs will write such software and build businesses around it. One example is 3DprinterOS, which wrote an operating system compatible with many consumer-grade 3D printers. Within four months of its launch, 4,700 users in 920 cities and eighty-three countries used the system to create 8,100 prints across more than two thousand 3D printers.[293]

Scanning

In their book, *Fabricated*, Hod Lipson and Melba Kurman paint a picture of a world, not too many years from now, when people will have their bodies scanned periodically. If they ever need a new limb, kidney, or hip, the measurements can be found in their own personal blueprint. If they need complex surgery, surgeons can practice on models 3D printed from the blueprint.

Scan Depot scanned all of ZeframWD's warp-drive parts and offered both the designs and 3D printed copies for sale. Their goal was to be a one-stop source of 3D printable blueprints for every land and space vehicle and industrial machine. If the original manufacturer will not provide them, Scan Depot will scan the part and create its own blueprints. Customers who formerly bought parts will buy scanners that enable them to make their own parts.

Archeologists scan priceless artifacts so they can examine and even destroy them, without damaging the original, such as the cuneiforms described in "From design to print" in chapter 2.

Personal scanners can be used today to scan toys, dolls, jewelry, and common household objects. They will get better and better.

Making and running scanners and creating scanning software will be major job generators in the 3D printing industrial revolution.

National security

The US military is actively examining what 3D printers can do. The army created a mobile fab lab for printing things as needed, where needed, when needed.[294] Projects include 3D printing uniforms,[295] weapons,[296] blast-proof vehicle parts,[297] and drones.[298] Logistics experts foresee using 3D printing to perform field repairs,[299] enable shipboard manufacturing,[300] and fabricate food for frontline troops.[301] Military medical scientists print models of human brains and skulls to study the effects of shock-waves[302] and traumatic injuries.[303] And research is underway to 3D print surgical instruments and materials,[304] including human skin.[305] All of these projects mean jobs, either for defense-contractor employees or military personnel.

Printers and materials

As the use of 3D printers grows, so will the demand for more machines, materials, and related software. The very existence of these machines will drive part and product design into uncharted territory. World leadership will belong to the countries that make the most powerful printers and the most versatile materials, that create the most robust designs, and that write the design and production software to make it all work.

Inventor to entrepreneur

America runs on small businesses, and 3D printing will create even more of them. Many of my examples relate to the infrastructure of the 3D printing industry, such as making and networking machines, securing digital blueprints, and supplying materials. Perhaps the largest number of new small businesses generated by 3D printing will be started by entrepreneurs who use 3D printing to create new products in virtually every industry. According to Melba Kurman:[306]

> 3D printing technologies are creating a new and growing marketplace, what I call consumer to consumer, or "C2C manufacturing." This is the world of moonlighting designers, online service providers, mom and pop 3D printing services, and energetic and creative solo inventors and entrepreneurs.

By making it much easier to design, prototype, and manufacture products, 3D printing's democratization of manufacturing enables any inventor or maker to become an entrepreneur. For example, entrepreneur Kegan Schouwenburg uses 3D printers to make her SOLS brand custom orthotics.[307] Her company partnered with WebPT, a web-based physical-therapy company, to bring SOLS 3D printed orthotics to a network of forty-three thousand physical therapists.[308]

Consumer-grade machines are currently limited in what they can make and the materials they use. But that has not stopped enterprising innovators like Mark Anderson, whose Artisan Instruments uses 3D printers to make replacement parts for pipe organs. Parts are unavailable for many old pipe organs and are difficult to make with traditional methods. Anderson makes the parts on consumer-grade machines with ABS. Similarly, Vadym Chalenko uses low-cost 3D printers to make his Beastgrip brand lens adapter and rigging system, which attaches a wide variety of lenses, filters, and photo and video accessories to smartphones, for "phoneography" aficionados. Dan Clark uses inexpensive 3D printers to make ear cups for his MrSpeaker high-end headphones. Robert Hughes, owner of Lucky Bug Lures, uses consumer-level 3D printers to make "Fish Be Warned!" fishing lures.[309]

DISRUPTION CHECKLIST

Because 3D printing democratizes manufacturing, it can disrupt almost any product-based company. Their old ways of operating may stop working when 3D printing eliminates barriers to entry, competitors flood the market, and customers become competitors. For this to happen, several pieces need to fall into place. I call these pieces the Market Disruption Checklist.

On the industrial side, two things are needed to trigger the disruption of any existing product-based market:

- The ability to build large things, and hence the need for 3D printers with large build platforms
- The ability to make either single items quickly or many items simultaneously—that is, speed or scale of production

On both the home and industrial sides, there are some additional requirements for market disruption:

- Advanced materials (including materials that may not yet exist) that enable the efficient printing of complex structures
- The ability to print complex, integrated structures, such as smartphones and blenders
- The ability to print very small things, such as the integrated circuitry of computer chips
- Hybrid machines that can perform the processes that a 3D printer cannot
- Innovators, especially the innovators of the future—namely, young people who grow up with 3D printing

WHERE DO WE STAND?

When anyone can 3D print things of almost any functionality, away from control, everything will change. But keep in mind that a home-printed smartphone may not look or feel like a smartphone of today. It need only have the functionality of a smartphone. Look and feel will be dictated—or freed—by the capacities of 3D printers and their materials. Thus, the ability to 3D print anything really means the ability to print a thing with virtually any functionality, even though the final product may look and feel very different from things we know today.

Where does the technology stand now?

Large build platform to make big things

There are plenty of 3D printers capable of making big things. And big things are being printed. Northwestern Polytechnical University in China printed a titanium aircraft wing spar.[310] Voxeljet 3D printed three replicas of James Bond's famous Aston Martin DB5 for the movie *Skyfall*.[311] Local Motors, Oak Ridge National Laboratory, and Cincinnati Inc. used Big Area Additive Manufacturing (BAAM)—essentially an enormous Material

Extrusion printer—to 3D print the ABS/carbon-fiber Strati automobile. Printed in Chicago in September 2014, the Strati was the first crowd-sourced, open-source automobile 3D printed in front of a live audience. The design reduced the twenty-five thousand parts in a normal production car to about sixty-four.[312]

Speed or scale to rival mass production

Neil Hopkinson of Loughborough University and Sheffield University in the United Kingdom developed a process called High Speed Sintering (HSS) that rivals the speed of injection molding.[313]

Attempting to break the 3D printing speed barrier, 3D Systems has poured money into R&D to develop its Continuous, High-Speed Fab-Grade Printer, which uses multiple stationary 3D printheads and a mobile, assembly-line print bed to mass-produce products.[314] One application may be modular smartphones for its joint Project ARA with Google.[315]

But the democratization of manufacturing, mass customization and mass personalization, and the ability to 3D print things with virtually any functionality, away from control, may reduce or eliminate the need for mass production and economies of scale in many industries.

Steps in this direction are HP's Multi Jet Fusion, Impossible Objects' Composite-Based Additive Manufacturing (CBAM), and HSS. Although these machines are much faster than other machines on the market, they are not as fast as mass production. But what if there were hundreds of thousands of these machines installed throughout the world? Would mass production still be needed?

Advanced materials

In "Morphing Manufacturing" (chapter 1), I described Carbomorph, gra-phene, chiplets, self-forming metals, and metals that are liquid at room temperature. 3D printers like the Stratasys Connex make "digital materials" by combining multiple materials as they print. MIT's 3D assemblers will use programmable materials, and Directed Energy Deposition printers, such as Optomec's Laser Engineered Netshaping (LENS) machines, can make metal alloys on the fly.

Despite these advances, there is a lot of room for innovation in the 3D printing materials space. 3D printing may create a golden age for materials scientists. As Terry Wohlers said, "Materials are key to the future success of 3D printing, particularly for production applications. Compared to conventional manufacturing, the selection of materials for 3D printing is limited. We will see growth in all the material segments."[316]

Ability to print complex structures
Developing the ability to print complex, integrated structures will have the greatest implications for the future of 3D printing. In "Morphing Manufacturing," we saw the Smart Wing drone, the first fully integrated 3D printed complex structure, printed by Stratasys and Optomec.[317] The Smart Wing was 100 percent 3D printed; Stratasys machines printed the structure and outer shell, and Optomec's machines printed the circuitry. Optomec also has done other cutting-edge electronics work, such as 3D printing integrated antennas.[318]

Disney is working on 3D printing interactive toys and 3D printed speakers that can be made in any shape and emanate sound from 100 percent of their surface area.[319] Princeton University 3D printed a bionic ear. 3D Systems' and Google's Project ARA expects to yield modular, customizable, 3D printed smartphones. MIT is developing 3D assemblers to build fully integrated complex products from programmable materials. CSIRO and Deakin and Monash Universities 3D printed a jet engine and Rocket lab 3D printed a rocket engine.

But 3D printing complex structures currently faces a major obstacle: no single machine or process can make an entire complex structure, such as a smartphone. To make parts, products, and machines of almost any functionality, the 3D printing industry needs to combine existing and new processes that, together, can produce such functionality.

In the meantime, creative companies are filling in the gaps that current 3D printers can't fill. For example, with current technology, only the outer shell and buttons of OwnFone's customizable cell phones can be 3D printed. But with its development kits, OwnFone will send you the phone's electronic innards, which you can assemble with the custom shell that you 3D printed.[320]

Microscale

Harvard University and the University of Illinois 3D printed a microbattery three hundred microns wide, about two to three times the thickness of a human hair.[321] A direct-write process called focused electron beam induced deposition (FEBID) is being used to 3D print at less than a hundred nanometers, which is roughly one-tenth the diameter of a human hair.[322] Northeastern University is developing the nanoscale offset printing system (NanoOPS), which can print nanoscale structures and circuits down to twenty-five nanometers onto flexible or hard substrates using conductive, semiconducting, or insulating nanomaterials.[323]

But to 3D print things of any functionality, machines must be able to print not only circuits but also semiconductors and microchips, and the ability to do so must be combined with all the other requirements on the disruption checklist into one machine.

Hybrid machines

Japan's Matsuura makes the Lumex laser sintering 3D printer and high-speed mill combo.[324] DMG Mori Seiki (Germany and Japan) combines laser deposition welding (a type of Directed Energy Deposition) with a five-axis CNC mill. Flexible Robotics Environments' (United States) VDK6000 Robotic Work Center combines several processes into a single machine. For 3D printing, it offers Powder Bed Fusion of metals, plastics, and ceramics, and a Material Jetting process called metal cold spray. For traditional manufacturing, it includes a CNC mill and grinding, drilling, and polishing functions. The machine mounts all of these functions on a six-axis robotic work center. The machine also includes a 3D laser scanner and ultrasonic inspection.[325]

Boston-based Voxel8, whose machines printed both a quadcopter's body and internal circuitry, plans to combine 3D printing with existing automated manufacturing technology, such as pick-and-place machines.[326]

The technology of innovative hybrid consumer-level machines will probably also trickle up to industrial machines.

These hybrid machines are a step in the right direction, but they have far to go. Before this item on the disruption checklist can be ticked off, 3D printer hybrids will need to integrate the structure and electronics of complex devices with the traditional manufacturing processes necessary to finish them.

Innovators

According to Engineering.com, skilled 3D printing–related jobs soared 1,384 percent from 2010 to 2014 and were up 103 percent from 2013 to 2014. The three jobs most in demand were industrial and mechanical engineers and software developers.[327] These jobs are being filled by the innovators of today. Tomorrow's innovators—who will fill the gaps in the disruption checklist—are kids today. They are just starting to be initiated into the world of 3D printing, using consumer-grade machines, the sales of which have skyrocketed from 1,816 units in 2009 to 140,000 in 2014.[328] Gartner predicts that worldwide 3D printer sales will double yearly and top 2.3 million machines by 2018, most of which will be consumer-level machines.[329] I am confident an abundance of 3D printing innovators will emerge and that this item of the disruption checklist can be confidently ticked.

3D PRINTING AWAY FROM CONTROL

I have talked a lot about the disruptive effects of 3D printing: making things in fundamentally different ways at lower costs and with smaller carbon footprints; designing parts and products without manufacturing restrictions; becoming makers again; democratizing manufacturing and driving regional and distributed manufacturing; shrinking companies; shortening and fundamentally changing supply chains; blurring lines between product designers, manufacturers, retailers, and customers; transforming companies and creating new types of businesses; repatriating jobs and filling new kinds of jobs. But as revolutionary as these effects are, they pale in comparison to 3D printing away from control.

Away from control means making things without anyone knowing about it or being able to control it. The democratization of manufacturing naturally leads to the ability to 3D print away from control. 3D printing's ultimate disruption will happen when it is possible to make things with virtually any functionality away from control.

ZeframWD got a little taste of 3D printing away from control when it realized that the Federation and other customers were printing their own warp-drive parts. But ZeframWD was not totally in the dark; when it learned what customers were up to, it began selling them blueprints before its business was destroyed.

On the industrial side of 3D printing, customers' ability to make or repair their own parts is not entirely away from control. If a customer stops buying parts and starts making them, the supplier may notice the lost sales. However, the supplier will have no way of knowing the extent of the customer's in-house parts printing and customization. More importantly, the customer can make or repair parts away from control because the supplier may have no way to stop or control the customer's in-house parts making.

On the consumer side, away from control means the ability to 3D print in any way that is not controlled and cannot be controlled, such as 3D printing at home from blueprints obtained peer to peer on the Internet, 3D scanning and 3D printing any object, printing or buying 3D printed products on the black market, obtaining pirated proprietary blueprints from an Internet website, such as Pirate Bay, or from the Deep Web or the Dark Web, or having personal blueprints printed at uncontrolled local shops or by Internet-based fabricators.[330] Some such printing may violate intellectual property rights. But as 3D printing commentator Michael Weinberg of Public Knowledge said, "Most of the physical world is not protected by any type of intellectual property."[331] Most personal 3D printing away from control will be perfectly legal.

When 3D print shops become as common as Starbucks, you will be able to have products printed down the street or around the block. Either the shop will print it for you from blueprints it stocks, or you will send your blueprints to one of the shop's printers in the morning, then pick up the print on your way home from work. The shop may not know if products being printed on its machines are protected by any IP rights. Many products printed in such shops will be legal. Others may not be. Either way, the company that once sold you such products will not know you are now 3D printing them and will not be able to control it.

You might also print products in your own home, on your own machine. Many people buying personal 3D printers today are using them to make products for home businesses. SmartTech Markets predicts that at least two million homes will have 3D printers by 2023.[332] I believe the numbers will be much higher. Eventually, as many homes will have 3D printers as have 2D printers today.

Some people believe there will never be a 3D printer in most homes. Reasons why they should never say never are discussed in "Why the experts are wrong," below. But even if most homes someday will have a 3D printer, they will not all have the same ability. Some home printers will be able to make almost anything. Some may be purpose-built, like the Mink women's makeup printer, a Disney teddy-bear printer, or a supersafe children's printer like the Printeer.[333] Some young kids may have printers that print only superheroes, and some older kids may have printers that print only tools. Some homes will have printers that print only plastics, others will have metal-only printers, and others will have composite printers. The homeowners with the biggest ride-on lawnmowers or best-equipped woodshops will own extremely versatile machines with footprints that fill a corner of the garage. Apartment dwellers will have desktop 3D printers that can only print small items, like earrings, necklaces, and bracelets, on demand. The average homeowner will own a printer that can make almost anything, with size and price being the only limitations.

Friend networks will expand the power of personal 3D printing away from control. Your printer may not be able to print something you want, but your friend's machine can. Maybe none of your friends' machines can print you a new modular lawnmower, but one friend's machine can print the engine module while your printer makes the frame module.

3D printing things with almost any functionality away from control is where the real disruption will happen. Anyone, or any group of friends, may be able to bypass the traditional supply chain and self-manufacture. Presently, the things that can be self-manufactured are limited, but this is a time problem: given enough time, anyone may be able to make almost anything, away from control.

Making things of almost any functionality away from control will change everything. You will no longer need most manufacturers' products because you will be able to make them yourself. Manufacturers will probably realize that it is no longer profitable to continue to mass-produce their products and will be forced to sell blueprints and customized products instead, as ZeframWD did. Retail outlets that formerly sold mass-produced products will vanish, just like camera stores vanished when photography went digital. Without product sales, states will be unable to collect sales taxes, and the federal government may be unable to collect customs duties or enforce embargoes. Governments will be unable to control product safety. These are just a few of the effects of widespread 3D printing of products with almost any functionality, away from control.

WHY WOULD ANYONE WANT TO MAKE THINGS THEY COULD GO OUT AND BUY?

I have already questioned why big companies would continue to mass-produce things if they could sell the digital blueprints, shift the manufacturing burden to others, and make only customized products. After customers began 3D printing their own warp-drive parts, ZeframWD's market for selling such parts started to dry up. It no longer made sense for ZeframWD to mass-produce warp-drive parts, but it made perfect sense for customers to make them in house. Customers were able to 3D print the parts they needed when and where needed, for less money than buying from ZeframWD.

But why would the average person want to start making things instead of simply buying them? There are many reasons, any one of which may be enough to cause a person to make, not buy.

The basic reason, which is coded into our DNA, is that we are all makers at heart. Making is in our bones. Being able to make things gives great satisfaction and feeds our souls.

I have also talked at length about customization. Making your own products gives you the ability to decide the look, shape, size, color, texture, and functionality that you want, not what some faceless product designer decided for you and millions of other people. If you could make a product the way you want it, wouldn't you do it?

And how many times have you been unable to find a product to satisfy some particular need? You were amazed that with so many products in the world, the product you needed did not exist. Imagine if you could 3D print such products. Wouldn't you do it?

Convenience is also a reason to make, not buy. Although it has become very easy to surf the Internet, order a product, and have it delivered to your door in a day or two, a day or two is not the same as now. Products can be 3D printed when you need them.

Everyone complains that personal privacy is vanishing. When you 3D print away from control, no one knows it and no one can control it. 3D printers are the ultimate privacy machine. For example, 3D printing away from control is perfect for adult toys. This is certainly why SexShop3D. com will sell you the blueprints for the toy of your choice, which you can print and customize in the privacy of your own home. Because the adult toy industry is worth $15 billion per year, this could be a major reason why many homes will have 3D printers.[334]

I have saved cost for last, although it may be the driving factor for many people to 3D print their own stuff. The Michigan Technological University found that 3D printing twenty-seven common household items—including an iPhone dock, jewelry organizer, showerhead, orthotics, safety razor, toys, and paper-towel holder—could save the average family $2,000 per year, and that was with 2013 technology.[335] By 3D printing products they need or want, people will save money. Although they will need to buy raw materials for their printers, they will not have to pay for a manufacture's advertising, packaging, transportation costs, and profits, and they can have the product customized the way they want it, when they want it.

WHY THE EXPERTS ARE WRONG

Some 3D printing industry experts predict that the development of 3D printing over the next number of years will be mostly on the industrial side, not the consumer side.[336] They also say that most homes will not have a 3D printer anytime soon, and that consumer-level 3D printers will remain relatively unsophisticated.[337] For example, the folks at IDTechEx Research say:[338]

> Others believe there will be a 3D printer in every home, which would equate to a trillion-dollar addressable market...Given the limited capabilities of today's 3D printers we feel that is a triumph of hope over reality.
>
> Consumer-level 3D printers are a kind of power tool...The addressable market is then a fraction of the global home power tool market which is growing at around 5% per annum, much slower than the 100% growth in sales of consumer-level 3D printers from 2013 to 2014. Therefore, we expect the consumer market for 3D printing to start to saturate in the next few years and never exceed the global home power tool market.

Some predictions are more negative. Terry Gou, president of Taiwan's Foxconn Technology Group, which makes smartphones for Apple, called 3D printing a gimmick, not suitable for mass production and without commercial value.[339] Korea's Samsung called consumer-grade 3D printers unmarketable (but quickly changed its tune).[340] I believe they are all wrong, just as IBM's founder, Tom Watson, wrongly believed there was a market for only five computers, and Digital Equipment Corporation's founder, Ken Olsen, wrongly said "There is no reason for any individual to have a computer in his home."[341]

Watson and Olsen were not the only ones to misjudge new technology. Thomas Edison said, "Fooling around with alternating current is just a waste of time. Nobody will use it, ever." Western Union concluded that the "telephone has too many shortcomings to be seriously considered as a practical form of communication." In 1899, *The Literary Digest* said the "horseless carriage is at present a luxury for the wealthy; and although its price will probably fall in the future, it will never, of course, come into as common use as the bicycle." Lord Kelvin, one of the most prominent scientists of Victorian England, said "radio has no future" and "I'd rather send a message by a boy on a pony." Charlie Chaplin said of movies "the cinema is little more than a fad." Twentieth Century Fox's cofounder, Darryl Zanuck, said, "Television won't be able to hold on to any market it captures after the first six months. People will soon get tired of staring at a plywood box every night." IBM said to Xerox's founders that "the world potential market for copying machines is 5000 at most." YouTube's cofounder said, "There's just not that many videos I want to watch." In 1908, Wilbur Wright said, "I confess that in 1901 I said to my brother Orville that man would not fly for fifty years. Two years later we ourselves made flights. This demonstration of my impotence as a prophet gave me such a shock that ever since I have distrusted myself and avoided all predictions."[342]

History shows that betting against technology is a losing game, and that experts who believe technology will not improve and spread are often dead wrong. It's more likely that new technologies will wiggle their way deeper and deeper into our lives, until one day we wonder how we ever lived without them. Experts who predict that new technologies will become ubiquitous are the better bets. For example, Disney International's chairman, Andy Bird, was probably right when he said in 2013, "Every home within ten years, probably less than that, will have its own 3D printer, just as many homes now have a 2D or laser printer."[343]

Inside the 3D printing industry, there are already at least 250 start-ups and established companies that want to sell you a home 3D printer.[344]

The relative unsophistication of consumer-level 3D printers is a short-term problem. Eventually, some company, which I call Company X, will want to sell consumers a 3D printer that can make things with almost any functionality. The proof for this is that companies want to sell you whatever they can convince you to buy. Why wouldn't some company, or many companies, design a printer that gives you the power to make almost anything?

Company X may be an existing company. Or it may be a company like Hewlett Packard, which said of 3D printing in 2013 that it will "lead this business."[345] Or it may be a Japanese or Korean consumer-electronics manufacturer, who are finding themselves with fewer and fewer products to sell as home stereo systems, VCRs, CD players, DVD players, and even cameras head toward the White Elephant Burial Ground. Traditional manufacturing companies from outside the 3D printing industry will start making 3D printers because there is money to be made in selling them.

No matter who Company X turns out to be, its printers will start out making fairly simple devices and products, like kitchen tools and running shoes, and will get better and better, faster and faster, and capable of making more and more complex things over time, like power tools and home electronics. When other companies see the market potential that Company X saw, they will want some of the action, and Company X will find itself with a lot of competition. That competition will spur the development of more and more sophisticated machines, until one day consumers will buy home 3D printers that will make almost anything.

Other experts say personal 3D printers will never be able to make a complex product like a smartphone because the printer would need to be able to print twenty or more materials, such as different plastics, metal alloys, and glass.[346] This is horse thinking. Today's smartphones look the way they do, and are made of the materials they are made of, because of the manufacturer's tradeoff between aesthetic design and the constraints of traditional manufacturing methods. A smartphone made by a personal 3D printer need not, and almost certainly will not, look or feel anything like the smartphones we know today. Functionality—the ability to do what smartphones do—will be its only requirement, while much of its look and feel will be customized. Its material composition will not be constrained by traditional methods; the printer will be able to make it do what a smartphone needs to do with only a few materials. In fact, graphene and Carbomorph alone have many of the characteristics a smartphone needs: transparency, conductivity, rigidity, and strength.

No products of personal, make-anything printers need to look or feel anything like the products we know now. With sufficiently versatile materials, a personal 3D printer need not be as complicated, or as capable of making complicated things, as you might think.

Other experts believe personal 3D printers will never be able to make products with almost any functionality because, they say, it will not be safe to process metals in the home. Anyone who does woodworking, home metalworking, or jewelry making knows that many homes are already filled with dangerous equipment. 3D printers don't need to be dangerous to work with metal. For example, the Vader metal inkjet printer contains a small, safe furnace to melt metals. The Mini Metal Maker makes things from metal clay.[347] Michigan Technological University is developing an inexpensive, open-source metal printer, which can be used safely in the home.[348] The North Carolina State University has developed a 3D printable metal that is liquid at room temperature.[349] A personal 3D printer that uses it would not need a furnace or other high-heat source. Also, simply because products we know today are made with metal does not mean that 3D printed home versions of such products must also be made with metal. If the metal is for conductivity, another material like graphene or Carbomorph may provide it. If the metal is for strength, composites can be just as strong, like the Markforged personal machine, which prints with carbon fiber.[350]

All of these machines contain the kernels of Company X's personal, make-anything printer. Other machines do, too. The RoVa3D simultaneously prints in five different colors and five different materials. Each printhead can be fitted with differently sized nozzles so that one head can make fine details while another prints internal support structures.[351] The Cartesian Argentum is a personal printed-circuitry printer.[352] Company X's machine could also be a hybrid that combines additive and traditional processes. For example, the FABtotum is a combination personal 3D printer, scanner, and cutting-and-milling machine that raised $589,000 in 2014 on Indiegogo.[353] The Luinar TriBOT combines 3D printing, CNC milling, and injection molding in a $5,000 machine for home use. Combine all of these kernels, and we are well on the way to a personal 3D printer that can make anything. When such a machine exists, who wouldn't want one, especially if that machine satisfies your need to create—including creating items that can be found nowhere else—and to customize those items at your own convenience, in total privacy, and for less money than buying retail?

Other experts say a personal make-anything 3D printer could never be cheap enough for most people to buy. I don't buy it. Americans spend billions of dollars every year on televisions, computers, printers, tablets, smartphones, lawn mowers, and shop equipment. If they want it, they find a way to buy it. Also, technology prices inevitably drop. Here I point to two numbers: $5 million and $400. Those are the costs of the most powerful computer in 1975 and a smartphone with the same computing power today.[354] As personal make-anything 3D printers are developed and widely adopted, their prices will drop to the point of affordability for most people, just like every other technology that has come down the pike.

Some experts believe that most homes will not even have simple 3D printers. This is also horse thinking. I agree that not every home will want or need a make-anything printer. But most homes without make-anything printers will have some kind of 3D printer for at least two reasons. The first is purpose-built printers. They will make having some products so convenient that you cannot live without them. The garage may have a hand tools printer, the playroom may have a dollhouse furniture printer, a toy train printer, or a dinosaur printer. Kitchens may have pasta printers, dinnerware printers, or kitchen gadget printers. The master bedroom may have a makeup printer, a jewelry printer, and maybe an adult toy printer.

The second reason is kids, which I believe will be the strongest driver for home adoption of 3D printers and the impetus for Company X to shift into high-gear development of a make-anything printer. Kids are already fascinated by 3D printers. They see them more and more at schools and public libraries. One day their homework will require them. Their friends will have them. Kids will demand home 3D printers. Parents will also want their kids to have them, to help prepare them for the future. Which will a parent prefer a child to do for hours on end: watch TV, play video games, or make things with a 3D printer? Kids' first printers will be simple and safe and will make simple and safe things. But as the kids grow, personal printers will get better and better and more and more capable of making complex things. Just as home computers and smartphones become obsolete in two to three years, 3D printers will need to be replaced with the newest, the fastest, the most capable.

3D printers will someday be in every home because we are heading into a new age. This may sound circular, but when 3D printing away from control changes everything, as I believe it will, *everything* will change. When a personal 3D printer can make almost anything, don't expect to be able to buy such things. The companies that made them may no longer exist or may have decided that the only way to survive is to sell digital blueprints instead of selling the things themselves. Owning a printer may be the only way to obtain certain products, making ownership nearly compulsory.

Over the past twenty-six years, the worldwide 3D printing market has grown at a compound annual growth rate (CAGR) of 27.3 percent. Its CAGR was 33.8 percent for 2012–2014.[355] Both printer makers and users are likely to see continued exponential growth, and 3D printers are likely to become more and more common in industry, the community, and the home. They are likely to get better and better and faster and faster, just as laptops, home computers, and cell phones have done in a short span of time.

WHEN WILL TOTAL DISRUPTION HAPPEN?

Everything will change when you can make anything. When will that be? For an answer, let's go back to the Market Disruption Checklist. On the consumer level, to be able to make anything, 3D printers need to make products with sophisticated functionality, using three or four materials, at most. To achieve high-level functionality *and* a custom look and feel will probably require machines that manipulate materials on the molecular or atomic level. MIT's Center for Bits and Atoms is working on such "3D assemblers."[356]

The printer also must be able to print complex structures that include integrated circuitry on the nano level. It must be able to perform secondary manufacturing processes, such as heat-treating, polishing, or picking and placing non–3D printed components (or 3D printed components made elsewhere). When personal 3D printers can do all of these things away from control, everything will change.

By 2025, 3D printing should be fully integrated into a vibrant US manufacturing economy. But how long will it be until you can print things with virtually any functionality, away from control? Bill Gates's famous statement applies here as well: "We always overestimate the change that will occur in the next two years and underestimate the change that will occur in the next ten."[357] I predict that by 2025 you will be able to make almost anything away from control. Gartner predicts full consumer adoption of 3D printing in five to ten years, but I'll stick with 2025 because time flies.[358] The McKinsey consulting firm seems to agree: "We estimate that consumer use of 3D printing could have potential economic impact of $100 billion to $300 billion per year by 2025."[359]

WILL MASS PRODUCTION GO THE WAY OF THE DINOSAUR?

The short answer is probably no. There will probably always be a place for mass production. But as 3D printing takes hold of consumers and industry, we probably will not need nearly as much of it, or may not need it on the huge scale we have today. There will still be companies that centrally mass-produce some products, like Coca Cola and toilet paper, and there will probably also be smaller-scale regional mass production. But 3D printing processes are getting faster, and researchers are working on mass-production 3D printing. Also, there is no reason why products cannot be mass-produced with a roomful of 3D printers or multiplatform printers that can print large quantities of the same product at the same time, in rooms the size of sports arenas. Don't think of 3D printers printing only one thing at a time. Here is a photo of stacks of hip-replacement cups printed by an Arcam Powder Bed Fusion 3D printer. Think how many of these cups could be made in an arena full of Arcam printers.

Photo courtesy of Arcam

But 3D printed mass production may only be needed on a smaller scale. As IBM said, "3D printing is expected to fundamentally transform the principles of global mass production."[360] We will have mass production, but it will be much different than we know it today.

Centralized mass production on the immense scale we know today is a remnant of the Industrial Revolution. It may not fit or be needed in a 3D printed world. I have discussed several of the reasons for this. The ability to customize parts and products at no additional cost is one of the great strengths of 3D printing. By comparison, no two mass-produced parts or products are different. Making them different substantially increases the price per part. As the expectation of customization grows, all of the factories that mass-produced such parts replaced by customized ones simply will not be needed. As IBM said, 3D printing "frees companies from the need to build standardized parts and pursue economies of scale."[361] This is an interesting twist, suggesting that companies only make standardized parts because economics forces them to do so. The implication is that if they are not forced to standardize, they will naturally want to customize. Mass production has no place in markets where the products become mass customized.

The democratization of manufacturing will have a similar effect. As small companies enter a market with 3D printed products, the mass producer loses market share. As it loses sales to its new competitors, its costs rise, forcing it to raise its prices, while its 3D printing competitors sell the product for less than the mass-producer's original price. As the manufacturing of any product is democratized, mass production of that product becomes unsustainable. Mass production has no place in a market for products whose manufacturing has been democratized, except maybe localized, smaller-scale mass production to meet regional needs. As McKinsey's Daniel Cohen observed:[362]

Multinational corporations could face the unenviable prospect of competing against countless start-ups that need only a computer, design expertise, and the ability to finance small production runs.

Regional and distributed manufacturing are also nemeses of mass production. 3D printing will shift manufacturing to the point of need. The factories that manufacture for a region will be smaller. Although parts and products may be mass-produced by 3D printing in large enough quantities to satisfy local needs, centralized mass production of such parts and products—like we have today—will not be needed.

The ability to make almost any product away from control will be a further nail in mass production's coffin, and probably the biggest one. The first industries to be affected will probably be toys because the machines to print them need not be capable of printing complex or refined structures. For toys and many other products used in the home, good-enough 3D prints may be good enough to kill the competition. 3D printers capable of printing reasonable copies of many toys exist today and are becoming better and better all the time.

Disruption of mass production in the toy industry may happen in several ways. Let's say father Frank and little Jimmy decide to 3D print a toy dump truck as a father-and-son project. They surf the Internet for dump truck blueprints. They find a digital blueprint that vaguely resembles a famous brand-name dump truck. They download the blueprint and print out a fully functioning toy. Every time this happens, the famous brand is one step closer to ceasing mass production of toy dump trucks. Moreover, because the blueprints for the brand-name dump truck were not available online when Frank and Jimmy searched for a truck to print, the brand also lost a blueprint sale. If it doesn't get its blueprints online fast enough, the market will simply move on without it, enabling countless father-and-son teams to print generic dump trucks.

This scenario raises an interesting question that only real-life market dynamics can answer in time: Why 3D print a brand-name dump truck—or any similar product—when a generic truck can be printed for less? The blueprints for the branded truck will certainly cost more than the blueprints for the generic. In fact, the latter may be free. Maybe there will always be some demand for branded products—and for digital blueprints for branded products—but probably not of the same magnitude that companies mass-produce actual products today.

The greatest potential disruption of mass production by 3D printing away from control is the elimination of the market protection provided by economies of scale. Take, for example, dinner plates. You probably have a set of eight dinner plates, salad plates, soup bowls, and cups and saucers. Let's assume they are not protected by any intellectual property rights, such as design patents or copyrights. Thus, anyone is free to copy the design and make identical dinner plates. However, the entry barriers to mass-producing such products protect the markets of the companies that make them. Companies using traditional methods cannot enter the dinner plates market unless they have enough capital to build a big factory, and they must make and sell millions of dinner plates to cover the cost of the factory and have some profit left over.

An old-line manufacturing company, Plates4-8, mass-produces millions of your plate design, using economies of scale. Plates4-8 will probably never switch its mass-production lines from traditional machines to 3D printers if the markets for its plates stay the same. But that is a big *if* because you will eventually own a 3D printer that can make many things, including dinner plates. Or you may have a shop down the street that can print your plate, or someone in your Friends Network may have a purpose-built dinnerware printer. Or an Internet 3D printing fabricator will offer to make your plate. If you have eight dinner plates and one breaks, you can print one to replace it. If you can print one plate, you can print eight (along with all of the other pieces that make up a set), and if you can print eight, you no longer need Plates4-8. Once you can do that, Plates4-8 may still have a market for plates, but it will probably be much smaller, and mass-producing plates may no longer be profitable. Plates4-8 may then change its production lines to 3D printers because it will be making far fewer plates and will probably be customizing them. In fact, every plate in a set may be a little different.

All of this eliminates the need for the mass producer and economies of scale. Thus, even if 3D printing does not replace mass production, it could disrupt or destroy the need for it. These are the reasons that people who ask if 3D printing will ever be capable of mass production may be asking the wrong question. More importantly, when people can 3D print almost any product away from control, mass production will be displaced by production by the masses.

6

Merging Science and Nature

PRODUCT DESIGN BONANZA

3D printers can make things that could not be made before, either because there was no way to make them with traditional machines or because it would cost too much. The elimination of manufacturing limitations and prohibitive production costs, coupled with the availability of advanced materials, is a bonanza for product designers, engineers, and customers, allowing them to think and design outside the box, way outside the box. 3D printing will rock the things we make, resulting in radically different mass-customized products with complex, elegant, and increasingly organic structures in which science and nature merge, both in appearance and reality.

MASS CUSTOMIZATION

One of 3D printing's great strengths is its ability to make one-of-a-kind products. Some of this mass customization will be of products that do not yet exist. But existing products will be customizable too. Consider again Plates4-8's dinner plates. Whether the manufacturer is faced with market disruption caused by personal 3D printing away from control or is looking for ways to use 3D printing to gain a competitive edge, Plates4-8 will offer customized dinner plates. For example, Plates4-8 may sell sets of 3D printed dinnerware that look handmade; every plate in the set will be a little different. Or Plates4-8 or its retailers may offer a web interface that allows customers to design their own plates, which are then printed by the retailer, by a local Plates4-8-approved fabricator, or by a consumer using a personal printer at home or in a Friends Network. In any event, Plates4-8 will shape its product line, customization tools, and printing options with the customer's design interests in mind. IBM observed that because of 3D printing, "[p]roduct design and retailing will be influenced greatly by interactions with customers."[363]

Customization is starting to happen. 3D Systems and Google announced Project ARA to 3D print mass-personalized modular smartphones.[364] Hasbro and 3D Systems partnered to bring Hasbro's vast inventory of toy designs, which include Mr. Potato Head, Playskool, Star Wars, Tonka, and Transformers to a 3D printer near you.[365] Hasbro also partnered with Shapeways, so that kids of all ages can create customized versions of Hasbro products, which Shapeways 3D prints and either sells for you or sends to you, on demand, starting with My Little Pony. Certain fans of Hasbro's Little Pony brand (known as Bronys, or Bros who like ponies) design and sell personalized Little Pony figurines through the Shapeways platform. The program is wildly successful. The Brony stables feature more than nine hundred ponies, with many more to come from designers licensed by Hasbro.[366] This is not only a great way to shift the company from making and selling products to designing and selling digital blueprints, but it is also an incredible way to get additional mileage from old toy brands. Hasbro and Shapeways will do the same with other Hasbro brands, such as Transformers, Dungeons and Dragons, Scrabble, Monopoly, and GI Joe.[367] I can't wait to print my own custom Rock'em Sock'em Robots that look like my wife and me.

Customization is already happening in the $15 billion adult toy industry. French Coqs' website allows customers to design customized adult toys, which the company 3D prints in medical-grade silicone and ships to you. The company will also make highly personalized toys from photos you provide, and its customization interface even allows you to improve on Mother Nature's endowment.[368] SexShop3D.com will sell you the blueprints for the toy of your choice, which you can customize (using dildo-generator.com) and print in the privacy of your own home.[369] Who says there will not be a 3D printer in every home?

Other custom 3D printing services may be a narcissist's dream. 3D Systems' 3DMe service allows customers to upload a personal headshot and profile, from which the company will print a selfie character of your choice, from chefs to baseball players, Mr. Spock to Santa, cowboys to personalized wedding cake toppers.[370] You choose the pose. Disney does the same at its theme parks, where you can make a Cinderella or Star Wars imperial stormtrooper selfie, or carbon freeze yourself as You Solo, in imitation of Harrison Ford's most enduring image.[371] Japan's Petfig will do the same for your Siberian Husky or house cat. Again, you choose the pose, from running dog to kitty couch potato.[372]

London start-up OwnFone's web-based platform allows you not only to design the outer shell of your own cell phone online but also to 3D print it at home and install inner electronics that the company mails in a kit.[373]

This type of customization is pretty simple: making personalized jewelry or dinnerware, putting your face on Mr. Potato Head or Obi-Wan Kenobi, or 3D printing a custom smartphone with your own family members' names on the buttons. But as customers push the limits of customization, new products will emerge. Eventually, customization tools may allow you to design entirely new products, which you can have printed or print at home. As Chris Anderson wrote in *Makers*, 3D printers enable the design and manufacturing of "products that the world wants but doesn't know it yet."[374]

IMPROVED PRODUCTS

Industry is starting to realize that 3D printing can make parts better than traditional methods can. Because parts can be 3D printed without regard to their complexity, product designers and engineers can design them to do what they want them to do, not what traditional methods allowed them to do. Thus, 3D printing allows part and product designs to be optimized for function. For example, the SOLS 3D printed robo-boot is outfitted with gyroscopes and sensors that control air pockets in the boot, which react to body movements and shape the boot accordingly.[375]

There is another side to optimization: structure. Ideally, structural design balances strength and flexibility in a lightweight product composed of no more material than necessary. Enter topological optimization, which uses mathematics to optimize product design.[376] Using topological optimization, product engineers can find the best design for the performance requirements of the part. Applying topological optimization to design for additive manufacturing will result in structurally optimized parts that look like they came from another planet. For example, in the photo below, a traditionally designed and manufactured structural node for a bridge is shown on the left. To its right are two topologically optimized, 3D printed, load-bearing, structural bridge nodes, designed by Arup, the global engineering firm. Ignoring traditional production constraints, a topologically optimized design concentrates metal where it is needed most, making the part stronger than its traditionally made counterpart. Maybe more importantly, the design prints no metal where none is needed, making the part lighter, too, and saving material.

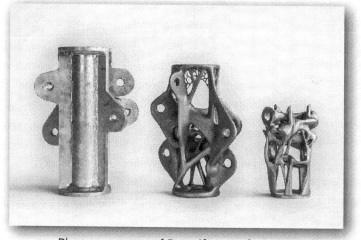

Photo courtesy of Davidfotografie/Arup

As Arup's Salome Galjaard said of the part's design, "This approach enables a very sophisticated design, without the need to simplify the design in a later stage to lower costs."[377] This complex design could only be made with a 3D printer.

3D printing will allow countless product designs to be improved in many ways that are hard to imagine today. Once designers and engineers realize that they can optimize product designs and manufacture complex parts with reduced weight, waste, and cost, we will see radical reinterpretations of existing products.

Airbus Defence and Space used topological optimization to transform the design of a structural bracket for the Eurostar E3000 telecommunications satellite, then 3D printed the bracket in an aluminum alloy. By 3D printing the bracket, Airbus reduced the number of parts from four to one, eliminated forty-four rivets, reduced weight by 35 percent, and improved stiffness by 40 percent.[378]

Photos courtesy of Airbus Defense and Space

The ultimate in 3D printed product improvement may be human repair and enhancement. As McKinsey observed:[379]

> In medicine, the ability to print body parts from the patient's own cells could improve transplant success rates and prevent deaths that occur due to patients having to wait for donor organs.

Several companies and universities are working on bioprinting human tissue and organs. Eventually, organs may be custom bioprinted to replace failing ones, or simply for human enhancement. We can only hope that 3D printed human replacement parts will be at least as good as the originals, and improvements would be ideal. Human joints are already being replaced by 3D printed ones. Mayo Clinic is offering customized joint replacements, and forty thousand replacement hip cups have already been installed in as many humans.[380] A Texas company, BioDevices, is developing bioprinted reconstructive breast implants.[381]

ENTIRELY NEW PRODUCTS

It is easy to think of mass customization and mass personalization resulting in 3D printed products tailored to customers' needs, such as shoes that perfectly fit your feet, glasses that fit your face, or tennis-racket grips designed for your hand. Or jewelry, dinnerware, doorknobs, and plumbing fixtures made to your design. Or a washing machine or sink that perfectly fits the space you have for it. Or customized toys for kids or adults. Or medicines customized by purpose and dose.[382] Or food.

3D food printers already exist (launched in 2014), and research that may have a great impact on 3D printing food is ongoing. One goal is customization. "It's very easy to add or remove a macro- or micronutrient [in] food," says Daniel van der Linden of the Dutch research institute TNO, which makes prototyping printers for the food industry. Their machines have printed pasta with extra doses of calcium or vitamins, but the customization could just as easily have been mushroom or garlic flavoring. Another objective is being pursued by the PERFORMANCE (PERsonalised FOod using Rapid MAnufacturing for the Nutrition of elderly ConsumErs) project, which received €3 million from the European Union to 3D print foods modified for therapeutic purposes. Daniel van der Linden has described 3D printing customized carrots and other vegetables that can be chewed and swallowed by people afflicted with dysphasia, a condition that makes swallowing difficult.[383]

All of these 3D printing–enabled projects make products the way consumers want them. However, the products themselves are not new;

they are just customized. It is harder to think of mass customization resulting in entirely new products, things that have never existed. But it will happen. As companies and customers push the limits of customization, entirely new products will emerge. A great example is Behnaz Farahi's 3D printed "Caress of the Gaze" garment, which looks like a mash-up between a soft porcupine and Van Gogh's "Starry Night," turned into a short, woman's poncho. Farahi, a designer and PhD candidate at the University of California, embedded motion sensing cameras that cause the garment to react to onlookers, altering its form and undulating in response to precisely where and how intensely the watcher is watching (see it in action at http://3dprintingindustry.com/2015/10/05/starers-beware-this-3d-printed-garment-knows-when-youre-looking-at-it/?utm_source=3D+Printing+Industry+Update&utm_medium=email&utm_campaign=b1bbb1fc77-RSS_EMAIL_CAMPAIGN&utm_term=0_695d5c73dc-b1bbb1fc77-60484669).[384] Imagine the black eyes that may result!

3D printing has great strengths that will lead to entirely new products. Traditional manufacturing methods have limitations that dictate product design, and therefore products are designed so that they can be manufactured by existing methods. Because 3D printing has no such limitations, design can aspire to structural optimization. For example, John Obielodan and Brent Stucker foresee 3D printing models of body parts with built-in sensors that record the location and pressure of cuts and punctures, to be used in training budding surgeons in the art of incisions and sutures.[385]

Everyone has seen the way ants work together in colonies. Imagine 3D printed robotic ants that work together to build things. Festo, the German engineering firm that invented an elephant-trunk robotic arm and a 3D printed robo-seagull (shown below in "Fundamentally different products"), did just that. Festo's robotic ants mimic the cooperative behavior of real ants by making individual decisions while working as teams toward a common goal. Each ant is about the size of a human hand, with a stereo camera in its head, grippers below its chin, and floor sensors that tell the ant where it is. Their circuitry is overlaid on their 3D printed bodies, which is a perfect job for direct-write Material Jetting systems. These ants will be factory workers of the future.[386]

Photo courtesy of Festo AG & Co. KG/ © Festo AG & Co. KG

Other roboticists are 3D printing fish—or something like them. A team at the Austrian University of Graz 3D printed a school of fish-like robots capable of learning individually and functioning as a group. The project's goal is to create interacting, cognitive, autonomous robots for ecological monitoring, searching, maintaining, exploring, and harvesting resources in underwater habitats.[387]

This project also shows how 3D printing can be used to upgrade existing technology. Here, the team cannibalized a toy submarine, then 3D printed new parts large enough to hold sensors and actuators, which enabled them to turn a cheap toy into a sophisticated scientific robot.

On a smaller scale, Professors Shoachen Chen and Joseph Wang of the University of California 3D printed microscopic fish-shaped robots designed to swim through the human body to flush toxins and deliver medicine.[388]

A problem with almost all products is that they break. Deloitte has suggested that products will be 3D printed with embedded strain gauges and sensors that will tell you if they are about to break or getting too hot, rusting, and so on.[389] America's aging infrastructure would benefit from such advances. The ability to know that a bridge is about to collapse could save lives and the commuter disruption caused by such catastrophic surprises.

Creating entirely new products takes more than just 3D printing. It also takes ingenuity, innovation, and vision. Because 3D printing will be able to make almost anything the human mind can design, it is a great tool for turning an inventive spark into reality.

NATURE-INSPIRED DESIGNS

The most exciting thing about 3D printers is that they can be used to make products that look and feel very different from products we know. Just because a product is made of twenty or twenty-five materials today doesn't mean it can't be 3D printed from three or four materials tomorrow. Just because we are accustomed to certain products being made of metal doesn't mean they can't be 3D printed from composites. Just because we think of products as looking a certain way doesn't mean that 3D printed versions of such products will not look very different.

The greatest and most powerful strength of 3D printing is that it allows companies, product designers, engineers, and customers to think outside the box in many ways. But this is extraordinarily difficult to do. According to University of Texas professor Carolyn Conner Seepersad, "Researchers in cognitive psychology and engineering have demonstrated that designers experience a powerful tendency to adhere to designs they have encountered previously."[390] We are very accustomed to thinking about things in certain ways, and old habits die hard. Even when we think we are thinking outside the box, we are probably still stuck inside some larger box.

I read an article in the early 2000s about how the Wright brothers designed flexible aircraft wings because they saw that birds' wings flexed in flight. The article said that "In years to come...morphing [aircraft] wings will be sophisticated structures that automatically reconfigure their shapes and surface textures to adapt to monitored changes in flying conditions."[391] 3D printing not only makes such designs buildable but also drives product design more and more toward organic designs, potentially merging science with nature.

We saw in "Improved products" the topologically optimized structural bridge node and telecommunications satellite bracket, which look more like they were grown than built. Product designs will tend to become more natural and organic because 3D printers make such designs not only realizable but are also easier to print than designs with traditional straight lines and square corners. In fact, the sooner product designers and engineers stop thinking in terms of T-squares and start thinking about how Mother Nature designs things, the sooner we will see both radically new product and part designs and radically new products. Some designers are already breaking the straight-line/square-corner paradigm. For example, design students Mario Coppola and Salvatore Gallo designed this tennis racket, which looks more grown than built.[392]

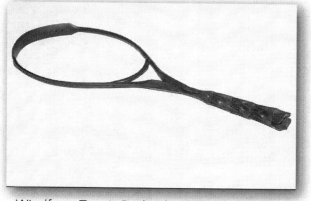

Windform Tennis Racket by CRP Technology/
Photo courtesy CRP Technology

Seattle's Pensar Developments designed a fully customizable 3D printed shoe. Taking its name from nature, the DNA shoe is customized not only to a customer's anatomy but also to his or her gait and the mechanics of how his or her foot actually works.[393]

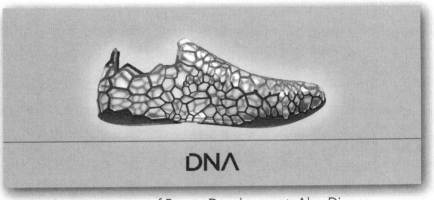

Image courtesy of Pensar Development, Alex Diener,
Mark Selander, Kristin Will, Spencer Denton

Ondra Chotovinsky designed this seashell-inspired speaker and Martin
Hreben 3D printed it.[394]

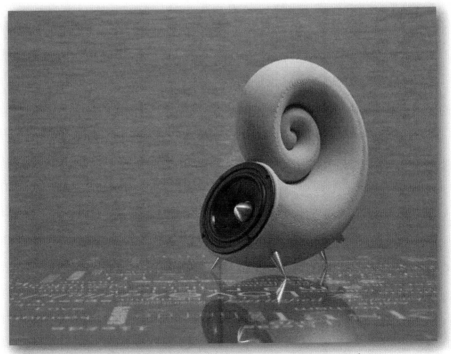

Photo courtesy Ondra Chotovinsky & Martin Hreben

Netherlands design student Lilian van Daal said of her nature-inspired 3D printed chair design, "In nature materials grow in different structures and that's the way a plant, for example, gains different functions. I love the idea of applying this concept to our human world."[395]

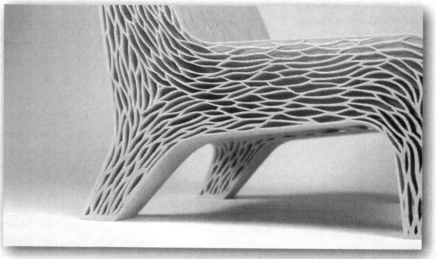

Photo courtesy of Lilian van Daal

These designs are examples of biomimicry creeping into product design.[396] This is happening not because designers suddenly discovered nature and want to mimic it, but because 3D printing frees them to design and build organic designs. As Fatima Qasim wrote:[397]

> Nature works on the principle of layer-by-layer amalgamation of matter to create a single unit. Geographical formations are made by a slow process of sedimentation, while human growth proceeds through the formation and development of cells. 3D printers thus clearly imitate nature.

Others, like Spanish designer Maximo Riera, are directly copying nature in their 3D printed product designs, such as Riera's whale tail, elephant, squid, rhino, and hippo chairs, which will enliven any living room.[398]

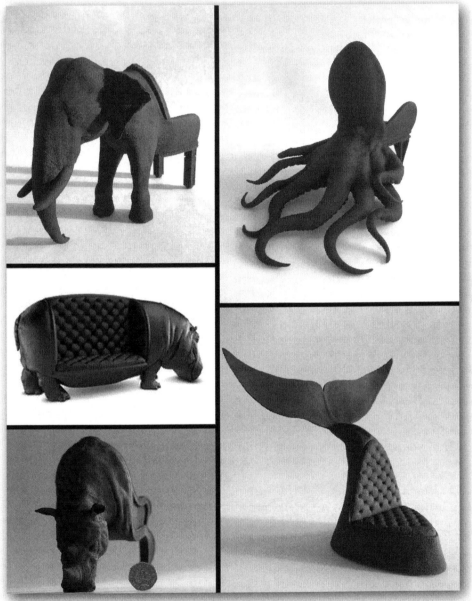

Photos courtesy of Maximo Riera

Florida-based Monad Studio fused science and nature to produce this hauntingly beautiful 3D printed electronic violin.[399]

Photo courtesy of MONAD Studio / Eric Goldemberg + Veronica Zalcberg
in collaboration with musician Scott F. Hall www.monadstudio.com

Biomimicry is also creeping into industrial product design. For example, EDAG, a leading automotive engineering service company, designed the Genesis 3D printed concept car, which evokes the design of a sea turtle.[400]

Photo courtesy of EDAG Group

A team of engineers and designers at Indiana and Purdue Universities drew from nature for their lightweight car design, which they call the Aerodynamic Water Droplet with Strong Lightweight Bone Structure, or WaterBone for short. The 3D printed aluminum-foam radiating rib frame was inspired by the aerodynamics of a water droplet and the structural stability and safety of the human ribcage.[401]

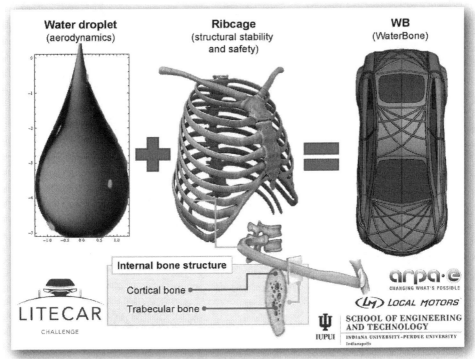

Images courtesy of Andrés Tovar, Indiana University–
Purdue University Indianapolis

Plumbing fixture manufacturer American Standard is mimicking nature in 3D printed faucet designs. In one design, fine structures of concealed waterways converge at the top, just before reaching the aerator, giving the impression that the water appears magically out of the faucet.[402]

Photo courtesy of American Standard

Biomimicry is also coming to robotics, which makes sense because the whole point of robots is to substitute for human labor. Festo, a world leader in automation technology, designed the 3D printed Bionic Handling Assistant, inspired by an elephant's trunk. The trunk's flexible pincers bend around objects on contact, just like a human finger.[403]

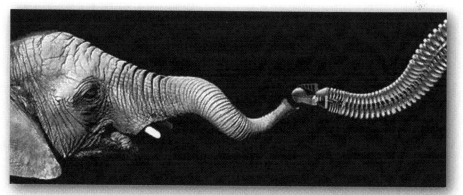

Photo courtesy of Festo AG & Co. KG/ © Festo AG & Co. KG

As the Wright brothers saw, aerial vehicles certainly could benefit from mimicking the designs of their feathered friends. Festo realized this and designed its 3D printed SmartBird robotic seagull drone. As Evan Ackerman observed, it "controls itself the same way birds do, by twisting its body, wings, and tail" and even turns its head to steer.[404] And they are much cleaner than the real thing.

Photo courtesy of Festo AG & Co. KG/ © Festo AG & Co. KG

The Robobird, a 3D printed remote-controlled flying machine designed by Netherlander Nico Nijenhuis, CEO of Clear Flight Solutions, is intended to be exactly what it looks like, a bird. Nico's intent is to put scarecrows out of work by chasing real birds away from places where they are not wanted, like airports and landfills. Nico says, "Birds are not only a nuisance, they can also be a serious threat to safety in aviation. The Robobird is an environmentally friendly solution for all your bird-related problems." What is important about the Robobird is not just that it looks like a bird. Designed with foam wings that deform upward and downward as they flap, it flies like a bird too.[405]

Photo courtesy of Clear Flight Solutions

These are examples of using biomimicry in mechanical structures. In other words, even though the designs mimic nature, most of them are being applied to what are essentially machines made from inorganic materials. Although Maximo Riera's nature-inspired chairs are not exactly machines, they are still made of inorganic materials. The most exciting thing about 3D printing is its potential to transform the product-design paradigm from inorganic structures to truly organic ones, to merge the human-made world with the natural world by combining 3D printers and bioprinters.

A step in this direction (literally) is the bioprinted running shoe designed by Shamees Aden and Dr. Martin Hanczyc. Printed from synthetic biomaterial called protocells, Aden's second-skin shoes perfectly fit the runner's feet. The protocells puff up to cushion the foot when needed and deflate when the pressure is off. If they tear, they heal themselves. At night, they rejuvenate in a jar of protocell slime. They can also be bioprinted in any color. According to Aden, "You would take the trainers home and you would have to care for it as if it was a plant, making sure it has the natural resources needed to rejuvenate the cells."[406]

MIT's Neri Oxman took 3D printing to a new level—combining nature and clothing—with her 3D printed, living wearable called Mushtari, which means something like "giant" in Arabic. Inspired by the human gastrointestinal tract, Mushtari contains 3D printed internal channels designed to host synthetic microorganisms that fluoresce in bright colors and photosynthesize biofuels. She envisions the living wearables fueling our bodies and repairing damaged skin. According to Oxman:[407]

The incorporation of synthetic biology in 3D printed products for wearable microbiomes will enable the transition from designs that are inspired by Nature, to designs made with and by Nature, to, possibly designing Nature herself.

As Barry Trimmer, the editor of *Soft Robotics* journal said of robotics, "We often take our cues from biology...Animals are living prototypes of what we want to build."[408] But animals are not the only models for future product designs. The natural world is a vast reference library from which product designers can draw.

4D PRINTING

Skylar Tibbits of MIT's Self-Assembly Lab is making materials that mimic nature. Using Stratasys's Connex multimaterial 3D printer, he is developing self-assembling multilayer smart materials by a process that he calls 4D printing. Tibbits has programmed materials on the particle level to self-assemble into specific shapes when they get wet. Although such smart materials are not organic, they act like living materials. A next step in 4D printing may be to bioprint organic smart materials that mimic nature because they are partially alive.

Inside-the-box applications for 4D materials are self-assembling furniture and toys. Imagine a chair that turns itself into a table. Imagine a box, launched into space, that transforms itself into a satellite.[409] Imagine a toy that knows that Tab A inserts into Tab B and does so itself, regardless of how unclear the assembly directions may be. Christmas mornings will be transformed. Outside-the-box applications include objects that adapt or respond to their environment and reshape, heal, evolve, or self-assemble over time. For example, BAE Systems is working on self-healing aircraft parts.[410] Tibbits gives this example: "Imagine if water pipes could expand or contract to change capacity or change flow rate; or may undulate...to move the water themselves."[411] Australia's Wollongong University has turned this idea into reality, 4D printing a self-operating water valve. When the water passing through the valve reaches a certain temperature, the structure of the valve changes its shape, closing the valve.[412]

In funding a joint research project between Harvard University, the University of Pittsburgh, and the University of Illinois, the US Army is thinking outside the box about 4D printing. The research team aims to develop materials that change their shape, properties, or function to adapt to their environment, as living materials do. Harvard's Jennifer Lewis said:[413]

> If you use materials that possess the ability to change their properties or shape multiple times, you don't have to build for a specific, one-time use...Composites that can be reconfigured in the presence of different stimuli could dramatically extend the reach of 3D printing.

Think about that: being able to design parts and products that can be 3D printed without regard to existing materials. Just as 3D printing frees designers and engineers to design products that cannot be built with traditional machines, 4D printing allows them to design products that cannot be made with existing materials.

Team member Ralph Nuzzo of the University of Illinois suggested more out-of-the-box applications:[414]

The ability to create one fabric that responds to light by changing its colour, and to temperature by altering its permeability, and even to an external force by hardening its structure, becomes possible through the creation of responsive materials that are simultaneously adaptive, flexible, lightweight and strong. It's this "complicated functionality" that makes true 4D printing a game changer.

My selfish hope from this technology is that my socks find their match in the dryer and stay together in the laundry basket and drawer.

FARTHER OUTSIDE THE BOX

This section is not directly about 3D printing. Its purpose is to inspire designers, engineers, and others to think outside the box and push the envelope of complex part and product designs that imitate the elegance of nature. Airbus is trying to do the same. Its concept design for a 2050-era aircraft with a visible bird-skeleton-inspired exostructure and transparent skin is not meant to fly but to "stretch the imagination of engineers."[415]

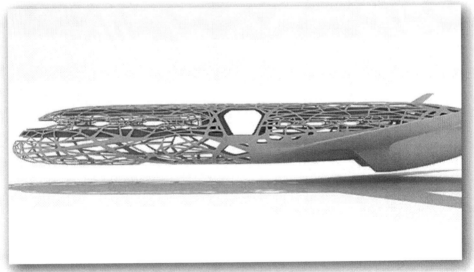

Photo courtesy of Airbus Group

Aerospace engineers can now push performance boundaries by creating ultralightweight parts with complex organic shapes.[416] As Airbus explained the structure of its design:[417]

> Future aircraft could be built using a bionic structure that mimics the bone structure of birds. Bone is both light and strong because its porous interior carries tension only where necessary, leaving space elsewhere. By using bionic structures, the fuselage has the strength it needs, but can also make the most of extra space where required. This not only reduces the aircraft's weight and fuel burn, but also makes it possible to add features like oversized doors for easier boarding and panoramic windows.

This is the essence of topological and structural optimization, which will drive human design closer and closer to Mother Nature's designs. 3D printing can turn such designs into reality.

BAE is also thinking outside the box with its self-dividing aircraft concept. Like a flock of birds that flies in formation while all is safe, BAE's aircraft divides itself into smaller aircraft when attacked or threatened.

Image courtesy of BAE Systems

Science-fiction movies, literature, and art are filled with images of aircraft, spacecraft, and products that copy nature. Alex Brady's artistic imaginings of the Swan Plane and Heavy Bomber merge science and nature in futuristic aircraft designs:[418]

Images courtesy of Alex Brady

Is this an accident or a coincidence, or is it simply inevitable that the imperfect nature of human designs should progress toward nature's perfection?

We are on the verge of great breakthroughs in design. Without 3D printing, complex, topologically and structurally optimized, organic designs would be stuck in two dimensions. Because 3D printers can (or will soon) turn any design into reality, designers and engineers are freed to design new versions of parts and products that look nothing like their present-day counterparts, and to design entirely new things.

But it can be difficult to break old design habits. To do so, follow these rules of design freedom for a 3D printed world:

1. Think outside the box.
2. Parts and products need not look or feel as they do today.
3. Design geometries can be as complex as form and function require, or as the designer desires.
4. Designs need not have straight lines or square edges or corners.
5. Parts and products need not be made of the same materials, or as many materials, as they are today.
6. Surfaces need not be solid; they can be transparent.
7. Topologically and structurally optimize the design.
8. As designs imitate the elegance of nature, they approach perfection.

7

What Does "Genuine" Mean?

HOW WILL YOU KNOW IF IT IS REAL?

Counterfeiting is a $1.7 trillion threat to world economies.[419] From 2002 to 2012, 325 percent more counterfeit goods were confiscated than in the previous decade.[420] NASA says counterfeiting is one of its biggest challenges. 3D printing is a perfect tool for counterfeiters.[421] The democratization of manufacturing driven by 3D printing may lead to counterfeiting on steroids because copies of genuine products can be made by professional counterfeiters or by well-meaning people who 3D print things away from control. As 3D printers get better, faster, and more consumer friendly, anyone will be able to make copies of genuine products. And counterfeiters will always invent ingenious ways to make products that appear to be genuine.

Even if people want to buy the genuine product, how will they know it is genuine in a 3D printed world? If a bicyclist cracks his skull using a 3D printed bicycle helmet, or a child chokes on a 3D printed toy part, how will the company or the victim know if it was genuine or a perfect knockoff? How will they know who to sue, or if anyone should be sued? In a world where companies sell 3D printed products, blueprints, or both; where blueprints can be obtained from many sources, modified, and remixed; and where such products and blueprints are sold and resold, how will you know if a product is genuine? How will you know if a blueprint is the real deal? In a 3D printed world, what does "genuine" even mean? As Connor

McNulty, Neyla Arnas, and Thomas Campbell observed in their white paper on 3D printing and national security, "The distinction between original idea and physical product becomes blurred."[422]

Intellectual property owners worry that their copyrights will not stop people from making their own Star Wars action figures, that their trademarks will not block homemade Tonka trucks or Caterpillar toy tractors.[423] Design patent and utility patent owners worry that their patents will not stop would-be customers from making products the patent owners would rather sell to them.

Perhaps more significantly, the ability to 3D print things with virtually any functionality may substantially reduce the need and demand for genuine products or their blueprints. 3D printing may lead to the copying of everything from silverware to smartphones, displacing mass production with production by the masses. But why print a genuine product when you can print a generic substitute, especially if the blueprint for the generic is free? Will people buy genuine branded products, or even mass-produced generic products, if they can more cheaply obtain blueprints and make (and customize) those products themselves? Maybe not everyone will print their own products—or maybe they won't any time soon—but never say never.

Companies may find their products competing not only with their traditional competitors' products but also with copies of their own products, with customized versions of their own products, with generic substitutes for their own products, and with customized versions of generic substitutes for their own (and their competitors') products. Such products could be made by professional counterfeiters, 3D print shops, industrial customers, or consumers. It won't be only the product companies who will have skin in the game. Insurance companies, product-safety lawyers, IP lawyers, government regulators, and tax collectors will have a stake in knowing if a product is genuine or fake.

As 3D printing regionalizes and distributes manufacturing, companies may have products made by local 3D printing fabricators or in their own local factories. Or the companies may sell "genuine" design blueprints (specifying the 3D printer to be used, materials, postproduction, etc.) for commercial customers or consumers to have printed by authorized print shops, or to print themselves. The companies will want customers to be confident that the product is genuine, or to be able to determine if it is genuine if a problem arises, especially if the product has changed hands.

ZEFRAMWD QUESTIONS WHAT IS REAL

Not long after ZeframWD started selling blueprints for warp-drive parts, it suffered a data breach. It wasn't clear what the hackers stole, but soon ZeframWD started to notice warp cores and blueprints for sale on StarBay, Astrobaba, Yoda's List, and other product resale websites. All of the ads claimed to sell genuine ZeframWD warp cores and blueprints. Suspicious, ZeframWD investigated. It soon realized just how complicated the question of what is genuine can be in a 3D printed world:

- ZeframWD's investigators found advertised for sale one used warp core made in its mass-production factory just before it closed and two others custom-made in its remaining bespoke factory.
- They found several warp cores advertised as new, never used. However, only one had been 3D printed by an authorized fabricator and included a guarantee that it complied with all ZeframWD specs.
- Another appeared to have been 3D printed from official blueprints, but ZeframWD would not warranty it because there was no way to ascertain who had printed the core or if the process had followed ZeframWD specs.
- Another core appeared perfect in every way but was priced so low that ZeframWD suspected it had been printed from a pirated design and inferior materials, and could explode at warp 2.

- Several other warp cores showed minor or major flaws resulting from a variety of production failures, such as improperly modifying ZeframWD blueprints, printing with unauthorized blueprints or materials, printing on the wrong type of machine, or failing to use ZeframWD's process controls.
- One warp core that had been printed by a ZeframWD customer appeared to comply with official specs but lacked certification. Another showed signs of having been printed from blueprints made by scanning a ZeframWD core.
- Investigators also found cores that boasted performance to warp 15, while ZeframWD's current models maxed out at warp 12. Further investigation revealed the cores had been 3D printed by an independent fabricator from blueprints offered by WormHoleLTD, a performance shop that specialized in souped-up warp cores custom-printed on its own machines. However, WormHoleLTD also sold altered versions of ZeframWD's blueprints, allowing customers to print high-performance cores on their own machines or by the fab of their choice. It was impossible to tell who had printed the warp-15-capable core.
- A final core had clearly been 3D printed on a lower-quality machine. The part was used and boasted three light years of service, which suggested it probably worked. But it lacked the polish of a ZeframWD-made part. The seller was an individual named Mudd who owned a low-end space-garage machine that investigators could not identify.

ZeframWD also found blueprints for sale, some claiming to be unmodified ZeframWD official warp-core blueprints and others claiming to improve on ZeframWD's blueprints. One claimed to be made from a scan of a ZeframWD warp core.

ZeframWD also investigated peer-to-peer platforms and black-market websites. They found hundreds of ZeframWD warp-core blueprints, some probably genuine, some safely modified and customized, others space time-bombs waiting to go off. Many were free.

After its investigation, ZeframWD realized that its customers really had no way of knowing if ZeframWD parts or blueprints were genuine, unless the customer obtained them directly from the company or an authorized fabricator. Yet very few of the parts and blueprints available for sale, or the blueprints available for free on peer-to-peer platforms, were genuine. ZeframWD also realized that if a customer or independent fab 3D printed a part from ZeframWD blueprints on the right machine with the right materials and used the right process controls, the part was no less genuine than a part made by ZeframWD or its official fabs.

IS IT REAL OR NOT?
How did ZeframWD know the warp core made by the independent fab was printed from official blueprints? How was it able to distinguish the warp cores made in its own factories or by authorized fabs from others that were not?

The answer to the first question is simple. ZeframWD included secret, nonfunctional signatures in its blueprints. ZeframWD found the signatures in the 3D printed warp cores, confirming that its blueprints were used. Unfortunately, there was no way to tell if the blueprints had been modified, resulting in potentially unsafe warp cores that did not match ZeframWD specs. The answer to the second question left ZeframWD's management scratching their heads, looking for a way to mark genuine products in a verifiable, reliable, and nondefeatable way.

A commercially available solution, currently used in other industries, is DNA marking: this technology, developed by a Stony Brook, New York, company called Applied DNA Sciences (ADNAS),[424] uses plant DNA to mark products with visible or invisible signatures that, when screened, identify the product as genuine. ADNAS has the necessary credentials. After a couple of military disasters involving two-dollar counterfeit parts, the US Defense Logistics Agency (DLA) discovered that the US defense supply chain is riddled with counterfeit parts.[425] In 2012, the DLA mandated that certain types of parts must be marked with DNA signatures.[426] ADNAS's DNA inks are also used to mark cash in transit, live copper rails in Sweden's national rail system (which have a pesky habit of disappearing because the high cost of copper makes them valuable on the black market), highly prized Japanese mackerel, and even entire burglary-prone neighborhoods in London.[427] The company's DNA inks are also used to mark cotton and wool fiber to assure fashion houses and high-end carpet and textile makers that the fiber they are buying is genuine.

According to ADNAS, its scientists[428]

have developed a precision-engineered mark based on botanical (plant) DNA. The engineered mark has not and cannot be broken. The conventional process used to sequence ("decode') native DNA is not possible with the engineered mark. Additional layers of protection and complexity are added to the mark in a proprietary manner. This engineering "secret sauce" is shielded by a portfolio of 21 patents and other intellectual property protection.

A gram of DNA ink can protect 100 billion DVDs,[429] and no evidence exists that DNA markings can be counterfeited with 3D printing.

Importing this technology into the 3D printing industry, a company could DNA-mark products made at its factories or authorized 3D printing fabricators could do so. The marking technology could be built into 3D printers, or applied to products separately. Products could be screened by authorized fabricators or licensed third parties to verify their authenticity or possibly by consumers with a smartphone app. Products not marked would be viewed as counterfeit, even if printed according to specifications.

Another possible solution is quantum dots, which are supersmall nano-crystal semiconductors.[430] Quantum Materials Corporation and Virginia Tech developed a system for embedding quantum dots in 3D printed objects, which gives them a unique and unrepeatable fingerprint.[431] Quantum dots could be used the same way as DNA marking.

The method chosen by ZeframWD remains a secret, for security reasons.

WHY WILL ANYONE CARE IF 3D PRINTED PRODUCTS ARE GENUINE?

The simple truth is that it will be much harder to tell genuine products from copies in a 3D printed world, and there will be far more copies—and types of copies, as ZeframWD discovered—than there are today. But will anyone care?

Companies like ZeframWD care very much whether customers buy genuine products or have them printed by authorized fabricators. Only by 3D printing proven designs with approved machines and materials under adequate process and quality controls, and by providing great customer service and a warranty, can ZeframWD ensure customer safety and satisfaction, and demand a premium price for its parts. ZeframWD can also demand a premium price for its blueprints if they include specs for how to 3D print parts that live up to its high standards. If the company provides means for independent fabricators and customers to mark the parts as "ZeframWD compliant," entrepreneurs may start third-party companies to certify parts as genuine and insure their users against losses.

Perhaps more importantly, ZeframWD worries about parts printed by customers or their fabs, or by independent shops, or by pirates, which do not match its specs or were printed on the wrong machine. ZeframWD does not know the source of the blueprints for such parts and has no control of the printing process. Some may have been printed from blueprints generated from inferior scans of a ZeframWD warp core. Defects in such parts could make them fail, with catastrophic consequences. Although ZeframWD can't prevent some or maybe even most of such parts from being 3D printed away from control, it can disclaim—in its blueprints—any liability for problems arising from printed parts that are not certified compliant with all of its specs. But that deals with only a small part of the problem.

If a part that looks like a ZeframWD warp core fails, ZeframWD may be blamed for it, and its first concern will be to determine if it is a genuine part or was made from genuine blueprints according to company specs. In some cases, this may be difficult or impossible. And, in other cases, a warp core printed by an independent fab or customer may match company specs but not be certified. If that part were to fail, ZeframWD could find itself in the sticky situation of admitting that the part is no different from a genuine part, even though it was not printed by ZeframWD or an authorized fab. Unscrupulous authorized fabs may even ship warp cores out their front door for market price and ship identical warp cores out the back door at a deep discount, as happens with name-brand clothing today. ZeframWD could be forced to warrant the back-door parts, or be blamed if they fail.

ZeframWD also cares about blueprints available for sale on the Internet or being shared peer to peer. Its reputation and freedom from legal liability depend on maintaining control of its product designs, its crown jewels. For standard blueprints and company-customized blueprints, ZeframWD can scan them against its library copies and determine if they are genuine. But there may be copies that did not originate from ZeframWD. For custom blueprints made with ZeframWD's customization tools, ZeframWD can tell if they are genuine by secret fingerprints hidden in the blueprints. It views all other custom blueprints as not genuine.

Mass customization presents an entirely different set of problems for determining what is genuine and what genuine means. Certainly custom parts made by ZeframWD or its authorized shops, or from ZeframWD custom blueprints according to official specs, would be warranted as genuine. But is a warp core genuine if it is printed from blueprints made from ZeframWD's own customization tools? The answer seems to be yes, if the part was printed according to specs generated by its customization tools. This raises a separate set of problems for ZeframWD: Can it tailor performance and manufacturing specs to customer-customized parts, and how can it certify that custom parts meet such specs? And can it warranty such parts?

Consumers may care about these issue, too. Law professors Deven Desai and Gerard Magliocca view the brand as a savior in a 3D printed world. They believe the added value that brand owners will be forced to provide (to survive) will lead consumers to continue to want and even demand authentic branded products.[432] Melba Kurman believes that "as manufacturing becomes more decentralized, ironically, consumers will demand more reassurance that the 3D printed goods they are buying are safe to use and will perform as advertised. The power of a brand name will increase in importance." She also believes that consumers may pay a premium for verified safety and performance.[433]

In my view, some will and some won't. On the industrial side, some customers will pay a premium for genuine standard or customized parts, or for genuine blueprints. Some will print the blueprints according to company specs to get the company's customer service and warranty, or simply because they have greater confidence in the genuine part. Others will buy secondhand parts, parts printed by independent fabs, parts made by pirates, and parts of uncertain provenance and performance. Others will print the parts themselves, some according to specs, some not. As always, price and other factors will affect each customer's decision. For example, a customer may 3D print parts from lower-quality material if the parts are sacrificial or are not mission critical, or are needed immediately.

On the consumer side, all of the same things will happen, but price and intelligence may play a bigger role in whether some consumers buy name-brand products or blueprints, and whether they print blueprints according to company specs. Some will want verified safety and performance, and others won't care. For example, although most cyclists may want a genuine bicycle helmet printed by a respected manufacturer or from company blueprints according to company specs, some will buy knockoffs or print them at home with unsafe materials and ignore the specs. For many parts consumers can 3D print, brand simply may not be important. But as in the industrial arena, makers of genuine consumer products and blueprints will be forced to prove that defective products are not genuine.

Many consumers will care more about price than whether or not a product is genuine. Visit any public market in Asia and watch Western tourists buying counterfeit CDs, DVDs, Levi's jeans, and North Face jackets. Or ask the average parents if they allow their kids to share music peer to peer on the Internet. Or notice how many women buy fake designer handbags from New York City street vendors, or how many men buy fake Rolex watches. For many products, people care only about price, not whether a product is genuine. There is no reason for this to change when 3D printed versions of almost any product—or generic substitutes—become commonly available, or when you can print them or have them printed away from control.

Some people may always want and pay a premium for brand names, but price, along with the human need to make, fueled by 3D printing and the power to make things away from control, will put great pressure on brands. Some companies will survive as product manufacturers. Some will switch to making custom products only. Some will start selling only blueprints. And some will fail when regional and distributed start-ups begin to sell copies and customized versions of products and blueprints, when generics are printed by new companies, and when blueprints for almost any product or generic substitutes become commonly available and are printed by industrial customers and consumers away from control. This last point is important: for consumer goods and industrial parts, traditional manufacturers will face competitive pressures not only from regional and distributed manufacturing, and from generics, but also from customers themselves, who 3D print away from control.

As 3D printing regionalizes and redistributes manufacturing, manufacturers will be forced to police the marketplace for copies of their products and blueprints, to find ways to identify genuine products, and to try to stop poor quality and dangerous copies (and copies that infringe their IP rights). They will also be forced to compete with good, legitimate copies and generics, and to compete with customers and consumers printing away from control. Determining what products are genuine will be much more complicated in a 3D printed world, and the question itself could eventually become meaningless.

8

The Dark Side: 3D Printing
New Kinds of Crime

THE DEVIL'S PLAYGROUND

3D printing has the potential to transform the world by simplifying manufacturing, shortening supply and distribution chains, democratizing production, creating and repatriating jobs, reducing waste, customizing products to our needs, and producing radically different products. But 3D printing can also be the devil's playground. Like anything else, 3D printing has a dark side, and some people will be drawn to it. It will soon be possible to 3D print almost anything away from control. Guns have already been 3D printed, some within control and some away from control. Thieves are using 3D printers to create new forms of crime. Counterfeiters, drug dealers, black marketers, gangsters, terrorists, and other criminals will not be far behind.

THE DARK SIDE TODAY

Almost everyone has heard about Texas law student Cody Wilson, who made headlines in 2013 by 3D printing a plastic gun and posting the blueprints on the Internet.[434] When I heard him speak at the Inside 3D Printing conference in New York, he was introduced as one of the most dangerous men in the world. During his speech, he said the fact that his gun may evade a metal detector was an accident and not the point of his "experiment." Although I did not understand him at the time, I have come to believe that Wilson's 3D printed gun was an experiment in 3D printing away from control. He could have chosen any item, and in fact may have made a more earthshaking impact if he had chosen to 3D print a smartphone away from control instead of a gun (imagine the fear this would have struck into the hearts of the top brass at Apple and Samsung). But he chose a gun, and the world caught its first glimpse of the dark side of 3D printing. The blueprints for Wilson's gun were downloaded one hundred thousand times before the US government forced their removal from the server.[435] But if it had not been Cody, it would have been someone else. In fact, the ZigZag plastic gun was 3D printed in Japan shortly after Wilson printed his.[436] Because Japan has strict antigun laws, the maker of the ZigZag gun was sentenced to two years in jail for 3D printing several guns and posting videos of the process on the Internet.[437] In 2015, police in Chiloquin, Oregon, made arrests for the illegal possession of an AR-15 assault rifle. Its lower receiver—the key to what makes it a weapon—was believed to have been 3D printed.[438]

US citizens have always been able to make guns, and it has always been legal to do so as long as they were detectable.[439] Detectability, of course, is what gives us comfort that our airplane seatmates are not carrying. In late 2013, an independent fabricator called Solid Concepts 3D printed the fully functioning reproduction of a classic Browning 1911 design, shown below, using stainless steel and a nickel-chrome alloy called Inconel.[440]

Photo courtesy of Solid Concepts

I have held this gun in my hand, and it is a beautiful example of what the current state of the art can do. Solid Concepts' 3D printed gun didn't scare people because it was printed on a high-end machine, is detectable, sells for just under $12,000,[441] and probably struck people as more of a rich collector's toy than a threat to public safety. Wilson's gun scared people by demonstrating that anyone with a 3D printer can make not just a gun but an undetectable gun. What really scared people was that terrorists and other crazy people might now make undetectable guns. Also, even though the law prohibits the sale of guns to convicted felons,[442] 3D printing allows felons to get guns without anyone knowing about it, away from control.

Detectable or not, guns can be made by 3D printers. Philadelphia, Pennsylvania, was the first US city to outlaw 3D printed guns.[443] Various other local governments have considered banning 3D printed guns, including California and the territory of Queensland, Australia.[444] The futility of doing so is illustrated by the plasma railgun made by an Imgur (www.imgur.com) user known as NSA_Listbot, who used a 3D printer and commonly available parts to make a handheld electromagnetic projectile launcher that fires rods made of Teflon/plasma, graphite, aluminum, and copper-coated tungsten at a speed of about 560 mph. It is not a gun in the traditional sense, but it is just as dangerous. Innovators are pushing the envelope of the types of weapons that can be 3D printed.[445] And accessories, too. An unidentified fabricator modified the digital blueprint for a commercial silencer, then 3D printed a cool-looking custom silencer on a Powder Bed Fusion machine. This is a great example of what independent fabs can do with 3D printing, away from control.[446] 3D printing away from control is, by definition, beyond the reach of legislation.

To date, no one has been shot by a 3D printed gun, although a man did use one to kill his wife in an episode of the Sherlock Holmes TV series *Elementary*.[447] But criminals have been exploring the potential of 3D printing. In a police raid in Manchester, England, police discovered 3D printed gun components with a 3D printer.[448] In another raid in Brisbane, Australia, police found 3D printed gun parts, but reported that the crude parts were probably more dangerous to the gunmaker than to his potential victims.[449] But gun-printing criminals are still thinking inside the box. Although the plastic guns 3D printed to date are not very pretty, they still look like guns. However, there is no reason why a 3D printed gun might not look like a shoe or a hairbrush or a soda bottle.[450] The same may be true of bombs. As 3D printing industry analyst Alex Chausovsky said, "Think of master bombmakers in the Middle East making new designs that look like everyday products."[451]

But should the 3D printing of guns be banned? There is no reason to ban the 3D printing of metal guns because it is legal to make them with traditional methods and because they are detectable. There is also no reason to ban the 3D printing of plastic guns because criminals will print them anyway. Banning any new technology is a knee-jerk reaction based on fear and on the incorrect assumption that the bad guys will obey the law. In the early days of radio, some people feared that the new invention would be used to explode bombs at a distance. Lucky for the future, no one banned radio because of such fears.

In developments surely being followed by the underworld and would-be Houdinis, a German hacker used 3D printers to reproduce handcuff keys for high-security handcuffs.[452] MIT students have CT-scanned locks, then used the scans to 3D print master keys.[453] Skilled lock-pickers Jos Weyers and Christian Holler 3D printed a bump key, which can be used to pick almost any pin tumbler lock.[454] In fact, all that is needed to make bump keys is a photo of the keyhole, the right software, and a 3D printer.[455] In a hilarious Radio Shack video ad, Jason of *Friday the 13th* fame 3D printed the store clerk's house key.[456]

Criminals have also been thinking of dark-side 3D printing applications beyond guns. A Frenchman 3D printed fake facades for cash machines, which cloned the data on users' ATM cards.[457] Criminals in Sydney,

Australia, used 3D printers to make attachments for bank machines that skim bank card information from unsuspecting ATM users. By using 3D printers, the criminals make the skimmers look like they are part of the ATM machines.[458] Organized crime is jumping on board. In coordinated raids against gangs in Malaga, Spain, and the Bulgarian cities of Sofia, Burgas, and Silistra, police seized equipment used to 3D print sophisticated skimming equipment, including fake card slots for bank machines.[459] A criminal who calls himself "Gripper" makes a skimmer by the same name, which he sells online. Gripper recruits other criminals to join his international network and offers round-the-clock tech support in Moscow, South Africa, the UK, and the United States. The Gripper boasts: "Bare [sic] in mind we have the power to mass-produce these ATM skimmers with the latest technology…We have all files needed and printing facilities in China. Also we have files to mass-produce MSRV [magnetic-stripe-reading] electronics." [460] The Gripper is a good example of the dark power of combining the Internet and 3D printing. The portability of 3D printers means illegal items can be made in constantly relocated stealth factories,[461] while the Internet can be used as the Illegal Information Superhighway.

THE WILD WEST OF 3D PRINTING

3D printed guns only scratch the surface of the dark side of 3D printing. 3D printers will be used to make many types of weapons. Certainly the military will be 3D printing weapons, but the bad guys will be 3D printing them, too. Some printed weapons will be primitive and others will be sophisticated, some will be detectable and others will not, some will be made by high-end metal printers and others will be made by inexpensive plastic printers. As personal 3D printers become better and better, anyone will be able to make high-quality weapons away from control.

Researchers at Louisiana Tech University and India's JRobotics Group have been working on 3D printing legal drug-delivery devices and pharmaceuticals,[462] and University of Glasgow chemist Lee Cronin is working on 3D printed legal prescription drugs.[463] Briar Thompson suggests it will not be long before 3D printers also will be used to print illegal drugs.[464] In his article "Can You 3D Print Drugs?," Chris Gayomali wrote:[465]

> But with all the useful and practical applications of 3D printed drugs comes an obvious dark side. Take, for instance, the potential for amateur organic chemists to engineer their own designer drugs. In *Drugs 2.0: The Web Revolution That's Changing How the World Gets High*, author Mike Power envisions a near future where DIYers (mostly college grads with chemistry degrees) are using highly sophisticated techniques—including 3D printers—to render "controlled substances" an obsolete relic of the past.

This will be a boon to organized crime, which will be able to print illegal drugs at the point of need, thereby eliminating the capital investment and risks of shipping and storing large quantities of drugs. And when personal printers are capable of printing your customized prescription at home, the same type of printers also will be used to make illegal drugs away from control. In fact, there is no reason why drug dealers will continue to sell drugs when they can sell the blueprints instead, which local dealers or users can print away from control. But of course drug dealers may also become obsolete relics of the past when free blueprints for illegal drugs become widely available for 3D printing away from control.

Briar Thompson has also suggested a dark use of 3D printing that will strike fear into governments and financial institutions everywhere: 3D printing cash.[466] One might question how 3D printing currency would be different from the ways that cash is printed today. The US dollar is printed on special linen-like paper with colored threads used to detect counterfeiting. Such paper would be a good candidate for 3D printing. Paper currency is also printed from plates, which would also be good 3D printing candidates. Perhaps most importantly, many countries rely on larger denomination coin currency far more than the United States. 3D printers are perfect tools to print counterfeit coins.

COUNTERFEITING

Cash is not the only thing 3D printers can counterfeit. In fact, 3D printing could lead to counterfeiting on steroids. You name it, and counterfeiters will be able to make it with 3D printers, or sell the blueprints. They will not be limited to Rolex watches and YSL handbags. Virtually any branded product will be counterfeited with 3D printers by printing it with or without the brand, or by printing a generic product with a band name on it. 3D printers will make it much easier for enterprising counterfeiters to enter the game, and counterfeiting will become democratized, distributed, and regional. It will also be possible to counterfeit at home or in Friends Networks, for personal use, away from control. And the only difference between a counterfeit and the real deal may be the source of the blueprints.

Brands are protected by trademarks covering the brand name and sometimes the look and feel of the product, such as its shape or color. Brands may also be protected by copyrights and patents. In those situations, brand owners will have tools to fight back against the counterfeiters, if they can find them. This problem will not be fundamentally different from brand counterfeiting today, except that it will be on a much larger scale, distributed throughout the world.

But brand counterfeiting will be a relatively small part of the problem. Counterfeit parts have been a serious problem for many years for car and airplane makers, and the entire US defense supply chain.[467] This problem will grow and become more distributed and regional with 3D printing. The problem will expand to virtually any type of product or part.

AWAY FROM CONTROL AND PRODUCT ANARCHY

In a world where thousands of small businesses can 3D print industrial and consumer products and parts of all types, where governments and companies print and customize all of their replacement parts, and where consumers can 3D print almost any product or part in their homes, through Friends Networks, at a shop down the block, or through thousands of small fabs around the world, words like "counterfeit" and "genuine" have less meaning. A more meaningful distinction in a 3D printed world may be "within control" and "away from control." Some products and parts will probably always be made within control but probably far fewer than are made today. Almost any product or part will also be 3D printable away from control by companies, consumers, and pirates, without anyone knowing about it or being able to control it. Products and parts made away from control may be inferior to their within-control counterparts, but they may also be just as good or better, and customized to boot. Thus, products and parts 3D printed away from control may or may not be counterfeits, but it will hardly matter. What will matter are quality, safety, performance, and cost.

I am hopeful that 3D printing will transform industry and economies in positive ways, but the results could also be disastrous. Unfortunately, 3D printers have the potential to cause complete product anarchy, where there is little or no product consistency, no safety or quality, no reliable brands, and no distinction between genuine and fake. As Hod Lipson and Melba Kurman observe:[468]

> The downside of widely available tools of production is an economic meltdown. Rampant counterfeiting erodes profit margins. Add to that the devastating effect of unrealistic intellectual property laws that attempt to enforce private ownership of ideas in an era when anybody can 3D print exact copies of anything.

Once-thriving companies may find it impossible to stay in business because they lose control of their products and blueprints. They may find that no one will buy their products because they can get substitutes (good or not) elsewhere, or make them away from control. They may find that no one will buy their blueprints because they can get copies of official blueprints, or blueprints for a substitute, elsewhere for free or on the cheap, or create their own from a CT scan. Governments may be unable to collect sales taxes because most products are made away from control. The ability to 3D print almost anything away from control could become so disruptive that economies break down.

THE REALLY DARK SIDE

It is impossible to predict how dark the dark side of 3D printing will get, but here are a few examples.

In 2014, the FBI's Terrorist Explosive Device Analytical Center (TEDAC) announced its intention to buy a 3D printer to study whether terrorists can use 3D printers to make bombs. It will probably find that the answer is "yes" and "soon." TEDAC's mission is solely to study improvised explosive devices made by terrorists.[469] The FBI must be credited for thinking ahead and preparing for this modern horror.

Various researchers are working to 3D print bacteria and viruses.[470] Just as this technology could be used for legitimate scientific purposes, the technology to 3D print bacteria and viruses could easily be adapted by terrorists, with catastrophic results. Germ warfare is nothing new. What is new is the ability to 3D print germs from blueprints available on the Internet or from other sources.

In *Fabricated*, Hod Lipson and Melba Kurman describe the black-market trade in 3D printed human organs "a few decades from now." They predict high demand from black-market organ makers for bioprinters cast off by hospitals and legitimate bioprinting companies, along with injuries to patients caused by faulty organ blueprints and shady organ fabricators who cut corners and fail to work in sterile environments.[471]

In their article entitled "Toward the Printed World: Additive Manufacturing and Implications for National Security," Connor McNulty, Neyla Arnas, and Thomas Campbell say that 3D printing may make nuclear proliferation harder to detect because countries and political groups who are not part of the "atomic club" may use 3D printers to make parts for nuclear weapons away from control.[472] In fact, rogue nations or groups may use 3D printers to make products they can't buy because of international sanctions and embargoes. As New America warfare expert Peter Singer observed, "3D printing could turn sanctions—which have been a crucial part of foreign policy for a generation or more—into an antiquated notion."[473]

THE DISARMING CORRUPTOR

Designed by University of London researcher Matthew Plummer-Fernandez, the Disarming Corruptor disguises 3D printable blueprints, allowing them to slip through filters meant to block them from design repositories. Plummer-Fernandez became frustrated when the iMaterialise design repository automatically blocked the upload of his artistic rendition of Mickey Mouse, and again when he learned that Thingiverse blocked blueprints for 3D printable weapons. "I was confronting all these taboos showing up in 3D printing around copyrighted material and 3D printed weapons, and I think these services are leaving their users out to dry," he said in a *Forbes* interview. His solution: a software tool that disguises the blueprint, making it unrecognizable by algorithms designed to block content that violates IP rights or is otherwise illegal or objectionable. Once disguised, any design can be uploaded to any 3D printing blueprint repository. The Disarming Corruptor also generates a password that can be shared independently of the repository, so that people who download the design can remove the masking and print the object.[474]

The Disarming Corruptor—and other tools like it—renders impotent any efforts to prevent the transmission of 3D printable designs that infringe third-party IP rights or violate laws that prohibit printing certain types of objects, like guns. As Cody Wilson commented, the Disarming Corruptor "explodes the idea that there will be certain shapes we can guard against. Information itself is plastic, and it can be molded and changed." Tools like the Disarming Corruptor are a 3D printing criminal's dream, enabling the sharing of designs for any and all products, legal or not. But dodging IP and other laws and transmitting gun blueprints is just the tip of this dark iceberg.

DON'T BLAME THE TECHNOLOGY

Some illegal 3D printed products, or their blueprints, will be bought, sold, or traded in physical or virtual black markets. Organized crime will find creative ways to profit from 3D printing, such as trafficking in 3D printed drugs and human organs. Terrorists will adopt the technology to further their misguided missions. It is impossible to predict how deeply such users will delve into the dark side of 3D printing. But don't blame the technology. As with many technologies, 3D printing can be misused but not because the technology is inherently flawed. People are flawed. Although the size of the problem could be huge, this is only because the technology is so revolutionary and disruptive. Governments, law enforcement, homeland security, and the military must assess the risks from the dark side of 3D printing and plan accordingly. However, the nature of the technology and the ability to make things away from control will limit governments' ability to regulate the dark side of 3D printing. In his article "Should Government Regulate Illicit Uses of 3D Printing?," Daniel Castro, a senior researcher with the Information Technology & Innovation Foundation, concluded that regulating such uses will be unlikely or impractical.[475]

9

3D Printing the Wheels of Justice

WIDESPREAD LEGAL DISRUPTION

Because 3D printing will have profound effects on stakeholders—companies, consumers, governments, and economies—it is bound to rock the law too. Intellectual property law is mentioned most often, but the legal effects of 3D printing will be much broader. 3D printing will certainly affect IP law, but challenges to product-safety and product-liability law will probably have more relevance to most people in a 3D printed world. As 3D printing away from control spreads, product-safety and liability issues will multiply, as will insurance claims and related legal issues.

Government regulators will also be challenged. Health care regulators will be faced with approving countless 3D printed medical devices, drugs, and human organs. Doctors who 3D printed the trachea splints that saved several newborn babies sought and thankfully obtained emergency FDA clearances.[476] Usually such approvals happen at a normal pace, such as the FDA's clearance of a bone tether plate 3D printed from a titanium alloy by MedShape of Atlanta, Georgia.[477]

Aviation regulators will face the same issues with 3D printed aircraft parts. Consumer products regulators will grapple with the safety of products made within control and away from control. 3D printing away from control will also challenge governments' abilities to collect income and sales taxes, and to control the export of technology that may be used for nefarious purposes. 3D printing new kinds of crime will challenge law enforcement, investigation, intelligence, military, national-security, and criminal-justice systems. It will strain intercountry relations and lead to calls for new laws to address the dark side.

Americans have two national pastimes. One is baseball and the other is suing each other. As companies and people are negatively affected by 3D printing, they will complain, then sue. Some will try to get Congress to enact new laws to protect their interests. Others will look for creative, positive approaches and trust in the free-market system. It would be nice to think that the stakeholders will work out their problems in proactive, creative, and amicable ways. As Hod Lipson and Melba Kurman wrote, "Wise companies will embrace 3D printing to enrich the users' experience, not embark on quixotic IP battles against their own customers."[478] Their wise words apply to all legal disputes in the 3D printing space, not only those involving IP rights. But it is more likely that 3D printing will be as much of a full-employment program for lawyers as the Internet has been.

INTELLECTUAL PROPERTY AND IP RIGHTS

Intellectual property is a type of personal property resulting from human creativity, such as inventions, books, music, and movies. In the United States, there are five kinds of government-given rights that protect IP:

- Utility patents, which protect inventions
- Design patents, which protect the nonfunctional designs of functional products, such as the aesthetic design of a smartphone
- Copyrights, which protect the concrete expression of ideas, such as books, movies, music, software, art, and sculpture
- Trademarks, which protect brand names, logos, and some product designs, such as the Coca Cola trademark, logo, and the old-style twist bottle design

- Trade secrets, which protect confidential business information, such as formulas (the most famous trade secret is the Coca Cola formula) and software source code

Most other countries have similar types of IP rights.

IP rights cover the processes, machines, materials, and software of 3D printing, as well as post-manufacturing steps. IP rights may also cover the parts and products made by 3D printers, which could be almost anything. Copying IP owners' products without permission infringes their IP rights, and they can sue to stop it. Intent is not necessary to infringe IP rights. If you copy a product, even accidentally, it can infringe IP rights. But as Michael Weinberg of Public Knowledge has correctly observed, "Most of the physical world is not protected by any type of intellectual property."[479]

IP principles apply to 3D printing just as they apply to any other type of technology. However, the potential scale of 3D printing may have profound effects on IP. 3D printing cuts across all types of IP, all types of technology, and almost all types of products. Eventually, anyone will be able to re-create almost any existing product design and manufacture and distribute it, or simply make and use it, away from control.

As industrial and personal 3D printers become capable of making more and more things away from control, infringement will proliferate and IP rights will become increasingly irrelevant. "Impotent" may be a better word. The Gartner group predicts that "by 2018, 3D printing will result in the loss of at least $100 billion per year in intellectual property globally."[480] Similar predictions, which turned out to be accurate, were made about the music industry in the mid- to late 1990s. Gartner's prediction seems to be based not only on infringement of IP rights by competing products but also on products that will never be bought. 3D printing may result in widespread copying, especially of consumer products, but perhaps more importantly, companies that formerly bought replacement parts will start making the parts themselves, or repairing them.

SOME PEOPLE DON'T LIKE IP

Until recently—except in the popular-music space—most people did not pay much attention to IP rights and had no strong feeling about them one way or the other. But in the 3D printing space, many people simply don't like IP rights, do not use them to protect their own creations, and are working together to dodge them or narrow their reach. IP rights opponents view IP rights as a closed system. The opponents of IP rights believe 3D printing, combined with the Internet and the open innovation movement, will eliminate or substantially narrow IP rights.

The growing opposition to IP rights became apparent to me with the publication of my article[481] describing the Electronic Frontier Foundation's[482] use of the Internet to crowdsource evidence to defeat pending patent applications relating to 3D printing.[483] Many people posted comments in response to the article.[484] Here is one of the kinder responses: [485]

> There is a persistent widespread belief that intellectual property law (and patents in particular) encourage innovation. This is intuitive[;] however, the evidence to the contrary is now overwhelming and the unavoidable conclusion is that intellectual property actually stifles innovation.

Some people see IP as a roadblock to much more than innovation. In his article "The Case for Open Source Appropriate Technology," Dr. Joshua Pearce, a professor of materials science and electrical and computer engineering at Michigan Tech, links the closed, IP-rights-based[486]

> model of technological development [to] the widespread poverty and environmental desecration seen around the globe, which is directly responsible for a morally and ethically unacceptable level

of human suffering and death. For example, more than 10 million children under the age of five die each year from preventable causes (WHO 2007). This waste of human life could be prevented by known (to humanity as a whole) technologies, many of which are simply not available to those that need it. Availability is restricted by both the cost of access (such as pay-to-view articles on renewable electricity generation under copyright by the IEEE) and by companies wielding patent law to maximize profit at the cost of human lives (e.g., restricting the sale of antiretroviral drugs to treat HIV in Africa) (Shantharam 2005). A solution to this general problem of access to critical information for sustainable development is the growth of open source appropriate technology.

Dr. Pearce sees open-source 3D printers as part of the solution to this problem.

The open tech movement opposes mainly patents and copyrights. There are strong philosophical forces at odds here. On the one hand, there is the US Constitution. Article I Section VIII grants to Congress the power "to promote the Progress of Science and useful Arts, by securing for limited Times to Authors and Inventors the exclusive Right to their respective Writings and Discoveries."[487] This is the basis of the US patent and copyright systems. On the other hand, there are IP opponents, who ask, "Are actions done in the name of protecting and encouraging innovation actually causing its destruction?"[488]

One IP opponent published an algorithm for locating evidence for defeating 3D printing patent applications.[489] There is also an organized effort to use the Internet and crowdsourcing to challenge 3D printing–related patent applications.[490] Those who oppose IP rights in the 3D printing space may come to the defense of defendants, crowdsourcing prior art to help defeat patents being asserted against them.

Even within the IP law establishment, this is an unprecedented time of anti-IP-rights sentiment. As a result of the America Invents Act and recent landmark court decisions, existing patents are being invalidated at a very high rate. Congress is currently hot to enact legislation to curb the ability of some patent owners to sue for infringement of their patents. The anti-IP-rights sentiment is not limited to patents. Courts have been issuing rulings for years that have gradually been strangling copyright owners' rights.

Nevertheless, IP rights are important to established companies. But within the 3D printing industry, there is a split between IP lovers and haters. This is a snapshot of some of the players in the 3D printing industry. Above the line are many of the major or important players. Below the line are some of the smaller companies and start-ups at various stages of development (there are many more).

Snapshot of 3D Printer Players

Industrial Printers	3DSYSTEMS, Stratasys, Arcam, OPTOMEC, RENISHAW, EOS, envisionTEC, mcor technologies, Materialise, Voxeljet, organovo, MakerBot, ExOne
Consumer -grade Printers	3D Kits, A1 Technologies, Ac123Dc, Afinia, Airwolf 3D, Asiga, B9Creations, BatBot, Bits from Bytes, Blue Printer, CB-Printer, Code-p, CSP, Cubify, Deezmaker, Essential Dynamics, Eventorbot, EZ 3D printers, Fabbster, Fablicator, Felix Printers, Formlabs, German RepRap Foundation, Hot Proceed, Hyrel 3D, Intelligent Machine Inc., Invent Apart, iRapid, Leapfrog, Lulzbot, Makemendel, Makerbot, Makergear, MaukCC, Mbot 3D, MendelParts, MendelMax, miniFactory, Mixshop, Multistation, NW RepRap, PP3DP, Printrbot, Rays Opitcs, RepRap France - eMotion Tech, RepRapPro, ReprapSource, Robo 3D, Robot Factory, Romscraj, Sharebot, Solido, Solidoodle, Sumpod, Tantillus, The Future is

Many of the companies above the line are publicly traded, or will be, or are candidates for acquisition. IP rights are very important to them. They have portfolios of patents and other IP rights and will continue to build them. The companies below the line may or may not value IP. Some may oppose IP rights. Some of them may believe in open technology. But the moment those companies rise above the line, IP rights and the ability to capitalize on and protect what is theirs becomes very important to them and they start building IP portfolios. This happened to MakerBot, which was born of the open-technology movement but now owns many patents and applications.

THE IMPORTANCE OF IP RIGHTS

IP rights give owners the right to stop others from using their IP for a period of time, limited by statute. This gives companies and even individuals, such as writers and musicians, a powerful competitive advantage. With the guarantee that no one else will legally be able to use their IP without permission, companies can invest in research and development, knowing they will be able to charge enough for their protected products to recover their R&D costs. To maintain their competitiveness and guard their investments, companies need strong and ever-growing IP portfolios, especially patents. If someone violates their IP rights, they will enforce them. IP litigation is common in industry and is a sign of success. If an industrial company has not been sued for IP infringement, it probably is not very successful or important. In other words, it has not become big enough or important enough to step on other IP owners' toes.

To date, there has been little litigation over IP rights in the 3D printing space. One reason may be that 3D printing is not just one process (as described in "3D printing is not just one process", chapter 1). Most of the major players compete for sales of 3D printers, but the processes used by their machines, and their applications, are mostly different, so they may not compete directly. For example, 3D Systems' sales of Vat Photopolymerization machines may not directly compete with Stratasys's sales of Material Jetting machines because different customers need different machines for different purposes. Some players have also licensed other players to use their technology, so they will not be suing each other over the licensed technology. The industry also is not yet large enough to support the degree of IP litigation common in many big industries. The result has been an industry in which the major players peacefully coexist and rarely sue each other for infringement of patents or other IP rights. There also seems to be a tacit understanding that IP litigation may hinder widespread adoption of the technology and industry growth.

HP's entry into the industrial 3D printing arena, along with the potential effects of Impossible Objects' CBAM process and Loughborough and Sheffield Universities' High Speed Sintering (HSS), may become good examples of how IP rights work. HP's Multi Jet Fusion, IO's CBAM, and Loughborough/Sheffield's HSS appear to be major innovations that will force other printer makers to innovate to keep pace with, or exceed, such technology. HP certainly has a portfolio of patents protecting Multi Jet Fusion, and CBAM and HSS are covered by some patents as well.

Although other 3D printer makers may try to avoid infringement by "designing around"—or dodging—such patents, HP and Loughborough/Sheffield will probably sue for patent infringement if they believe that any of the 3D printer makers' attempts to innovate step on their toes. (HP may or may not be open to licensing its technology to the industry; HSS is available for licensing.) IO may or may not have the resources to sue infringers and may find that it makes more sense to license its technology rather than litigate its patents.

If HP's process and patents prove to be a competitive threat to other 3D printer makers, IO and Loughborough/Sheffield may become the belles of the ball as suitors seek to license their technology, as alternatives to Multi Jet Fusion. The result will be that other 3D printer makers will develop innovative technology, some of which may infringe HP's, IO's, or Loughborough/Sheffield's rights, some of which may not, and some of which may use the technology under license. Thus, HP's, IO's, and Loughborough/Sheffield's patents will give them a competitive edge and force other companies to travel down R&D paths they may not otherwise have taken, or to knock on HP's or the Belles' doors, looking for licenses.

HISTORY REPEATS ITSELF

Although IP rights give many companies a competitive advantage, they can also clash. Think of downloading music on the Internet. The ability to share music on the Internet was an incredible technological innovation, but it clashed with the traditional method of protecting music owners' rights: copyrights. The ease of downloading songs has changed the way that industry operates. After a dark period of suing students and single mothers, the music industry shifted to business models that no longer rely on copyright infringement lawsuits to prevent people from trading in illegal copies of songs. The same may happen to traditional manufacturers of things when it becomes possible to 3D print things with virtually any functionality away from control because IP rights will be impotent to stop it.

So history may repeat itself. In the 1980s the movie industry fought the VCR and lost.[491] In the 1990s the music industry fought digital taping.[492] In the 2000s the Internet changed the music industry forever. When IP infringement away from control becomes common, industry will fight to protect IP rights because the Internet and 3D printing are powerful tools for disrupting and avoiding IP rights. In their 3D printing article, law professors Deven Desai and Gerard Magliocca say we don't learn from our mistakes:[493]

> There is no reason for patent and trademark law to repeat the mistakes of copyright, but there is every reason to think that these mistakes will be repeated.

While there has not been much IP litigation in the 3D printing space, as 3D printing becomes increasingly ubiquitous and the market capitalization of the industry rises, the risk of IP infringement battles will increase. When the day comes that enough money is at stake—and it will come—the scale of the 3D printing IP wars, which will probably be mostly patent wars, will be as big or bigger than the smartphone patent wars.

THE FIVE IS

IP rights and rights holders have the most to lose from widespread 3D printing away from control. Although IP principles apply to 3D printing the same as they apply to any other technology, 3D printing has the unique potential to threaten the value of IP rights and their ability to give companies a competitive edge. Combined with democratized manufacturing, 3D printing has the power to make IP rights impotent.

As powerful personal 3D printers become common, as more and more independent fabs open their doors and install better and better printers, and as industrial customers begin to realize they can make replacement and spare parts in house, or repair existing parts, democratization of manufacturing will increase away from control. When anyone can 3D print things with virtually any functionality, away from control, IP rights will suffer the Five Is (pronounced "five eyes"):

Infringement: when anyone can 3D print things with virtually any functionality, the risk of IP infringement away from control will become increasingly high.

Identification: infringement away from control will be increasingly difficult to identify.

Impractical and Impossible: it will be increasingly impractical and impossible to enforce IP rights against infringement away from control, and some products may entirely lack effective IP protection.

Irrelevant: IP rights will become increasingly irrelevant; they will exist and be enforceable for 3D printing infringement within control, but will be largely irrelevant for 3D printing infringement away from control.

Although I have focused the Five Is on IP infringement, they apply equally to other types of illegal activity. As 3D printing away from control becomes widespread, all relevant laws may suffer the 5Is.

The risk to IP rights (and other laws) posed by 3D printing depends on the degree of democratization of manufacturing away from control. For products that are unlikely to be 3D printed away from control, IP rights will probably continue to work effectively, much as they do today for traditional manufacturing methods. But as the democratization of manufacturing increases away from control, IP rights are likely to become increasingly irrelevant or impotent.

Design remix will also contribute to IP's impotency. Designs that are clearly derivative of other designs may lead to claims of IP infringement, assuming that the original design was protected by some type of IP rights in the first place. But if an IP-protected design is remixed to the point that it is unrecognizable as a derivative of the original design, any IP rights covering the original design may be impotent to challenge the remixed design.

RISK TO THE IP SYSTEM

The democratization of manufacturing may threaten the IP system in any industry where 3D printing can be used to make parts and products, including aerospace, automotive, and health care. In the aerospace industry, customers, especially government customers, may start to 3D print their own parts, as the Federation of Planets started printing its own warp-drive cores. In the auto industry, consumers, Friends Networks, and independent fabs will eventually print replacement parts, such as fenders and door panels, fuel injectors and other engine parts, air filters, bumpers, and headlights. Many of these aerospace and auto parts may be covered by one or more utility or design patents.

In health care, domestic and offshore black markets and other types of printing away from control could result from the democratization of manufacturing, and therefore threaten IP rights that protect 3D printed health-care products. For a compelling near-future scenario involving black-market 3D printed human organs, see Hod Lipson's and Melba Kurman's book *Fabricated: The New World of 3D Printing*.[494] However, the IP issues of such a market pale in comparison to the product-safety and liability issues.

The IP implications for 3D printable materials are essentially the same as in the aerospace, automotive, and health-care industries. However, the risk to the IP system may be relatively low because democratized manufacturing of patented materials away from control may not be common, especially for complex and advanced materials. Most people will probably buy their 3D printing materials through traditional supply chains, within control.

INFRINGEMENT AWAY FROM CONTROL INVOLVES ALL TYPES OF IP RIGHTS

According to Melba Kurman, "3D printing infringement will impact only a few, specific industries, and even there, 3D printed manufacturing will have a gradual and localized effect."[495] Her reasons are that 3D printing is slow, it is not as easy to make a thing as to copy a music file, consumer 3D printers print in only one material, and 3D printing can't compete with mass production. She may be right, but only for the short term, because the reasons she gives are probably only short-term shortcomings of 3D printing. And Kurman recognizes this: "Once it matures, truly multimaterial printing of currently incompatible raw materials (e.g., ceramics and metals) will have the potential to disrupt some types of manufacturing."[496]

Certain industries are ripe for infringement from 3D printing away from control, such as toys and figurines, adult products, tools, models (such as model trains, boats, and planes), and plastic replacement parts. 3D Systems makes Star Trek selfies from photos you supply. Disney offers the same for Cinderella and Star Wars selfies. Hasbro is making some of its toys and games available for legal copying. All of these products probably will be infringed soon, maybe by blueprints made from scanning or from leaked copies of genuine blueprints, all shared peer to peer on the Internet.

Let's look at how each type of IP right may be affected by 3D printing away from control.

Copyrights

Copyright is fundamentally at odds with the open-technology movement, some of which is made up of Makers. To quote an advertisement for the May 2013 Bay Area Makers' Faire: "You are going to be thrilled with [this] talk on the legal rights of makers and how to fight the copyright laws that are on the horizon."[497] Many people believe that copyrights, which protect original expression, like music, movies, and writing, sometimes stand in the way of technological innovations.

As 3D printers become capable of making almost anything, copying things away from control will become as easy as downloading illegal music. However, most 3D printable objects are not copyrightable. Things like dolls, toys, and sculptures may be copyrightable, but common things like dinner plates, kitchen tools, hand tools, and remote controls are not. So copyright is not a tool to prevent people from 3D printing most things.

Copyright will be important for protecting software used in the 3D printing industry, such as for design, scanning, manufacturing and machine control, machine networking, streaming of blueprints, file authentication and security, digital rights management (DRM), and file management. But the digital blueprints for things may or may not be copyrightable. If the blueprint is for a noncopyrightable object, then the blueprint may not be copyrightable either. If the blueprint resulted from scanning an object, it also may not be copyrightable.[498]

For copyright infringement within control, the Digital Millennium Copyright Act will be used as a tool to remove from the Internet digital blueprints that allegedly infringe copyrights. The DMCA provides a procedure requiring website operators to remove content that copyright owners accuse of infringing their rights. If the website operators do so, they are protected from copyright infringement claims. Of course even if a design or product is taken down, anyone with the blueprint can still print and share it in other ways.

Copyright infringement by 3D printing within control can be stopped just like any other type of copyright infringement. But copyrights infringed away from control will be subject to the Five Is. In time, industrial- and consumer-grade 3D printers will be able to make almost anything that is copyrightable, away from control.

Trademarks

It will become easier and easier to counterfeit brand-name products away from control, which will lead to widespread trademark infringement and counterfeiting of branded products—a category of goods especially vulnerable to the Five Is. And because the meaning of "genuine" will be eroded, buyers of branded parts and products may have no way of knowing if they were made or authorized by the brand owner.[499]

Trademarks also carry with them an implied guarantee of consistent quality and authenticity. You can walk into any McDonald's in the world and the name itself guarantees that the quality of the food will be consistent. 3D printing away from control eliminates the trademark owner's ability to control the quality of things bearing its trademark and even eliminates the implied guarantee that a trademark-bearing product was made or authorized by the trademark owner. In a 3D printed world, there may be no reason to assume that a branded product is authentic. Thus, the presence of a brand name on a product will be no guarantee of anything.

Perhaps more significantly, the ability to 3D print things with virtually any functionality may substantially reduce the need and demand for branded products and kill the companies that make them. Why print a trademarked product when you can print a generic substitute, especially if the blueprint for the generic is free? And if you can print the generic, why buy the brand, especially if you can tweak the digital blueprint for the generic product to look just like the branded one, and even include the brand name or logo? Although it will always be possible to enforce trademarks infringed within control, 3D printing—both within control and away from control—may erode the number of branded products and, therefore, the need to enforce trademarks within control or the brand owners' ability to do so.

Utility patents

Products and processes may be covered by one or more utility patents. A utility patent that covers how a product is made is called a "product-by-process" patent. Such a patent is valid only if the product itself is patentable, regardless of the process. A product that is not patented (either because its patent expired or it was never patentable) does not become patentable by 3D printing it.[500] So it is not possible to make an old product patentable by filing a patent for the process of 3D printing it. Also, if the old product is already covered by a product-by-process patent for the traditional way of making it, the patent is not infringed if the product is 3D printed.[501]

3D printing may stress the patent system the same way that the Internet and the digital revolution have stressed the copyright system.[502] Enforcing patents against infringing products 3D printed away from control will become increasingly challenging because of the Five Is, and more and more things will be 3D printed away from control. It will also be difficult to enforce patents against digital blueprints for products that infringe patents within control. Because many companies may choose (or be forced) to sell blueprints rather than physical products, their inability to enforce patents against blueprints may prevent them from stopping infringement.

Some IP attorneys have proposed that Congress enact a law like the Digital Millennium Copyright Act, but for patents.[503] Although such a law may provide patent owners with a way to stop some patent infringement within control, it will have little or no effect on infringement away from control. Other IP attorneys may favor extending patent protection to digital blueprints, or making the 3D scanning of parts illegal. The former could happen, but such patents would have little effect on 3D printing away from control. Making 3D scanning illegal probably won't happen because scanning is a type of reverse engineering, and reverse engineering has been protected under the law for a long time.

Professors Desai and Magliocca, along with legal commentators Davis Doherty and Carlos Rosario, have suggested an exemption from patent infringement liability for personal manufacturing or personal use. As Desai and Magliocca wrote, "It is unclear why personal 3D printing should be unlawful, especially given the futility of enforcement."[504] They do not seem to realize that the enactment of such a law could sound the death knell for patents, and for any company that makes products that can be made away from control. When consumers start making patented products instead of buying them, a personal exemption from patent infringement would excuse most infringing manufacturing. Although patent owners' ability to enforce their patents would be subject to the Five Is, the potential to enforce them in appropriate situations would be better than having no right to do so because of a personal exemption from infringement. Moreover, such an exemption really isn't necessary. If infringement away from control becomes common, it will be impractical or impossible to sue infringers.

Design patents

Design patents have long been a neglected sister of IP law, but 3D printing could make them the Cinderella of IP rights. It is fairly easy to "design around" a design patent, meaning to change the design so that it does not infringe the patent. Thus, design patents will probably be useful for products with unique designs, such as the 3D printed violin shown in "Nature-inspired designs" (chapter 6), and products for which customers are unlikely to accept a substitute with a different design. For example, car owners may want to replace a bumper only with a bumper for their car's model, so it would be worthwhile to patent the bumper's design. But this may only be true of new cars or certain models. Owners may not care if a replacement bumper is authentic to their model if the car is old or inexpensive. If the design of a part is not important to the customer, he may not care that a replacement part looks different from the original. Because it is usually easy to redesign a part so that it does not infringe a design patent, design patents for such parts may not be worth the paper they are printed on.

Trade secrets

Mass customization and mass personalization are hallmarks of 3D printing, but it is difficult to protect such products with patents and copyrights. This may not be a problem for IP owners because the customization itself will provide protection. Trade secrets may be the IP right best suited to protecting the ways that a company customizes products. In fact, the secret sauce of customization may be the savior of companies that find themselves selling designs rather than products and competing against widely available designs for the same or substitute parts. For example, ZeframWD's customers pay a premium for authentic blueprints because, along with providing the blueprints themselves, ZeframWD licenses its secret know-how for 3D printing its warp drives and other parts.

INFRINGEMENT AWAY FROM CONTROL WILL MUSHROOM

3D printing away from control will not be limited to garages, basements, and Friends Networks. Although there will be increasingly sophisticated 3D printers in most homes, thousands if not tens of thousands of independent fabricators will spring up all over the world, and they will have 3D printers capable of making almost anything. There will be several near you, and they will be as accessible as a convenience store. You will be able to select from products they offer to print, walk in with a blueprint on a USB drive, or email them a blueprint, and they will print it. Companies and governments will also buy their own 3D printers. They will 3D print their own replacement parts or have them made by independent fabs. Much of the latter will be done under confidentiality agreements, away from control.

3D printing away from control will become pervasive and will involve almost all types of products. Many of the products that will be 3D printed away from control will be covered by one or more of the five types of IP rights, but those rights will be irrelevant because of the Five Is. More importantly, many of the products will have no IP protection at all, making them free to copy without even the technical risk of infringing anyone's IP rights.

Widespread 3D printing away from control will change everything, and IP rights will have little effect. If someone 3D prints a product away from control and tries to sell it, IP rights owners may sue for infringement. But such products will no longer be away from control and will be only a small part of the problem. The immense power of 3D printing away from control will be wielded by consumers, industrial customers, and governments who become makers, making or repairing the things they need for their own use rather than buying them.

GOOD GUYS AND BAD GUYS

Most infringement by 3D printing away from control will probably be unintentional. Consumers who 3D print products may not be aware that IP rights are involved. And if it becomes so routine to copy things—using a combination of 3D scanners, printers, and widely available blueprints—that rights-owners throw up their hands in defeat, then such infringement may become the norm. This has already happened to music, where seventy percent of online users see nothing wrong with online piracy and ninety-five percent of downloaded music is illegal.[505]

But some infringement will be intentional. There will always be bad guys out there, and 3D scanners and printers are great tools for counterfeiting almost anything. Some users will scan objects with blatant disregard for IP rights and either use, sell, or freely share the blueprints. Some will use tools that mask files, such as the Disarming Corruptor,[506] so that they can be exchanged without triggering IP alarms. Others will trade infringing files peer to peer online or upload and download them on black-market websites, such as Pirate Bay, or exchange them on the Dark Web. Today's hacking and data breaches for personal data may yield to hackers who steal or sabotage digital blueprints.[507] Some of the intentional infringement will not be away from control, so IP rights owners may try to stop it, as they try to stop counterfeiting of other products today, but even today this is hard to do because counterfeiters operate in the shadows. Attempts to stop 3D counterfeiting away from control will probably be less successful.

WHAT TO EXPECT FROM THE LAW

Whether IP infringement within and away from control is intentional or not, IP rights-owners will face massive and widespread challenges. Suing their customers will not be palatable and suing thousands of fabs will not be possible, assuming they can even identify infringement away from control. And there will be far more infringers than when music companies tried to sue consumers. As MIT's Neil Gershenfeld said, "You can't sue the human race."[508] IP enforcement didn't work in the music arena, and it will not work for infringement away from control.

Companies that make products and parts are in essentially the same position as the music industry in the late 1990s. The music industry did not proactively plan for the disruption that the Internet caused. It maintained its long-standing copyright-based business model well into the period when millions of people downloaded and shared infringing copies of music files without regard to copyright. When the industry started to feel enough pressure from dropping revenue, it stepped up its enforcement efforts. At the end of those efforts, the industry reached a point of desperation, suing college students and parents, and received a lot of bad publicity. Apple then introduced the iTunes business model, which essentially saved the music industry, or to be more accurate, reduced its losses. Music companies now sell digital files. iTunes is not physical-product based, and it is not IP-rights based. Music companies make far fewer physical media than they did ten years ago, and most brick-and-mortar music stores no longer exist, at least in the United States. The iTunes model does not rely on copyrights or enforcement against individuals who copy and share files. Although copyright is just as important as it once was for commercial infringers who produce enough infringing copies to make enforcement cost effective, the likelihood is low that the industry will sue individuals for sharing a few music files.

Companies threatened by 3D printing are likely to follow this same path, spending a lot of money on traditional IP rights protection and litigation that ultimately will not solve their problem and, in the end, possibly suing customers and generating bad karma. One important difference between the music industry and the parts industry is that most music is protected by copyright. Parts may or may not have any viable IP rights protection.

Current IP laws probably will be inadequate to address the challenges of 3D printing. IP rights-owners will petition legislators for new laws, for example, to protect blueprints and products printed from them and will try to protect their IP with technical measures known as digital rights management (DRM). More laws rarely solve these kinds of problems, however, and DRM rarely works.[509] DRM also does not prevent 3D scanning products with ever more sophisticated 3D scanners, tweaking the resulting blueprints away from control, and then 3D printing the products and sharing the blueprints. As Hod Lipson and Melba Kurman said, "DRM technologies may be a futile attempt to stem the tide. DRM technologies create an ongoing arms race between consumers and companies."[510] And as Kurman observed, "Pirates bent on IP infringement will likely remain one step ahead of any technological solution."[511]

IP laws will probably become narrower, not broader, because existing IP laws are increasingly seen as hindering innovation. Any new laws should protect IP while simultaneously enabling rapid innovation and leaving the markets to operate as freely as possible. As the IBM study recommended:[512]

> Prepare for IP reform and digital rights management by protecting businesses, but balance this with enabling innovation by disruptive technologies and open source platforms—start by considering the revision of stifling legacy regulations.

Referring to the constitutional basis for the US patent and copyright laws, Desai and Magliocca expressed a similar reluctance to beef up IP laws:[513]

> 3D printing should be lightly regulated, because it enables precisely the kind of creation and progress of the useful arts and sciences that intellectual property is supposed to foster.

In this regard, it is worth noting that although the US Constitution gives Congress the power to grant IP rights like patents and copyrights, it does not require them to exercise that power. And in recent years, Congress and the courts have been chipping away at IP rights.

To survive, many companies will transition to non-IP-rights-based business models, like iTunes, which makes music files available easily and cheaply enough that many consumers are enticed to buy rather than steal their music. Companies will sell 3D printable, value-added proprietary blueprints instead of physical parts and products. With the right business model, customers may be more likely to buy the blueprints than to download bootlegged copies or generic substitutes. In effect, instead of trying to beat the infringers, they will join them, or, to be more accurate, beat them at their own game. Although the revenue per part will be lower than for selling physical parts, profits per part may be comparable to present models because overhead is essentially eliminated after the part is designed and translated into a blueprint. This is what ZeframWD did. It not only worked very well, but saved the company.

An alternative is customization, which is a variation on the iTunes model. The parts in question may or may not lend themselves to customization, but 3D printing is ideal for mass customization. The ability to offer and provide customized parts—either as physical parts or proprietary blueprints—becomes, in effect, the protection for the part. The infrastructure that enables the customization is also protectable by traditional means. For example, patents and trade secrets may protect the customization process, and copyrights may protect the underlying software.

TAXATION AND CUSTOMS

A world dominated by distributed and regional manufacturing will involve fewer imports and exports because supply and distribution chains will be shorter, and things will be made near the point of need. This may result in more products sold locally, but it will also involve more 3D printing away from control. Instead of shipping products, many companies will transmit blueprints digitally. Some of this will be within control, but much of it will not. Fewer imports mean governments will collect fewer customs duties. Fewer sales of products within control mean lower sales-tax collections. Even sales within control mean lower sales-tax revenues if most sales are of blueprints, not products. As the IBM study concluded:[514]

Global trade will become less physical and more digital. New global trade flows will require evaluation of imports, duties, taxes and customs, including sales of digital data across national borders.

The digital transmission of blueprints and the manufacture of products away from control will challenge governments to capture taxes from commerce related to 3D printing. As Briar Thompson observed, governments' inability to capture taxes and customs duties from 3D printing commerce means tax revenues will drop.[515]

Although everyone likes the idea of paying fewer taxes, the taxing authorities will need to make up the losses somewhere. Two obvious targets will be taxing 3D printers and materials. Taxing the former will not make up the shortfall, and taxing the latter will have its limits. An alternative to lower sales tax and customs revenue will be higher income taxes, but that will have its limits, too. In a 3D printed world, governments will find it harder to generate revenues that are politically acceptable to the populace.

PRODUCT SAFETY AND LIABILITY

The purpose of product-safety laws is to prevent injuries. The purpose of product-liability laws is to compensate people who have been injured. These areas are almost entirely unexplored in the 3D printing space and are a potential legal minefield.

Product-safety law is the reason that the first few pages of most product-operating instructions warn of every conceivable danger related to using the product. Such warnings are intended to encourage consumers to use products safely and to reduce manufacturers' potential liability for injuries caused by using the products. Although you may see disclaimers of liability, the courts often reject them unless they are very clear and can't be missed by the user. But even warnings carefully crafted by the world's best product-safety attorneys will not shield a manufacturer from liability for injuries caused by defective products.

Consumer product-safety incidents cost the US economy $1 trillion per year.[516] And this is without 3D printing. Because 3D printing blurs the lines between manufacturer, designer, and customer, it may not always be clear who is responsible for 3D printed product safety and who will be liable for 3D printed product injuries. As 3D printers become common in industry and homes, they will create a worldwide spiderweb of design and manufacturing, and the question "Is this product genuine?" will become harder to answer and possibly meaningless.

Industrial and consumer designers' 3D printing blueprints will compete with those of original equipment manufacturers, and the hottest designs will be printed by thousands of different fabs or millions of different consumers, sometimes using machines with the proper capabilities and safeguards, and sometimes not. Some products will be made within control. Many will be made away from control, and then enter the stream of commerce. Some such products will be safe, but others will hurt people. Sometimes it will be possible to identify the designer, the fab, and the machines involved, but sometimes it may be impossible to determine who is to blame. Many designs will be open source or crowdsourced, resulting from the input of many designers. The pedigree of many 3D printed products may be so uncertain that people injured by the design will be faced with two choices: sue everyone or no one.

In product-liability lawsuits, the injured party will usually sue everyone in sight: the product manufacturer, the companies that made the machines that made the product, the distributors, and so on. For 3D printed products, the list of potential defendants may be much longer, and it may be difficult or impossible to figure out who should be on the list.

A new problem will arise in product-liability lawsuits involving 3D printed products: some faulty products will have been made by consumers running personal machines or by hobby businesses, not by manufacturing companies. It has long been the law that the manufacturers of defective products are "strictly liable" for injuries caused by their defective products. They can also be liable if the injuries were caused by the manufacturer's negligence. These rules apply to products 3D printed by companies just the same as they apply to any other manufactured products. But the rules may be different for products 3D printed by consumers, and most consumer makers will not even be aware of the product-safety laws that apply to product manufacturers. As 3D printing industry observer Scott Grunewald wrote, "By removing the manufacturing step from the process you remove all of the safety, quality and manufacturing standards that are currently in place."[517]

If someone is injured by a consumer's 3D printed product, the consumer who made the product, the company that made the 3D printer, the designer of the product blueprint, and the material supplier could be lawsuit targets. If the consumer injures himself with his own 3D printed product, he may want to sue the 3D printer company or the designer. Stanford Law School professor Nora Engstrom, who is an expert on product-safety and liability law, believes that consumers, 3D printer companies, and blueprint designers probably will be safe from strict liability for injuries caused by most products consumers 3D print and sell or use themselves, unless they become "commercial sellers," which means product companies rather than hobbyists who occasionally sell a 3D printed product. Of course she recognizes that courts could "end up softening lines and blurring boundaries in order to impose strict liability on hobbyist 3D inventors and digital designers,"[518] and they could also be liable for negligence.[519]

On the product-safety side, the government will probably issue safety standards for machines and materials to ensure public safety.[520] On the product-liability side, the courts will wrestle with whom to blame for product-related injuries, and whether to blame anyone at all.

INSURANCE

3D printing presents new risks to companies and consumers. The purpose of insurance is to protect against risk. 3D printing magnifies some risks that have been around for ages, such as counterfeiting and the magnitude of the risks relating to IP rights infringement. It also creates some entirely new risks, such as the product-safety risks and the potential liability attaching to 3D printer makers, product designers, fabricators, materials suppliers, and makers, as well as the difficulty of identifying genuine products. These risks are opportunities for insurance companies; they can sell insurance to protect against the risks. But because the risks are new, insurance companies have no experience with the type of claims that may be made, how frequently they may be made, the amount of such claims, or their long-term liability for such claims. As the director of CFC Underwriting, Graeme Newman, wrote:[521]

> The use of mass-market 3D printing technology will create an army of back bedroom manufacturers. Much of the process will be devoid of the usual rigorous testing found in the traditional manufacturing process with product safety likely to rapidly decline as a result. As new techniques and ink technologies are introduced, latent defects will appear in products that were previously unimaginable and many will not emerge for years, if not decades, after this process has become mainstream.

In addition to the army of bedroom manufacturers, industrial customers will become manufacturers, as they make or repair products and parts they formerly bought. Colin Bradbury, director of commercial underwriting at RSA, sees the risk for customer-printed products:[522]

> Pushing the manufacture out to the customer...puts more onus on the control of the design specifications. Companies have traditionally relied on a combination of specification control at the front end and quality control after production to ensure there isn't a problem, but this second stage is removed when the production is completed by the customer.

The designs for such products and parts may come from the manufacturer or from independent or unknown designers; they may be open source or crowdsourced, or they may result from customers scanning existing products. Such products and parts may fail, and they may cause injuries. Insurance companies will insure for such risks, after they figure out how to avoid losing money doing so.

Zurich Insurers predicts that insurance companies may start issuing product-recall insurance for 3D printed products. Zurich also sees employer risk for fabricators because "the raw materials used are sometimes powder based, so there is potential for respiratory issues for employees operating the machines." [523] Insurance lawyers William Knowles and Kathleen Grohman see employer risk because "certain additive processes have been found to emit ultrafine particles or aerosol emissions, which have proven to be toxic in animal testing."[524] Graeme Newman believes professional liability insurance will be crucial for designers, as their blueprints are printed across the globe by unknown printers they do not control. Newman also sees insurable risk in accidental IP infringement arising from parts printed by company employees, which bypass proper procurement and contracting. [525] Ageas Insurance sees risk in the 3D printing process:[526]

> Items can take a long time to print, so there's the potential for unattended overnight processing. Coupled with the heat that some of these printing processes can generate, this could increase fire hazard risk.

Insurance and insurance-law experts are just starting to consider the effects of 3D printing. As 3D printing rocks the world, it will create risk and therefore insurance opportunities in every area it touches. But such opportunities will also bring risks for the insurers themselves, litigation of disputed claims, and new laws and government regulation of the insurance industry.

THE NEED FOR BALANCE

As the dark side of 3D printing comes to light, the courts and federal and local governments will grapple with new kinds of legal problems. If it is not currently illegal to 3D print false fronts for ATM machines and provide 24-hour support for criminals who use them, it soon will be. Although I don't generally favor more laws of any kind, probably no one would disagree that outlawing such things is OK. The question is how far should the law go in addressing such problems?

One risk to the development and adoption of 3D printing is that governments will try to regulate the machines themselves. For example, there have already been calls to require 3D printers to recognize and refuse to print gun parts. Such efforts are the wrong approach. When the Industrial Revolution led to the mass production of weapons, governments did not react by requiring that machines be rendered technically incapable of making gun parts. Instead, they regulated the sale and use of such weapons.

Trying to control what types of things 3D printers are technically capable of printing is also horse thinking and ultimately doomed to failure. Guns need not look like guns, so any efforts to make 3D printers incapable of making things that look like guns would render them incapable of making anything. The better approach is to regulate the use of illegal objects that emerge from them. Although 3D printing away from control could rob such laws of some of their bite, such an approach makes people responsible for their actions without trying to control what the machines can and can't do.

The same is true of any potential uses of 3D printers that society finds undesirable. 3D printing industry analysts fear that court decisions and statutes relating to intellectual property rights could hinder innovation. The same could be true of the judicial and legislative response to any legal issues raised by the technology. New laws could evolve so as to foster the technology, or to stifle it. As Melba Kurman observed:[527]

The bad news is that as more design and manufacturing migrates "away from control," the temptation arises to encourage the passage of laws whose primary intent is to blindly protect today's established "brick and mortar" business models. Instead, our goal as legal professionals, policymakers, businesspeople, academics and 3D printing experts and enthusiasts should be to seek disruption. Ideally, the correct legal framework would actually accelerate the development of a 3D printed manufacturing economy so it can live up to its full disruptive potential.

I agree with Kurman: seek disruption, which is another way of saying "seek change." Most people fear change, especially if it may upset their apple-carts. 3D printing may upset many applecarts, but an incredible amount of good can come of it. New laws will not protect the apples anyway. The very nature of 3D printing away from control is that it can't be controlled, so new laws to prevent 3D printing away from control would be futile.

Where safety is an issue, balanced legal efforts to make 3D printed products safe is probably good for society. But for issues other than safety, keeping legal noses out of 3D printing and allowing the marketplace to decide may be better for society.

10

Rocking Kids' Futures: Paving the Roads to Tomorrow

KIDS ARE THE KEY

3D printing will rock the world in many ways, but will we be ready? Many companies probably will be unprepared. But the opposite may be true of educators and government policy makers. The former seem to see that tomorrow's workforce needs to learn about 3D printing today, and the latter are hopeful that 3D printing can revitalize manufacturing. For both, kids are the key, and schools and governments around the world are getting serious about 3D printing.

Kids are just starting to use simple, inexpensive, consumer-grade 3D printers today. They are the early adopters, and machines that are good enough today will become better and better, faster and faster, and capable of making more and more things. Kids will not only grow up with the technology, the technology will grow up with the kids because they will contribute to its advancement. Today's young innovators will 3D print our future. To some extent they will learn by using their own machines, teaching themselves, and improving the machines as they go. But they will also need access to advanced machines, processes, and materials. Schools and governments are beginning to pave the roads that kids will follow, from printing toys at home today to making high-tech parts and products in the factories of tomorrow.

TURN ON THE STEAM

There is a lot of talk about the importance of STEM education. Recently, the issue became hotter when STEM became STEAM: Science & Technology interpreted through Engineering & the Arts, all based in Math.[528] According to the US Bureau of Labor Statistics, the United States will have about 9.2 million STEM jobs in 2020. But according to the National Science Foundation, there will not be enough qualified graduates to fill those jobs.[529] Geopolitical expert George Freedman believes the United States will have a severe labor shortage beginning no later than 2020, which will accelerate in that decade.[530]

But there is hope. According to a joint international report spearheaded by the Institute of Electrical and Electronics Engineers (IEEE) Education Society, 3D printing will significantly enhance STEM+ education within a few years.[531]

INSPIRING KIDS TO LEARN

Adults often ask: "If I had a 3D printer, what would I do with it?" In my 3D printing lectures, I answer this question with a brilliant insight I learned from Mark Trageser, an independent toy designer who uses 3D printers to prototype and make toys. He says, "Don't ask me what to do with a 3D printer, tell me what to do with it."[532] I love it. Many adults need a little help to see how 3D printers can fit into their lives, at least today. But kids don't ask this question. They seem to be born with the innate ability to use technologies available to them. Hand a kid a 3D printer, and he or she will figure out what to make with it. Some of the things they make may not impress you, but I guarantee you that kids will push the envelope, not only of the things they make but of what the machine can do. Kids will do things with 3D printers that we may not think are possible. Why? Because they are not burdened with adult prejudices. Kids don't know what can't be done.

It isn't always easy to get kids interested in learning. But 3D printers inspire kids to learn simply because they exist. Put them in the same room together, and great things will result. I hear story after story of how kids are drawn to 3D printers as if they contain superstrong kid magnets that pull back their eyelids, exposing bulging eyes. Is it that these machines empower them to make things they want, without depending on adults, or that they tug at the maker strings deep inside them, or that they know with some sixth sense that these machines have a fundamentally different ability to transport them to places they could reach in no other way?

Adults can help the learning process. It is the adults' responsibility to bring 3D printers to the kids or to bring the kids to the printers. In "Coming to a school near you" and "Coming to a school not so near you," I give examples of how kids are being exposed to 3D printers in schools and libraries all over the world. Learning takes place for everyone, every hour of every day, everywhere we go. This goes double for kids, and the BBC gets it. In the UK, the BBC is trying to inspire young viewers with new TV shows, online learning, games, and contests involving 3D printing and other technology. In one show, *Nina and the Neurons: Go Digital*, the characters get hands-on experience with 3D printers. As 3D printing industry writer Michael Molitch-Hou said, the new shows are like "*Sesame Street* for the digital era."[533]

Anything that connects kids and 3D printers is good, especially if it meets kids on their own ground. The more kids are exposed to 3D printing, the more they will be inspired, the faster the technology will be adopted and improved, and the more prepared they will be for the future.

COMING TO A SCHOOL NEAR YOU

A joint report by the New Media Consortium, the Consortium for School Networking, and the International Society for Technology in Education ("New Media Report") predicts that 3D printing will be fully adopted in K–12 education by about 2019.[534] An amazing array of public and private initiatives is making this happen.

One is the Obama administration's program to bring fully equipped makerspaces into a thousand US schools.[535] Another is M.Lab21, which is bringing high-school shop classes into the twenty-first century by adding 3D printers and scanners, and developing advanced-manufacturing curricula. Its founding members, America Makes, 3D Systems, and the Society of Manufacturing Engineers (now called SME), will be supported by the likes of Deloitte, GE, Intel, Johnson Controls, Lockheed Martin, and NIST, which are all in the forefront of industrial 3D printing adoption.[536]

Consumer 3D printer maker MakerBot launched the MakerBot Academy to put a MakerBot 3D printer in every American high school. For colleges, MakerBot launched MakerBot Innovation Centers. The first center, at the State University of New York at New Palz, is making more than thirty 3D printers available for free use by students and faculty. As industry visionary and MakerBot cofounder, Bre Pettis, explained:[537]

Class projects can be brought to life through 3D printing and scanning. Product prototypes can be created, refined and finalized at a much faster and affordable pace. Schools can train future innovators and be ahead of the curve when it comes to preparing students for the real world.

3D printing software powerhouse Autodesk earmarked $250 million to improve STEAM education in America's twenty-seven thousand middle and high schools with its Design for the Future program. According to president and CEO Carl Bass, "Our customers have unfilled, high-paying positions due to the lack of qualified US high school and university graduates." The program gives teachers the tools they need to prepare students for STEAM careers.[538] Consumer 3D printer maker Airwolf is implementing a similar idea close to home: teaching Orange County California teachers how to use 3D printers in the classroom.[539] To help teachers know what to teach, teacher J. J. Johnson's SeeMeCNC offers a complete 3D printing curriculum.[540]

How do these efforts translate into the schools? One example is Charlottesville, Virginia's, school-within-a-school concept, where "lab schools" within area middle and high schools give students work experience in advanced manufacturing. Garnering international TV coverage, Buford Middle School launched the program with a 3D printing workshop, where students made their own stereo speakers.[541]

Grassroots efforts are bringing 3D printers to places that big dollars don't reach. Erin Wincek, librarian for the Saxonburg, Pennsylvania, public library, was bitten by the 3D printing bug. She wanted to build a 3D printing lab at the library but had no money. Chatting up anyone who would listen in her town of seven thousand, she finally secured a private donation. Printer time is now booked solid by library patrons.[542] 3D printers are popping up in other libraries all over the world.

These and other programs are putting 3D printers into young students' hands, to see what happens. Many of the programs teaching kids about 3D printing are outside the traditional school setting. At Pennsylvania Cyber Charter School's 3D printing summer camps, STEAM-oriented high-school students build their own 3D printers.[543] The Robert C. Byrd Institute operates similar summer camps for middle schoolers in West Virginia, Kentucky, and Ohio.[544] The free GoEngineer Kids Camps in California, Oklahoma, Texas, and Utah, for kids ten to eighteen, teach computer-aided design and 3D printing as foundations for advanced manufacturing careers.[545]

3D printers are also coming to a college near you. T. J. McCue, who spent eight months traveling the United States to see firsthand how 3D printing is changing America, reports that over two hundred universities and colleges offer 3D printing coursework.[546] MIT and the New York City College of Technology offer industrial 3D printing courses to scientists, engineers, and architects.[547] Florida Polytechnic University opened a 3D printer–equipped Rapid Application Development Makerspace Lab.[548]

Purdue University opened a 3D printing lab for students in its College of Technology.[549] The Wohlers Report lists over one hundred academic and research institutions with active 3D printing development projects. As the report observes, "more new ideas are developing than researchers can manage and money support."[550]

COMING TO A SCHOOL NOT SO NEAR YOU

Efforts to inspire kids with 3D printing and to train them for tomorrow's jobs are not limited to the United States. Down under in Australia, a shop on wheels called The Maker Machine is traveling the vast country, visiting schools, libraries, and youth clubs to teach STEAM with 3D printers and other tech tools.[551]

Finland is buying 3D printers for schools in Helsinki and three other cities. They can't supply all schools yet because the demand far exceeds the budget. As one school principal said, "3D printing fits well into education because the children are born curious towards new things. Also the creative work increases their self-esteem."[552]

The group behind Israel's first open-source 3D printing lab, the Reut Institute, is sponsoring Communal Tech Spaces "from the far south to the far north, so that Israel's periphery will have access to 3D printers now."[553]

Japan, which has been trailing the West in the development of 3D printing, budgeted $44 million in 2014 to prepare future workers for additive manufacturing by putting 3D printers into students' hands today.[554]

In the Netherlands, its homegrown Leapfrog 3D printers are teaching K–12 teachers how to teach students to use 3D printers.[555]

In New Zealand, K–12 students will have access to 3D printers,[556] and in Singapore undergraduate and graduate students at the Nanyang Technological University are using industrial 3D printers and bioprinters in its $30 million Additive Manufacturing Centre.[557]

Then there is the United Kingdom, which understands that education equals jobs and made a major commitment to use 3D printing to educate tomorrow's workers and to revitalize its manufacturing. Using 3D printers will become part of the standard curriculum in UK schools.[558] Renishaw, a UK-based maker of industrial 3D printers, teamed with Young Engineers to inspire young people to become engineers.[559] UK consumer 3D printer maker Ultimaker has a similar goal: to bring its CREATE Education Project to UK schools, inspiring kids with its motto "Imagine it-Make it."[560] Loughborough University partnered with the Kirklees Directorate for Children and Young People and the Open University to hook primary school kids on engineering by giving them access to 3D printers. Loughborough professor Russ Harris said, "The highly visual nature of immediately transforming their ideas and designs into parts which are then 'grown' in a very short time really captured the interest and inventiveness of the children."[561]

STEAMING UP THE CLASSROOM

The beauty of 3D printers in the classroom is that they not only prepare kids to work in the factories of the future and inspire them to be makers but also help bring abstract concepts to life. 3D printed models STEAM up the classroom like no other teaching tool. If a picture says a thousand words, a model you can handle and examine from all angles—and that you made yourself—says a million.

S and T are for science and technology

Of course 3D printers **are** technology. By using them, students learn how things are made. More importantly, they learn how things can be made, since 3D printers make things in a fundamentally different way than traditional machines and make things that could not be made before. They learn about design and structure and support and materials, hands on. The New Media Report observes that 3D printers in schools enable[562]

more authentic exploration of objects that may not be readily available to schools. In science and history classes, for example, students can make and interact with models of fragile objects such as fossils and artifacts. Through rapid prototyping and production tools, chemistry students can print out models of complex proteins and other molecules.

Students can print models of mechanical devices to see how they work, dinosaur bones to see how they make up a dinosaur, and anatomical models to learn how organs work. 3D printers in the classroom may even improve long-term health. Imagine the potentially positive health effects of having kids 3D print both a healthy and a diseased human heart, to show them the effects of a lifetime of French fries or smoking.

Kids can use home and classroom 3D printers to print really cool stuff, have fun, and learn at the same time, and even help other students to learn. For example, the National Institutes of Health created the 3D Print Exchange, which is a free online community-contributed library of 3D printable blueprints (http://3dprint.nih.gov/). Students who visit the website can download and print tangible models of things like proteins, pathogens, and DNA strands.

There is nothing like studying a physical 3D model. Imagine studying genetics by holding DNA strands that you printed yourself. According to a video on the NIH website, researchers who studied computer models of DNA strands for decades have made important advances faster by studying real, physical 3D models of the strands.[563] Students can also upload their own 3D printable blueprints, so other students can learn from their models.

Using 3D printers to inspire kids with science knows no bounds. Budding fourth-grade entomologists at one California school are designing and printing their own insects in teacher Clark Barnett's 3D printed entomology class. Their assignment: invent an insect living in the classroom, define its characteristics and habitat, draw it, 3D print it, photograph it in its classroom habitat, take stop-motion movies of the insect's movements, then upload the videos to YouTube.

Barnett says, "Entomology requires students to know a lot about insects and their parts. Instead of having them memorize this I used experiential education. When they are designing an insect the kids want to know what the parts are called. In my opinion, this is a much better way for them to learn, as opposed to rote memorization."[564]

E is for engineering

With a 3D printer, anyone—or even a whole class—can become a mechanical engineer. Eighth graders at Swanson Middle School designed and 3D printed a device to help a disabled student operate the touch-screen interface on his wheelchair.[565]

The 1,650 elementary school students at the Walt Disney Magnet School in Chicago use the 3D printers in their Makers Lab to make objects with braille labels to teach blind students at a neighboring school to read braille.[566]

University of Warwick's Dr. Simon Leigh sees Carbomorph as a great educational tool: "I can see this technology having a major impact in the educational sector, for example, allowing the next generation of young engineers to get hands-on experience of using advanced manufacturing technology to design fairly high-tech devices and products right there in the classroom."[567]

Engineering with 3D printers is not confined to the classroom. In 2012, puppeteer Ivan Owen and carpenter Richard Van As started the Robohand project. With the help of a 3D printer donated by MakerBot, they designed a 3D printable prosthetic hand and posted the blueprints on Thingiverse, free for anyone to use and improve. Richard was motivated by the loss of fingers in a woodshop accident. Ivan says, "It's truly uplifting to see the level of involvement and the number of people out in the world who have taken this idea as their own and are using it to help others." A new Robohand design is now available, which snaps together like Lego bricks.[568]

Some kids can be cruel. Nine-year-old Matthew Shields, born with-out fingers on one hand, had been teased by the cruel ones, and it was starting to get to him. Then, in stepped seventeen-year-old family friend Mason Wilde, a maker. After finding the blueprints for a mechanical hand through the Robohand project, Mason 3D printed a mechanical hand for Matthew at the local library, at a cost of about sixty dollars in materials and parts. Matthew can now open and close his mechanical fingers with a twist of the wrist. Now he can write and play catch with his brothers. With his new hand, the other kids now think he's cool.[569]

While a high-school sophomore, Easton LaChappelle took the Robohand project to the next level, combining 3D printed parts with a Nintendo telemetric Power Glove. His prosthetic hand won second place at the Intel International Science and Engineering Fair. At the fair, Easton met a girl with an $80,000 prosthetic arm that she was outgrowing. This spurred Easton to design a new, 3D printed version with the same func-tionality but at a cost of only $250.[570]

If kids like Easton and Mason had access to more sophisticated ma-chines, maybe they could do more amazing things. But maybe they are better off without them. After all, necessity truly is the mother of invention. The limitations of consumer-grade 3D printers are forcing true innovation in their young users, and kids are just starting to tap the engineering pos-sibilities of 3D printing.

A is for art

I'm not sure if the A in STEAM stands for fine art or liberal arts, but I will assume it means both. Certainly 3D printers can be used to make art, such as jewelry and selfies in the image of Star Wars characters or BoxTrolls.[571] But they can also be used to print geological formations, historical battlefields, great works of architecture, Leonardo da Vinci's models, dinosaur bones, ancient stone tablets, and models of Imperial Rome.[572]

Visual aids always help teaching. 3D printing a model of a Roman aqueduct and running water through it—as a class project—gives students a much better understanding of the history, engineering, and architecture than an artist's drawing in a textbook. Handling 3D printed dinosaur bones gives kids an even greater connection to the prehistoric beasts than they already have. Playing with Leonardo da Vinci's models of submarines, helicopters, and human wings will surely inspire kids to design things that never existed. 3D printers are teaching machines of unparalleled power.

M is for math

3D printers are also being used to turn math into models, which allows students to use their eyes and hands to learn geometry and calculus.[573] This 3D printed math was created by Henry Segerman, Saul Schleimer, Drew Armstrong, and Kenneth Baker.

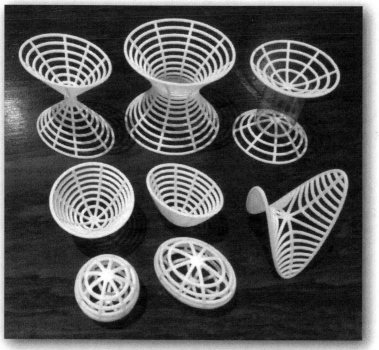

Photo courtesy of Henry Segerman

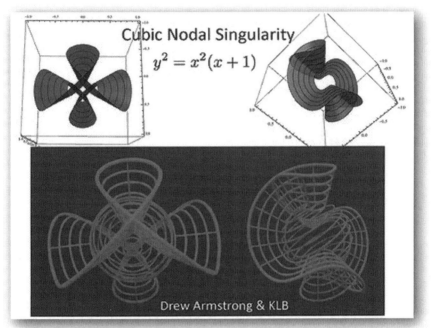

Image courtesy of Kenneth L. Baker/3D model design
by Drew Armstrong and Kenneth L. Baker

Photo courtesy of Henry Segerman/Design by
Saul Schleimer and Henry Segerman

I don't know about you, but I wish I'd had such models when I was learning math and geometry.

Dr. Laura Taalman, professor of mathematics and statistics at James Madison University, worked with her colleagues to build one of the first 3D printing classrooms in the United States, open to all students. Its printers run 24/7. Dr. Taalman uses the machines to teach a branch of applied math called knot theory. Unlike knots tied with rope, mathematical knots cannot be untied because they have no loose ends.

Before 3D printing, such knots were confined to the mind and drawings in the 2D world. Now students 3D print them, then examine them from all sides. As Dr. Taalman said, "It's pretty exciting for the students and really gets their attention. I think that having them look at and handle the knots adds to their comprehension of the concepts." Her courses— "Fabrication of 2D and 3D Mathematical Objects" and "Knot Theory Research and 3D Printing"—are sellouts.[574]

SELF-EDUCATION THROUGH MAKING

Kids also have an amazing ability to teach themselves. In fact, most of what they learn, and many of life's really important lessons, they learn outside the classroom. When I was a kid, I tinkered with parts of an old Bell Telephone switching system my father found in a junkyard and taught myself electronics by building simple circuits. I had my whole room wired from a central control panel. My friends were makers too. We learned construction techniques by trial and error by building forts in the woods and tree houses in unlucky trees.

Today, kids' lives are much more structured, but they have access to an unprecedented array of tools that allows them to feed their maker nature, including 3D printers. In fact, most consumer-grade 3D printers owe their existence to makers. Makers are making 3D printers, which are enabling the makers to make better 3D printers, along with other things. Today's young makers are tomorrow's engineers and entrepreneurs.

One resource available today, which I lacked as a kid, is maker and hackerspaces and fab labs. According to MIT's Neil Gershenfeld, the number of fab labs is doubling every eighteen months.[575] These spaces give kids the tools they need to make whatever they want and the freedom to do it their own way, on their own time, with the influence and support of their peers, and away from control. As Dr. Gershenfeld aptly observed,[576]

> The real strength of a fab lab is not technical; it is social. The innovative people that drive a knowledge economy share a common trait: by definition, they are not good at following rules. To be able to invent, people need to question assumptions. They need to study and work in environments where it is safe to do that.

Maker and hackerspaces allow kids to get away from authority, talk their own jargon, and give their creative minds free rein with the tools around them. As more and more of these spaces open their doors, more and more unusual, unexpected, and out-of-the-box creations will result.

Self-education need not happen away from home, and adults can and should be involved. What better way to build family ties and mentor young minds than for parent and child to make something together? 3D printers are the perfect family project machines. Take, for example, a dump truck. From finding and downloading the blueprints or scanning an old, broken toy, to customizing it, to printing it and learning the best way to orient it in the build chamber, learning the printer's quirks, cleaning up the print, and maybe painting the finished product, each step of the process is a learning experience for parent and child, and an experience both will remember. Similarly, the Digital Dollhouse allows kids to design and customize dollhouse furniture and then 3D print it.[577] Of course, the printer can also make the dollhouse itself. A dollhouse and furniture 3D printed by parent and child is not only a great tool for awakening the maker spirit and forging filial bonds, it will be a family heirloom fully furnished with great memories.

Kids with an entrepreneurial spirit will not stop when things come out of their machines. Some will turn them into businesses. One such kid is teenage Netherlander Maarten van Gelderen, who started his own 3D printing marketplace, Dhreams, for things to print at home. According to van Gelderen,[578]

> I want to make 3D printing more visible for the normal people. I have always been interested in 3D printing, but only the major companies were visible for me as a normal person. And they were companies who offer services to print products. What I was missing was a visible place for 3D printable designs. So I founded dhreams.com.

I wonder how old Maarten will be when he makes his first million.

PAVING THE ROADS TO TOMORROW

Carping about the government is part of living in any society on this planet. Of course, governments can always do more, and they can always do better, but at least in 3D printing they are starting to see its value to their people and to take proactive steps to make it part of education, manufacturing, business, and culture. Many governments recognize that 3D printing may bring the workers of today immediate benefits and build strong job markets for tomorrow's innovators.

The US government seems to be leading the charge. In 2012, President Obama proposed investing $1 billion in the National Network for Manufacturing Innovation.[579] America Makes, in Youngstown, Ohio, is the Obama-inspired innovation institute dedicated to accelerating the industrial adoption of 3D printing and the creation of related jobs. Its mission is to foster collaborative R&D and the exchange of ideas; to develop and improve 3D printing technology, design, and materials; to help companies and schools train tomorrow's workforce to use it; and to stimulate 3D printing–based start-ups.[580] America Makes is doing on a government level what TechShop and other makerspaces and hackerspaces are doing on a grassroots level. There is an obvious common goal here, driven by our maker spirit.

In addition to creating America Makes to reinvigorate American manufacturing, in 2014 the United States committed to invest at least $320 million private and public dollars in advanced manufacturing.[581] Youngstown, Ohio is the home of America Makes. Other innovation centers have been launched in Chicago, Detroit, and Raleigh-Durham, North Carolina.

The US government, which sponsors at least twenty-one national research laboratories[582] and contracts for the design and manufacture of parts and products throughout its alphabet soup of agencies, could become a major source of 3D printable blueprints. A White House memo instructed federal agencies to make 3D printable blueprints available to the public. The Smithsonian offers its Smithsonian X 3D platform, where you can find the blueprints for things like Abraham Lincoln's head (http://3d.si.edu/browser). The National Institute of Health (NIH) offers its 3D Print Exchange (http://3dprint.nih.gov/). And NASA offers its 3D Resources page, with blueprints for many spacecraft, space probes, and planetary crawlers (http://nasa3d.arc.nasa.gov/models/printable).[583]

Image from NASA 3D Resources (http://nasa3d.
arc.nasa.gov/models/printable)

Some members of Congress also seem to see the makers' handwriting on the wall. Congressmen Tim Ryan (D-OH), Steve Stivers (R-OH), Mark Takano (D-CA), and Mick Mulvaney (R-SC) formed the Congressional Maker Caucus. Rep. Ryan said:[584]

Experts tell us that the economy of making things is five times larger than the digital economy and the Maker Caucus will help us advance the right policies to keep our manufacturing sector thriving. I am happy to join my colleagues...in working on behalf of these new industries that will transform the way we make things in the United States—as well as bring in large numbers of new entrepreneurs to the process...

I want people to see the power of empowering individuals to build, make, create, design their own life—the products in their own life—and I think that tapping into the creativity and entrepreneurship of every single citizen is a powerful, powerful thing.

Although the US government is proactively fostering the advancement and adoption of this incredibly powerful technology, America lacks a national 3D printing strategy. The beginnings of such a strategy, however, may emerge from the US Comptroller General's Additive Manufacturing Forum, in which I participated. The forum was held in Washington, DC, in late 2014 to provide input by experts from the 3D printing industry for a report to Congress. Among other ideas, the experts suggested the formation of a task force to develop the strategy, as well as a plan to implement it. Ed Morris, the Director of America Makes, believes as I do that 3D printing should be integrated into every part of what he calls a "pre-K through gray" curricula in American schools because, as Morris says, the technology "is that ubiquitous."[585] I also believe America needs trade schools, possibly run through America Makes, to train workers to use 3D printing machines and design tools, and to develop software for the 3D printing industry.

Promoting 3D printing is not just a federal thing. States also want in. Like many states, Maryland wants to become a 3D printing hub. According to Jan Baum, executive director of 3D Maryland:[586]

> We have a very real opportunity to build Maryland into a hub for 3D printing and additive manufacturing, increasing Maryland's competitiveness, bottom line, and driving economic growth.

Because 3D printing will distribute and regionalize manufacturing, other countries are working toward making 3D printing a central part of their industrial policies.

Taking its cue from America Makes, Canada launched a national network dedicated to the adoption and development of 3D printing called Canada Makes. Like America Makes, it is a public-private partnership. Like many countries, Canada sees 3D printing as a potential job generator. Jason Meyers, president of the Canadian Manufacturers and Exporters

Association, said, "The global competitiveness of the Canadian manufacturing sector depends on the broad adoption of additive technologies and on the training of the next generation of designers and engineers."[587]

The European Union is investing about $60 million in various 3D printing projects. In addition, the European Space Agency is investing $13 million in its AMAZE program, which stands for Additive Manufacturing Aiming toward Zero Waste and Efficient Production of High-Tech Metal Products.[588]

The UK government is investing an ever-increasing mountain of pounds sterling in 3D printing. Its 3D printing R&D competition, called "Inspiring New Design Freedom in Additive Manufacturing," seeks to improve the technology and speed its adoption, build the United Kingdom's position in this space, and bring new 3D printed products and business models to market.

Having lost about 4.5 million jobs over the past thirty years,[589] the UK is banking on 3D printing to revitalize its economy and jobs market. As the Right Honorable David Willetts said:[590]

> Building on £20 million of previous Technology Strategy Board support for additive manufacturing innovation, [Inspiring New Design Freedom in Additive Manufacturing] will help secure more of this game-changing high value activity for the UK, driving economic growth and enhancing quality of life.

Similarly, UK Business Secretary Vince Cable said:[591]

> Investing in tomorrow's technology will bring jobs and economic growth throughout the UK. That's why...the Government announced the biggest ever investment in the work of the Technology Strategy Board (now called "Innovate UK"). With £440

million of funding they will support new manufacturing techniques to maintain the UK's position as a world leader in technology and design. This joint investment with the Research Councils highlights the commitment from across the sector to boost manufacturing in the UK.

The UK also plans to build a national center for 3D printing in Coventry and to inject £15 million into its existing Manufacturing Technology Center, which already uses 3D printing, to make aerospace parts.[592]

In a 2012 policy paper, Andrew Sissons and Spencer Thompson recognized that distributed and regional manufacturing driven by 3D printing could be a boon for the UK economy.[593] But the authors recognized that "time is of the essence; there may be big first mover advantages for countries that adopt 3D printing early, and the United Kingdom has an opportunity to lead the world in this area."[594] The paper also recognizes that the government could screw up this opportunity: "Get the policy response wrong, and the UK could easily stifle much of the potential of 3D printing before it takes hold."[595]

Of course, China is also intensely interested in 3D printing; it is investing about $33 million to build ten 3D printing innovation centers in ten different cities.[596] The Anhui Province and the cities of Hefei and Bozhou are investing about $245 million to develop 3D printing technologies and five publicly traded Chinese companies invested another $554 million to make 3D printers and materials.[597]

Japan also sees 3D printing as an important way to shore up its industrial competitiveness. A joint R&D project between the Japanese government, universities, and industry plans to develop 3D printing technology to produce end-use metal parts.[598] According to a report from Research and Markets, the Japanese 3D printer market will grow at a compound annual growth rate of 21 percent through 2018.[599]

Singapore plans to invest about $400 million to develop 3D printing technologies, and the Nanyang Technological University is building a $30 million 3D printing research center.[600]

South Korea plans to turn itself into a 3D printing industry power-house with its ten-year plan to provide almost six thousand public schools and over two hundred libraries with 3D printers by 2017, train ten million people (about one-sixth of the population) to use 3D printers by 2020, and transform manufacturing for the automotive, medical, and electronics industries. Although planners requested $15 million for the first five years of the plan, the government gave them almost twice that. In 2014, the government invested about $2.3 million to give small and medium businesses access to 3D printers.[601]

Governments should be commended for these efforts, which together with kids' inquisitive nature can build a bright future of thriving economies worldwide.

Afterword
What Will Really Happen?

EVERYTHING WILL HAPPEN

There is a lot of hype about 3D printing. Some people say it is difficult to separate the hype from reality, but doing so is actually quite simple. Anything that sounds farfetched probably isn't, but it will probably take longer to happen. Some people also believe the hype around 3D printing is bad. I disagree. It helps to spread awareness and adoption of the technology.

Experts, industry observers, and analysts differ about the extent to which 3D printing will be adopted and change the world. Some believe almost every home will have a 3D printer. Some believe independent fabs will 3D print most of what we want or need, and others believe large companies will use 3D printers to do so. Some believe 3D printers will replace mass production, and others believe 3D printers will simply be one more machine on factory floors. Some believe companies will sell designs rather than products, and others believe companies will make mass-customized products or send their designs to their own local factories for printing. Some believe 3D printers will create jobs, and others believe they will destroy them.

It is entirely possible that all of this will happen—and more. A world full of 3D printers that can make almost anything away from control will probably be an almost inconceivably complex place, where products and blueprints are designed, scanned, customized, made, and sold by an uncountable number of companies and home printers offering a dizzying array of products.

Will we really use 3D printers to make most of the things we need or want, rather than buy them? The answer to this question depends on four things: the ease of use and sophistication of home machines, the development of advanced materials, the availability of blueprints for the things we need or want (or the ease of duplicating them with scanners), and how deeply our maker spirit takes hold. There is also a middle ground between making and buying: customizing products and having them made by someone else, or having things we need or want made by a local fabricator.

STEAM ENGINES AND 3D PRINTERS

3D printers today are like steam engines in 1765, when James Watt took that invention, which had been around for many years, and made it an efficient, useful, working machine. Like the steam engine at the dawn of America, 3D printers have a long way to go. Today's machines have limitations. They are slow, and parts can vary from machine to machine. Almost all of today's machines are also one-trick ponies. Although they may do what they do very well, they currently do only one thing, such as making high-grade metal parts of great complexity. They make parts, not products. A single machine cannot print an entire complex product containing both structure and electronics (with rudimentary exceptions). But that time is coming.

As the Atlantic Council report observed, "The 3D printing revolution is occurring at both the high end and the low end, and converging toward the middle."[602] Consumer-grade machines that are already trying to combine 3D printing with traditional manufacturing processes will teach the industrial 3D printing ponies a few tricks, making them more and more capable of making products, not parts. And the technology of industrial-grade machines will trickle down to consumer-grade printers, making them more and more capable of making almost anything in the home. Industrial machines and consumer machines will become more like each other, leading to both industrial and home machines that can make almost anything.

It is impractical to think that this technology will not advance on both the high and low ends, that its advantages will not be developed and exploited, and that 3D printers will not be used for increasingly more manufacturing as time marches on. But the 3D printers, 3D fabricators, 3D assemblers, Star Trek replicators, or whatever they are called in the future will resemble today's machines about as much as a jet engine resembles Watt's steam engine. I am certain that I have barely scratched the surface of conceiving where this technology will go or what it will look like in a hundred years, but I am confident that it will profoundly rock the world.

Acknowledgments

Thanks to Hod Lipson, Michael Weinberg, Alan Meckler, Ed Morris, and Sarah Alexander for giving their time to review my manuscript and provide comments.

Thanks also to Tracy Albert, Chuck Alexander, Sarah Alexander, Tyler Alvarado, Gary Anderson, Bob Appleton, Paul Banwatt, John Barnes, Tyler Benster, Andres Bienzobas, Michele Boldrin, Bill Bonstra, Milan Brandt, Dan Brean, Ryan Brinks, Paul Brody, Joerg Bromberger, Dennis Carmen, Alex Chausovsky, John Cheek, Mark Cola, Patrick Comerford, Tony DeCarmine, Phill Dickens, John Dogru, Miss Donnameek, Nora Engstrom, Phil Eskeland, Beth Ferrill, Francis Flavin, Charlene Flick, Bob Frank, Gene Garbaccio, Michael Garcia, Slade Gardner, Todd Grimm, Richard Grylls, Stephan Gulizia, Michael Guslick, Peter Harter, Mark Hatch, David Hills, David Holden, Mark and Adele Horsburgh, George Iati, Troy Jensen, Gavin Jerome, Eric Johnson, Lawrence Kaplan, Penny Karas, Isaac Katz, Alexandra Kingsbury, Alan Kirschner, Melba Kurman, John Knapp, Adam Liberman, Ulf Linde, Hod Lipson, Stephen Liteplo, Mike Lotus, Allison Mages, Jim Malackowski, Frank Marangell, Alan Meckler, John Murray, Don Manzullo, Joni Mici, Wim Michiels, Mikoddy, Ed Morris, Peer Munck, James Orrock, Joshua Pearce, Janalyn Peppel, Michael Peretti, Bill Pratt, Stewart Quealy, Francis Rabuck, Juan Miguel Ramirez, Michael Raphael, Dan Remba, Cheryl Ann Richardson, Myles Riner, Keith Roberson, Jeff Roberts, Carlos Rosario, Lou Salerno, Tony Serventi, Scott Schiller, Joseph

Scott, Nitin Sharma, Karen Sinclair, Ryan Sybrant, Tuan TranPham, Dean Thomas, Briar Thompson, Paul Thompson, Marc Trachtenberg, Mark Trageser, Ken Tyler, Michael Vasquez, Turlif Vilbrandt, Carlton Washburn, Sunny Webb, Michael Weinberg, Andre Wegner, David Wells, Alex West, Neil Wilkof, Terry Wohlers, Bob Wood, Arthur Young-Spivey, and Severine Zygmont for stimulating discussions about 3D printing.

Thanks to Hod Lipson for valuable advice about the publishing industry. Thanks also to Ed Morris for making sure I got the facts straight on America Makes, and for being a sounding board. Thanks to Melba Kurman for her analysis of my work. Thanks to Tim Shinbara and Amber Thomas for inviting me to be a juror for the Association for Manufacturing Technology Additive Manufacturing Award, and to my fellow jurors for the rewarding experience. Thanks to the National Academies for inviting me to participate in the U.S. Comptroller General Forum on Additive Manufacturing, as well as Ana Aviles, Richard Hung, Tim Persons, and the other folks at the U.S. Government Accountability Office for a great report.

Thanks to the following for permission to use the images appearing in this book: Airbus Defense and Space and Airbus Group; American Standard; Arcam; Drew Armstrong and Kenneth L. Baker; Arup/Davidfotografie; BAE Systems; Alex Brady; Ondra Chotovinsky and Martin Hreben; Clear Flight Solutions; CPR Technology; CSIRO; Deakin University; EDAG Group; Festo AG & Co. KG; University of Graz Artificial Life Lab; Eric Harrell; Isaac Katz; Local Motors; Matthew Plummer-Fernandez; MONAD Studio/Eric Goldemberg and Veronica Zalcberg in collaboration with musician Scott F. Hal; Monash University; Nanyang Technological University; Oak Ridge National Laboratory; Optomec; Pensar Development, Alex Diener, Mark Selander, Kristin Will, Spencer Denton; Maximo Riera; Rocket Lab; Andrés Tovar/Indiana University–Purdue University Indianapolis; Henry Segerman; Solid Concepts; and Lilian van Daal.

Thanks to everyone who has published my stuff, including Michael Molitch-Hou, Ari Honka, and Eeetu Kuneinen of *3D Printing Industry News*; Sandra Helsel; Trevor Little of the *World Trademark Review*; Peter Livingstone of *Financier Worldwide*; Sophie Mohin, Craig Ryan, and all the folks at *3D Printing and Additive Manufacturing Journal* and Mary Ann Liebert, Inc.; William New of *IP Watch*; Maura O'Malley and Thomas Philips of *Intellectual Property Magazine*; Kristen Orlando, Stephanie Nguyen, Nellie Amjadi, Joe Ferrari, and Wesley Dodd of the Santa Clara Law Review; Rachel Park; Larry Plonkser of the Licensing Executive Society and *Les Nouvelles*; Aric Rindfleisch and Vishal Sachdev of the University of Illinois Champaign/Urbana; Laurel Ruma of O'Reilley; Sunny Sun of Recharge Asia; *Wired Innovation*; Evelyn Zhang of *3D Printing World* and Recycling Times; and Lijie Grace Zhang of George Washington University.

Thanks to Alan Meckler and Stewart Quealy for giving me a forum at the Inside 3D Printing conferences. Thanks to everyone else who has given me the opportunity to share my vision with an audience, including Cliff Allen, Michael Atlas, Monica Barone, Ivy Caro, Alayne Farrar, David Long, and Joanne Montague of the organizing committee of the AIPLA 2015 Mid-Winter Institute; Mark Belkin of the New York State Bar Association; Gidget Benitez, Alexandra el-Bayeh, and Michael Carroll of the American University Washington College of Law Intellectual Property Brief; Beth Benson, Duncan Ferguson, Albert Ferraloro, Mark Horsburgh, Alan Moyle, Mark Pullen, Karen Sinclair, Paul Thompson, and all of my other friends in the Licensing Executives Society Australia New Zealand; Brian Bishop, Mark Cola, Linda Holmes, and Shawn Kelly of the Additive Manufacturing Consortium; Anne-Josée Delcorde, Paul Banwatt, and Ashlee Froese of the 2013 webinar organizing committee of the Intellectual Property Institute of Canada; J.Scott Evans of Adobe and Etienne Sanz de Acedo, Sarah O'Connell, Ann Ang, and Margaret Rees of the International Trademark Association; Crystal Everson of the Global Strategic Management Institute; Jeff Fan of Select Biosciences;

Nichole Ferree of Thomson Reuters/ Thomson CompuMark; Francis Flavin, John Mansfield, and the Cosmos Club; Chris Foley and the Virginia State Bar IP Section Fall 2014 CLE Seminar organizing committee; Noni Goh of K2B International, Singapore; Elizabeth Goode, Gary Rabinovitz of Reebok, Mark Barfoot, Todd Grimm, and the rest of the Board of the Additive Manufacturing Users Group (AMUG); Rachel Gordon of IDTechEx; Jean-Claude Alexandre Ho of FORUM Institut für Management GmbH; Mississippi Attorney General Jim Hood, Noreen Leahy, Judith McKee, and Erin Schechter of the National Association of Attorneys General; Jason Keehn, Erin Dolleris, Alicia Dailey, Matthew Masongsong, and the other folks at Infocast; Yash Khanna and the other folks at Innoplast; Chris Kogler of Narrative IQ and Thought Leaders in Business, and Marty Katz of Synapse Partnership and Thought Leaders in Business; Lori Kraft, Dimity Orlet, and the other folks on the bus of the All Ohio Annual Institute on Intellectual Property; John Learmouth and Kelly McCarthy of Deanbridge Media; Deborah Lickness of John Deere and the Licensing Executives Society Aerospace & Transportation Committee; Jameson Ma of the AIPLA 2013 webinar organizing committee; Lauren McGinley and the Noblis speaker series; Karen Michael and Lakeisha Hill of Strafford; Susan Montgomery and Shaun Keough of Northeastern University; Stephanie Reid of the National Constitution Center; Aric Rindfleisch, Vishal Sachdev, and Kimberly Warpecha of the University of Illinois Champagne/Urbana; Sunny Sun of Recharge Asia; Dean Thomas of JNK Securities; and Michael Tobin, Monika Patel, and Victoria Wesolowski of Clear Law Institute.

Thanks to my law partners at Finnegan, Henderson, Farabow, Garrett & Dunner LLP for over 34 great years of practicing IP law in the best IP law firm on the planet, and for supporting the development of the firm's 3D printing practice. Thanks also to Susan Benesh, Anita Bhushan, Beth Ferrill, Steve Hennessy, Christopher Kent, Daniel Klodowski, Kai Rajan, Dan Roland, Carlos Rosario, Ben Sirolly, Kara Specht, Robert Stanley, Andrew

Vance, Robert Wells, Shaobin Zhu and the other members of Finnegan's 3D Printing Working Group, past and present.

Last but not least, many thanks to the editors and designers at Amazon Create Space, which is the future of publishing.

Notes

1. Robert Strohmeyer, "The 7 Worst Tech Predictions of All Time," *Tech Hive*, December 31, 2008, http://www.techhive.com/article/155984/worst_tech_predictions.html.

2. Apple II advertisement, "The Home Computer That's Ready to Work, Play and Grow with You," *Modern Mechanix*, September 1977, http://blog.modernmechanix.com/introducing-apple-ii/1/.

3. "3D Printing," *Wikipedia*, http://en.wikipedia.org/wiki/3D_printing.

4. Shanie Phillips, "USPS 3D Printing Revenue Not So Significant, Says Brookings," *Inside 3DP*, July 23, 2014, http://www.inside3dp.com/usps-3D printing-revenue-significant-says-brookings/.

5. Howard Smith, "You Must Make the New Machines," *3D Printing News and Trends*, April 4, 2013, http://3dprintingreviews.blogspot.com/2013/04/you-must-make-new-machines.html.

6. "3D Printing and the Future of Manufacturing," *Leading Edge Forum* (Fall 2012): 5, http://lef.csc.com/3D printing-and-the-future-of-manufacturing (Leading Edge Forum).

7. Paul Brody and Veena Pureswaran, "The New Software-Defined Supply Chain," *IBM Global Business Service Executive Report*, IBM Institute for Business Value, 2013, 4 (IBM Report).

8. David H. Freedman, "Layer by Layer: With 3D Printing, Manufacturers Can Make Existing Products More Efficiently—and Create Ones That Weren't Possible Before," *MIT Technology Review*, December 19, 2011, http://www.technologyreview.com/featuredstory/426391/layer-by-layer/.

9. Peter Zelinski, "The Future of Manufacturing," *Modern Machine Shop*, July 3, 2012, http://www.mmsonline.com/articles/the-future-of-manufacturing.

10. Sandra Helsel, "Johnson Controls Experiments with 3D Printing for Manufacturing," *Inside 3D Printing*, August 11, 2014, http://inside3dprinting.com/johnson-controls-experiments-with-3D printing-for-manufacturing/.

11. David L. Bourell, David W. Rosen, and Ming C. Leu, "The Roadmap for Additive Manufacturing and its Impact," *3D Printing and Additive Manufacturing* 1, no. 1 (2014): 6.

12. Mark Cotteleer and Jim Joyce, "3D Opportunity: Additive Manufacturing Paths to Performance, Innovation, and Growth," *Deloitte Review* 14 (2014), 7.

13. *Wohlers Report: 3D Printing and Additive Manufacturing State of the Industry Annual Worldwide Progress Report* (Fort Collins, CO: Wohlers Associates, 2014), 175 (Wohlers Report 2014).

14. Cotteleer and Joyce, "3D Opportunity," 7; *Wohlers Report: 3D Printing and Additive Manufacturing State of the Industry Annual Worldwide Progress Report* (Fort Collins, CO: Wohlers Associates, 2015), 122 (Wohlers Report 2015); Wohlers Report 2014, 111–12.

15. IBM Report, 3.

16. David del Fresno, "Revolutionary 'Smart Wing' Created for UAV Model Demonstrates Groundbreaking Technology," *Optomec*, March 1, 2013, http://www.optomec.com/revolutionary-smart-wing-created-for-uav-model-demonstrates-groundbreaking-technology/.

17. "Case Study: Heat Exchanger: Heralding a New Era for Engineering Design," *Within*, http://withinlab.com/case-studies/index11.php.

18. Gary Anderson, "The Future of 3D Printing with Terry Wohlers," *Engineering.com*, September 9, 2013, http://www.engineering.co m/3DPrinting/3DPrintingArticles/ArticleID/6294/The-Future-of-3D printing-With-Terry-Wohlers.aspx.

19. ASTM F2792-12a: Standard Terminology for Additive Manufacturing Technologies 1, 2, *ASTM International*, http://www.astm.org/search/ fullsite-search.html?query=standard%20terminology%20for%20 additive%20manufacturing&resStart=0&resLength=10&toplevel=pr oducts-and-services&sublevel=standards-and-publications&.

20. Juho Vesanto, "3D Printed Aston Martin DB5 Replicas," *3D Printing Industry News*, November 16, 2012, http://3dprintingindustry. com/2012/11/16/3D printed-aston-martin-in-james-bond-skyfall/.

21. Michael Molitch-Hou, "Mazak Adds Hybrid Metal 3D Printer to Machine Tool Lineup," *3D Printing Industry News*, November 4, 2014, http://3dprintingindustry.com/2014/11/04/mazak-hybrid-metal-3d-printer/?utm_source=3D+Printing+Industry+Update&u tm_medium=email&utm_campaign=44932d528d-RSS_EMAIL_ CAMPAIGN&utm_term=0_695d5c73dc-44932d528d-60484669; "Efesto: A Metalworking Revolution," *Efesto*, http://www.efesto.us/ company/.

22. David Sher, "NASA Is 3D Printing Multiple Metals Simultaneously with New Radiant Deposition Technique," *3D Printing Industry News*, August 7, 2014, http://3dprintingindustry.com/2014/08/07/nasa-3D printing-multiple-metals-simultaneously-new-radiant-deposition-technique/?utm_source=3D+Printing+Industry+Update&u

tm_medium=email&utm_campaign=cf2922a220-RSS_EMAIL_ CAMPAIGN&utm_term=0_695d5c73dc-cf2922a220-60484669.

23. Michael Molitch-Hou, "Sciaky's Giant 3D Metal Printers Available for Sale," *3D Printing Industry News*, July 11, 2014, http://3dprintingindustry.com/2014/07/11/sciakys-giant-3d-metal- printers-available-sale/?utm_source=3D+Printing+Industry+Updat e&utm_medium=email&utm_campaign=74d8a5f86b-RSS_EMAIL_ CAMPAIGN&utm_term=0_695d5c73dc-74d8a5f86b-60484669.

24. "Technology Mapping: The Influence of IP on the 3D Printing Revolution," *Creax*, July 14, 2014, http://www.creax.com/2014/07/ technology-mapping-influence-ip-3D printing-evolution/.

25. Chris Spadaccini, "Designer Engineered Materials," *Lawrence Livermore National Laboratory*, https://manufacturing.llnl.gov/ additive-manufacturing/designer-engineered-materials.

26. Kyle Maxey, "3D Printer from Optemec [sic] Prints Embedded Electronics onto almost Any Substrate," *Engineering.com*, January 27, 2015, http://www.engineering.com/3DPrinting/3DPrintingArt icles/ArticleID/9470/3D-Printer-from-Optemec-Prints-Embedded- Electronics-onto-almost-Any-Substrate.aspx.

27. Michael Molitch-Hou, "Neotech's Electronics 3D Printing System for Sale," *3D Printing Industry News*, July 22, 2014, http:// 3dprintingindustry.com/2014/07/22/neotechs-electronics-3D printing- system-sale/?utm_source=3D+Printing+Industry+Update&u tm_medium=email&utm_campaign=6e991b41f8-RSS_EMAIL_ CAMPAIGN&utm_term=0_695d5c73dc-6e991b41f8-60484669.

28. Kyle Maxey, "Optomec Awarded Patent for Electronics Printing Technique," *Engineering.com*, March 11, 2014, http://www.

engineering.com/3DPrinting/3DPrintingArticles/ArticleID/7297/ Optomec-Awarded-Patent-for-Electronics-Printing-Technique.aspx; John Graber, "Camtek to Begin Inkjet-Based, PCB 3D Printer Sales," *3D Printer World*, April 5, 2014, http://www.3dprinterworld.com/ article/camtek-begin-inkjet-based-pcb-3d-printer-sales.

29. Cotteleer and Joyce, "3D Opportunity," 9, n. 13; Wohlers Report 2014, 15.

30. Michael Molitch-Hou, "Fonon Announces New 3D Metal Printer," *3D Printing Industry News*, August 30, 2014, http://3dprintingindustry. com/2014/08/30/fonon-announces-new-3d-metal-printer/?utm_so urce=3D+Printing+Industry+Update&utm_medium=email&utm_ campaign=cc77099874-RSS_EMAIL_CAMPAIGN&utm_ term=0_695d5c73dc-cc77099874-60484669.

31. Staff writer, "FACTUM High Speed Sintering 3D printer Makes a Part in Less Than a Second," *3ders.org*, March 25, 2014, http:// www.3ders.org/articles/20140326-factum-high-speed-sintering-3d-printer-makes-parts-in-less-than-a-second.html; David Sher, "Additive Manufacturing Could Take the Injection Moulding Market, Says HSS Inventor Neil Hopkinson," *3D Printing Industry News*, April 25, 2014, http://3dprintingindustry.com/2014/04/25/3D printing-hss-inventor-neil-hopkinson/?utm_source=3D+Printing+Industry+Update&u tm_medium=email&utm_campaign=bb7f906a23-RSS_EMAIL_ CAMPAIGN&utm_term=0_695d5c73dc-bb7f906a23-60484669; Simon, "Sheffield University to Build a £1m 3D Printer That Will 3D Print Parts as Fast as a Production Line," *3ders.org*, June 3, 2015, http:// www.3ders.org/articles/20150603-sheffield-university-to-build-3d-printer-that-will-3d-print-parts-as-fast-as-a-production-line.html.

32. Shane Taylor, "New Dimension for Fabrisonic's Ultrasonic Printing," *3D Printing Industry News*, October 30, 2013, http://3dprintingindustry.

com/2013/10/30/new-dimension-fabrisonics-ultrasonic-printing/?utm_ source=3D+Printing+Industry+Update&utm_medium=email&utm_ campaign=4f6b3858a3-RSS_EMAIL_CAMPAIGN&utm_ term=0_695d5c73dc-4f6b3858a3-60484669; Hannah Rose Mendoza, "Ultrasonic 3D Printing Allows for Electronics to be Embedded in Metal via Sound," *3Dprint.com*, August 17, 2014, http://3dprint.com/12075/ ultrasonic-3D printing-uam/.

33. "Chuck Hull," *Wikipedia,* http://en.wikipedia.org/wiki/Chuck_Hull.

34. Spadaccini, "Designer Engineered Materials."

35. "Technical White Paper: HP Multi Jet Fusion Technology," *Hewlett Packard*, October 2014, http://h10124.www1.hp.com/campaigns/ ga/3dprinting/4AA5-5472ENW.pdf.

36. Michael Molitch-Hou, "Impossible Objects Secures $2.8 Million for Composites 3D Printing," *3D Printing Industry News*, December 17, 2014, http://3dprintingindustry.com/2014/12/17/impossible-objects-2-8-m-composites-3d-printing/; Impossible Objects Application International Additive Manufacturing Award, AMT/The Association for Manufacturing Technology, December 2014.

37. Sandra Helsel, "First Russian 3D Bio-Printer to be Unveiled in Moscow," *Inside 3D Printing*, September 26, 2014, http:// inside3dprinting.com/first-russian-3d-bio-printer-to-be-unveiled-in-moscow/?utm_source=Inside%203D%20Printing%20Latest%20 News&utm_campaign=cd84e39730-Inside_3D_Printing_Daily_ News_9_26_2014_9_25_2014&utm_medium=email&utm_term=0_ 861dc04374-cd84e39730-226645849; "What Is BioAssemblyBot?" *Advanced Solutions*, http://www.bioassemblybot.com/; Sandra Helsel, "University of British Columbia-Based Aspect Biosystems

Developing a 3D Bio-Printer," *Inside 3D Printing*, September 25, 2014, http://inside3dprinting.com/university-of-british-columbia-based-aspect-biosystems-developing-a-3d-bio-printer/?utm_source=Inside%203D%20Printing%20Latest%20News&utm_campaign=f012b96019-Inside_3D_Printing_Daily_News_9_25_2014_9_24_2014&utm_medium=email&utm_term=0_861dc04374-f012b96019-226645849; *Bio3D Technologies*, http://bio-3d.com/; *Cyfuse Biomedical K. K.*, http://www.cyfusebio.com/en/; Michael Molitch-Hou, "EnvisionTEC Launches Educational 3D Bioprinter," *3D Printing Industry News*, May 1, 2014, http://3dprintingindustry.com/2014/05/01/envisiontec-launches-educational-3d-bioprinter/?utm_source=3D+Printing+Industry+Update&utm_medium=email&utm_campaign=32b423799; *N3D Biosciences*, http://www.n3dbio.com/; Shane Taylor, "Generating Interest: A Regenerative 3D Bioprinting Breakthrough," *3D Printing Industry News*, April 25, 2014, http://3dprintingindustry.com/2014/04/25/regenerative-3d-bioprinting-breakthrough/?utm_source=3D+Printing+Industry+Update&utm_medium=email&utm_campaign=bb7f906a23-RSS_EMAIL_CAMPAIGN&utm_term=0_695d5c73dc-bb7f906a23-60484669; Andrew Wheeler, "Japanese Researchers Pursue Next Gen Bio-3D Printer for Skin, Bones, and Joints," *3D Printing Industry News*, January 22, 2015, http://3dprintingindustry.com/2015/01/22/japanese-researchers-bio-3d-printer/?utm_source=3D+Printing+Industry+Update&utm_medium=email&utm_campaign=4e33dc4b5a-RSS_EMAIL_CAMPAIGN&utm_term=0_695d5c73dc-4e33dc4b5a-60484669.

38. Brit Liggett, "Printer to Create First 'Printed' Human Vein," *Inhabit*, March 22, 2010, http://inhabitat.com/scientists-use-3d-printer-to-create-first-printed-human-vein/; "Organovo, Tissue Made to Order," Progressive Engineer Company Profile, http://www.progressiveengineer.com/company_profiles/organovo.htm.

39. "Using Inkjet Technology to Print Organs and Tissue," Wake Forest School of Medicine, http://www.wakehealth.edu/Research/WFIRM/Our-Story/Inside-the-Lab/Bioprinting.htm.

40. Matthew Braga, "Looking for Ways to Get 'Skin' in the Game," *Smart Shift*, July 16, 2013, http://business.financialpost.com/2013/07/16/looking-for-ways-to-get-skin-in-the-game/?__lsa=cf55-be22.

41. Michael Molitch-Hou, "The 'Six Million Dollar' Ear," *3D printing Industry News*, May 6, 2013, http://3dprintingindustry.com/2013/05/06/the-six-million-dollar-ear/?utm_source=3D+Printing+Industry+Update&utm_medium=email&utm_campaign=cd0759105c-RSS_EMAIL_CAMPAIGN&utm_term=0_695d5c73dc-cd0759105c-60484669.

42. Michael Molitch-Hou, "Anatomically Accurate Aorta Cells 3D Printed at Sabancı University in Turkey," *3D Printing Industry News*, March 14, 2014, http://3dprintingindustry.com/2014/03/20/3D printing-aorta-cells-turkey/?utm_source=3D+Printing+Industry+Update&utm_medium=email&utm_campaign=d340f2a8af-RSS_EMAIL_CAMPAIGN&utm_term=0_695d5c73dc-d340f2a8af-60484669.

43. Todd Halterman, "3D Printing Used to Make Heart Problem Detector," *3D Printer World*, February 28, 2014, http://www.3dprinterworld.com/article/3D printing-used-make-heart-problem-detector.

44. Brian Krassenstein, "3D Printed Human Heart By 2023, Says Top Scientist," *3DPrint.com*, March 11, 2014, http://3dprint.com/869/3D printed-human-heart-by-2023-says-top-scientist/.

45. Rachel Park, "New 3D Manufacturing Process—Materialising Micro Lattice Structures," *3D Printing Industry News*, July 17, 2013, http://3dprintingindustry.com/2013/07/17/new-3d-manufacturing-process-materialising-micro-lattice-structures/?utm_source=

3D+Printing+Industry+Update&utm_medium=email&utm_campaign=8eb3631a0c-RSS_EMAIL_CAMPAIGN&utm_term=0_695d5c73dc-8eb3631a0c-60484669.

46. Spadaccini, "Designer Engineered Materials."

47. "Self-Assembly Lab," *Self-Assembly Laboratory*, http://www.selfassemblylab.net/index.php; Neil Gershenfeld, "How to Make Almost Anything," *Foreign Affairs* 91, no. 6 (Nov.–Dec. 2012): 51–52.

48. Thomas A. Campbell, Skylar Tibbits, and Banning Garrett, "The Programmable World," *Scientific American*, November 2014, 65.

49. Michael Molitch-Hou, "NASA Awards Project for 3D Bioprinting Anything You Want," *3D Printing Industry News*, August 1, 2013, http://3dprintingindustry.com/2013/08/01/nasa-awards-project-for-3d-bioprinting-anything-you-want/?utm_source=3D+Printing+Industry+Update&utm_medium=email&utm_campaign=8de265df90-RSS_EMAIL_CAMPAIGN&utm_term=0_695d5c73dc-8de265df90-60484669.

50. Kelsey Campbell-Dollaghan, "Why Is the US Army Investing in 4D Printing," *Gizmodo*, October 9, 2013, http://gizmodo.com/why-is-the-us-army-investing-in-4d-printing-1442964294.

51. Michael Molitch-Hou, "CEO Jennifer Lewis on the Future of Electronics 3D Printing and Voxel8's Huge $12M Funding," *3D Printing Industry News*, July 24, 2015, http://3dprintingindustry.com/2015/07/24/voxel8-ceo-jennifer-lewis-on-how-12m-in-funding-will-fuel-the-future-of-electronics-3D printing/?utm_source=3D+Printing+Industry+Update&utm_medium=email&utm_campaign=293d6d5a74-RSS_EMAIL_CAMPAIGN&utm_term=0_695d5c73dc-293d6d5a74-60484669.

52. Wohlers Report 2014, 32, 39–40, 45, 52; "Hot Isostatic Pressing," *Wikipedia*, http://en.wikipedia.org/wiki/Hot_isostatic_pressing.

53. *Matsuura*, http://www.matsuura.co.jp/english/contents/products/lumex.html.

54. *Fabtotum*, http://www.fabtotum.com/.

55. Shane Taylor, "The TriBot Combines 3D Printing, CNC and Molding in One Machine," *3D Printing Industry News*, September 24, 2014, http://3dprintingindustry.com/2014/09/24/tribot-combines-3D printing-cnc-molding-one-machine/?utm_source=3D+Printing+Industry+Update&utm_medium=email&utm_campaign=62d27c16af-RSS_EMAIL_CAMPAIGN&utm_term=0_695d5c73dc-62d27c16af-60484669.

56. "High-Volume, Customized Manufacturing Becomes a Reality," *3D Systems*, June 16, 2014, http://www.3dsystems.com/ru/node/6708; staff writer, "3D Systems Releases First Details of High-Speed 3D Printing Assembly Line for Google's Project Ara," *3ders.org*, June 17, 2014, http://www.3ders.org/articles/20140617-3d-systems-high-speed-3D printing-assembly-line-google-project-ara.html; "The Future of Customized Fab-Grade 3D Printing," *3D Systems*, June 13, 2014, https://www.youtube.com/watch?v=UFb3TkC7OMo.

57. Molitch-Hou, "CEO Jennifer Lewis on the Future."

58. Mark Solomon, "3D Printed Electronics: Next Phase of the Additive Manufacturing Revolution?" *Advanced Manufacturing Insight*, February 12, 2015, http://www.advancedmanufacturinginsight.com/archived-articles/item/3D printed-electronics-additive-manufacturing?utm_source=Solomon3DPrintedElectronics&utm_medium=Newsletter021915&utm_campaign=Newsletter.

59. Wohlers Report 2014, 124.

60. Laura Griffiths, "Unilever Cuts Production Times By 40% with 3D Printing," *TCT*, January 20, 2015, http://www.tctmagazine.com/3D printing-news/unilever-cuts-production-times-by-40-with-3D printing/.

61. Alec, "Swiss Watchmaker TAG Heuer Adopts 3D Printing for Watch Design and Development," *3Ders.org*, May 19, 2015, http://www.3ders.org/articles/20150519-tag-heuer-turns-to-3D printing-for-saving-time-money-during-development.html?utm_source=Daily+3D+Printing+News&utm_campaign=022df24901-Latest_3D_Printing_News_05_20_2015_5_20_2015&utm_medium=email&utm_term=0_861dc04374-022df24901-226645849.

62. "How 3D printing Will Continue to Transform Manufacturing," Stratasys, 4–5, http://www.google.com/url?sa=t&rct=j&q=&esrc=s&frm=1&source=web&cd=1&ved=0CCAQFjAA&url=http%3A%2F%2Fwww.techbriefs.com%2Fdl%2F2014.php%3Fi%3D20972%26d%3D1&ei=RWzFVO2cNMzOsQSM74L4CA&usg=AFQjCNHHvRh-ncl2dCY51L8KH9LGkOhMZg&sig2=B8vlfjnMyKBfLdE-Mz-JPQ.

63. Michael Swack, "3D Printed Thermoplastics Versus Metal: Why Volvo Trucks Chose Additive Manufacturing for 30 Engine Assembly Tools," *Blog for a 3D World*, March 18, 2015, http://blog.stratasys.com/2015/03/18/volvo-trucks-additive-manufacturing/?utm_source=Daily+3D+Printing+News&utm_campaign=d1001138f6-Latest_3D_Printing_News_03_19_2015_3_19_2015&utm_medium=email&utm_term=0_861dc04374-d1001138f6-226645849.

64. James Manyika, Michael Chui, Jacques Bughin, Richard Dobbs, Peter Bisson, and Alex Marrs, "Disruptive Technologies: Advances That Will Transform Life, Business, and the Global Economy," McKinsey

Global Institute, May 2013, 111, http://www.mckinsey.com/insights/business_technology/disruptive_technologies (McKinsey Report).

65. "How 3D printing Will Continue to Transform Manufacturing," 10.

66. Staff writer, "3D Printed Pasta Carbonara Please!," *3D Printing Industry News*, August 20, 2012, http://3dprintingindustry.com/2012/08/20/3D printed-pasta-carbonara-please/.

67. "3D Printing," *Wikipedia*, http://en.wikipedia.org/wiki/3D_printing.

68. Staff writer, "Ceramic 3D Printing at Medalta," *3D Printing Industry News*, July 13, 2013, http://3dprintingindustry.com/2013/07/13/ceramic-3D printing-at-medalta/?utm_source=3D+Printing+Industry+Update&utm_medium=email&utm_campaign=be28217756-RSS_EMAIL_CAMPAIGN&utm_term=0_695d5c73dc-be28217756-60484669.

69. *ExOne*, http://www.exone.com/materialization/systems.

70. Leading Edge Forum, 7; staff writer, "LAYWOO-D3: 3D Printed 'Wood,'" *3D Printing Industry News*, September 18, 2012, http://3dprintingindustry.com/2012/09/18/laywoo-3d-the-latest-on-3D printed-wood/.

71. Megan Molteni, "Our 3D Printed Universe," *Popular Mechanics*, February 2015, 25, http://www.popsci.com/our-3D printed-universe.

72. *Wohlers Report: 3D Printing and Additive Manufacturing State of the Industry Annual Worldwide Progress Report* (Fort Collins, CO: Wohlers Associates, 2013), 30 (Wohlers Report 2013).

73. Jamie Ducharme, "MIT Produces Synthetic Bone With 3D Printing," *Boston Magazine*, June 18, 2013, http://www.bostonmagazine.com/

health/blog/2013/06/18/3d-printers-bone/?utm_source=
iContact&utm_medium=email&utm_campaign=Hub%20
Health&utm_content.

74. Staff writer, "3D Printers Could Create Customised Drugs on Demand," *BBC New Technology*, April 18, 2012, http://www.bbc.co.uk/news/technology-17760085.

75. "Printable and Flexible Electronics," *PARC*, http://www.parc.com/services/focus-area/flexible-and-LAE/; Susan Wilson, "Printing of High Quality Transistors Gets Closer Thanks to the University of Cambridge," *Blorge*, November 25, 2011, http://green.blorge.com/2011/11/printing-of-high-quality-transistors-gets-closer-thanks-to-the-university-of-cambridge/.

76. Sarah Zhang, "Scientists 3D Printed Self-Assembling Wood and Carbon Fiber," *Gizmodo*, October 14, 2014, http://gizmodo.com/scientists-3D printed-self-assembling-wood-and-carbon-f-1646263682?utm_source=Inside+3D+Printing+Latest+News&utm_campaign=dfc8793cb5-Latest_3D_Printing_News_10_17_2014&utm_medium=email&utm_term=0_861dc04374-dfc8793cb5-226645849.

77. Kyle Maxie, "Liquid Metal 3D Printing," *Engineering.com*, July 11, 2013, http://www.engineering.com/3DPrinting/3DPrintingArticles/ArticleID/5988/Liquid-Metal-3D printing.aspx

78. Staff writer, "Chinese Test Self-Forming Liquid Metal, Seeing a Terminator-like Future," *3ders.org*, March 4, 2014, http://www.3ders.org/articles/20140304-chinese-test-self-forming-liquid-metal-seeing-a-terminator-like-future.html.

79. Eetu Kuneinen, "3D Printing Personal Electronics in the Future with 'Carbomorph'?" *3D Printing Industry News*, December 20, 2012, http://3dprintingindustry.com/2012/12/20/3D printing-personal-electronics-

in-the-future-with-carbomorph/; Dan Thomas, "3D Printed Carbomorph Circuit Boards," *Engineering.com*, May 2, 2014, http://www. engineering.com/3DPrinting/3DPrintingArticles/ArticleID/7539/3D printed-Carbomorph-Circuit-Boards.aspx.

80. James Lee, "Investing in Graphene—the Nanomaterial of the Future," *The Futurist*, June 19, 2012, http://www.wfs.org/blogs/ james-lee/investing-graphene-nanomaterial-future; John Fleming, "In a Future of 3D Printing and Graphene, Nothing and No-One Will Be Safe from Becoming Outdated," *Huffington Post*, December 18, 2011, http://www.huffingtonpost.co.uk/john-fleming/in-a-future-of-3d-printin_b_1017194.html; Rachel Park, "The Guys Behind RepRap—Always Thinking Ahead and Now It's Graphene," *3D Printing Industry News*, March 21, 2013, http://3dprintingindustry. com/2013/03/21/the-guys-behind-reprap-always-thinking-ahead-and-now-its-graphene/?utm_source=3D+Printing+Indust ry+Update&utm_medium=email&utm_campaign=21b86e56a1-RSS_EMAIL_CAMPAIGN; staff writer, "First Demonstration of Inkjet-Printed Graphene Electronics," *MIT Technology Review*, November 24, 2011, http://m.technologyreview.com/view/426196/ first-demonstration-of-inkjet-printed-graphene-electronics/.

81. Graphene Flagship, http://graphene-flagship.eu/?page_id=5.

82. Gary Anderson, "The Best 3D Printing Stock to Buy Now is Graphene 3D Lab," 3DPrintingStocks.com, August 11, 2014, https://3dprintingstocks.com/best-3D printing-stock-ggg/.

83. Michael Molitch-Hou, "Kibaran Resources Joins 3D Group to 3D Print Graphene," *3D Printing Industry News*, June 25, 2014, http://3dprintingindustry.com/2014/06/25/kibaran-resources-joins-3d-group-3d-print-graphene/?utm_source=3D+Printing+Ind

ustry+Update&utm_medium=email&utm_campaign=e39ac8253d-RSS_EMAIL_CAMPAIGN&utm_term=0_695d5c73dc-e39ac8253d-60484669.

84. Rachel Park, "Chiplets—3D Printed Electronic Micro Materials," *3D Printing Industry News*, April 10, 2013, http://3dprintingindustry.com/2013/04/10/chiplets-3D printed-electronic-micro-materials/?utm_source=3D+Printing+Industry+Update&utm_medium=email&utm_campaign=80c0d3d9f3-RSS_EMAIL_CAMPAIGN; http://inside3dprinting.com/parc-moves-closer-to-3D printing-electronic-components-within-objects/.

85. Anderson, "The Future of 3D Printing with Terry Wohlers."

86. Wohlers Report 2014, 186–88.

87. Michael Molitch-Hou, "Consumer 3D Printing More Than 5 Years Away from Mainstream Adoption, Says Gartner," *3D printing Industry News*, August 20, 2014, http://3dprintingindustry.com/2014/08/20/consumer-3D printing-5-years-away-mainstream-adoption-says-gartner/?utm_source=3D+Printing+Industry+Update&utm_medium=email&utm_campaign=899ff4ba4a-RSS_EMAIL_CAMPAIGN&utm_term=0_695d5c73dc-899ff4ba4a-60484669; https://www.gartner.com/doc/2816917.

88. Jeremy Hsu, "Why 3D Printing Matters for 'Made in USA,'" LiveScience, December 5, 2012, http://www.livescience.com/25255-3D printing-made-usa.html; Paul Davidson, "3D Printing Could Remake U.S. Manufacturing," *USA Today*, July 10, 2012, http://usatoday30.usatoday.com/money/industries/manufacturing/story/2012-07-10/digital-manufacturing/56135298/1; Wohlers Report 2014, 19, 170.

89. Leading Edge Forum, 10.

90. Freedman, "Layer by Layer: With 3D Printing, Manufacturers Can Make Existing Products More Efficiently—and Create Ones That Weren't Possible Before," *MIT Technology Review*, December 19, 2011, http://www.technologyreview.com/featuredstory/426391/layer-by-layer/.

91. Alex Chavers, "3D Printed Rockets? NASA Shows What 3D Printing Technology Is Capable Of," *News Ledge*, September 2, 2014, http://www.newsledge.com/3D printed-rockets-nasa-shows-what-3D printing-technology-is-capable-of-9221.

92. Michael Molitch-Hou, "3D Printing Under the Fire: Platinum Thruster Part Seems Space-Ready," *3D Printing Industry News*, June 17, 2015, http://3dprintingindustry.com/2015/06/17/3D printing-under-the-fire-platinum-thruster-part-seems-space-ready/?utm_source=3D+Printing+Industry+Update&utm_medium=email&utm_campaign=471fdbb24f-RSS_EMAIL_CAMPAIGN&utm_term=0_695d5c73dc-471fdbb24f-60484669.

93. "SpaceX Completes Qualification Testing of Superdraco Thruster," SpaceX, May 27, 2014, http://www.spacex.com/press/2014/05/27/spacex-completes-qualification-testing-superdraco-thruster.

94. Staff writer, "Airbus' 3D Printing Transformation," *3D Printing Industry News*, June 14, 2014, http://3dprintingindustry.com/2014/06/14/airbus-3D printing-transformation/?utm_source=3D+Printing+Industry+Update&utm_medium=email&utm_campaign=c2249c64d9-RSS_EMAIL_CAMPAIGN&utm_term=0_695d5c73dc-c2249c64d9-60484669; Leading Edge Forum, 10.

95.   Brian Krassenstein, "New Airbus A350 XWB Aircraft Contains over 1,000 3D Printed Parts," *3D Print.com*, May 6, 2015, http://3dprint. com/63169/airbus-a350-xwb-3d-print/?utm_source=Daily+3D+P rinting+News&utm_campaign=10c0f8bf74-Latest_3D_Printing_ News_05_07_2015_5_6_2015&utm_medium=email&utm_ term=0_861dc04374-10c0f8bf74-226645849.

96.   Rachel Park, "Going Large on 3D Printed Aerospace Parts," *3D Printing Industry News*, January 24, 2013, http://3dprintingindustry. com/2013/01/24/going-large-on-3D printed-aerospace-parts/.

97.   Leading Edge Forum, 8.

98.   "GE Aviation Acquires Morris Technologies and Rapid Quality Manufacturing," GE Aviation, November 20, 2012, http://www. geaviation.com/press/other/other_20121120.html.

99.   Zelinski, "The Future of Manufacturing," *Modern Machine Shop*, July 3, 2012, http://www.mmsonline.com/articles/the-future-of-manufacturing; Peter Zelinski, "Why Did GE Aviation Acquire Morris Technologies?" *Modern Machine Shop*, January 2, 2013, http://www. mmsonline.com/columns/why-did-ge-aviation-acquire-morris-technologies.

100.   Travis Hessman, "Fear, Frenzy and the Birth of an Industry at GE's 3D Printing Lab," *Industry Week*, February 13, 2014, http://m. industryweek.com/blog/fear-frenzy-and-birth-industry-ges-3D printing-lab?NL=IW-02&Issue=IW-02_20140214_IW-02_449&YM_ RID=shelby@hudsonfasteners.com&YM_MID=1449934&sfvc4ene ws=42&cl=article_1; Wohlers Report 2014, 241.

101.   Wohlers Report 2014, 15, 23.

102. Zelinski, "The Future of Manufacturing," *Modern Machine Shop*, July 3, 2012, http://www.mmsonline.com/articles/the-future-of-manufacturing; Zelinski, "Why Did GE Aviation Acquire Morris Technologies?"; David Sher, "3D Printed, Mass Produced Parts to Give GE's New Jet Engines an Extra Boost," *3D Printing Industry News*, August 11, 2014, http://3dprintingindustry.com/2014/08/11/3D printing-ge-jet-engine/?utm_source=3D+Printing+Industry+Updat e&utm_medium=email&utm_campaign=3ff2d4b00c-RSS_EMAIL_ CAMPAIGN&utm_term=0_695d5c73dc-3ff2d4b00c-60484669.

103. "Product Advances That Rival Mother Nature," *The Doorway* 44, no. 3 (Summer 2007): 8–9, http://www.thegillcorp.com/public/ mcg_msds/doorway_file/Product_Advances_That_Rival_Mother_ Nature.pdf; *Airline Pilots Forum*, http://www.airlinepilotforums. com/archive/index.php/t-12052.html; Joshua Zumbrun, "Green Skies," *Forbes*, June 3, 2008, http://www.forbes.com/2008/06/02/ aviation-airlines-fuel-biz-logistics-cx_jz_0603aviation08_greening. html.

104. Andrew Wheeler, "GE Aviation's First 3D Printed Engine Component for GE 90 Engine," *Engineering.com*, April 15, 2015, http://www. engineering.com/3DPrinting/3DPrintingArticles/ArticleID/9957/ GE-Aviations-First-3D   printed-Engine-Component-For-GE-90- Engine.aspx.

105. Michael Molitch-Hou, "Turbomeca Opens 3D Printing Facility for Helicopter Engine Parts," *3D Printing Industry News*, January 14, 2015, http://3dprintingindustry.com/2015/01/14/turbomeca-opens-3D printing-facility-helicopter-engine-parts/?utm_source=Daily+3D+ Printing+News&utm_campaign=f144462ef1-Latest_3D_Printing_ News_01_15_2015_1_15_2015&utm_medium=email&utm_ term=0_861dc04374-f144462ef1-226645849.

106. Staff writer, "3D Printing Could Revolutionize War and Foreign Policy," *Space Daily*, January 5, 2015, http://www.spacedaily.com/reports/How_3D_printing_could_revolutionise_war_and_foreign_policy_999.html.

107. Staff writer, "Australia's Monash University 3D Prints An Entire Aircraft Engine," *3ders.org*, February 25, 2015, http://www.3ders.org/articles/20150225-australias-monash-university-3d-prints-an-entire-aircraft-engine.html?utm_source=Daily+3D+Printing+News&utm_campaign=e69c8e403e-Latest_3D_Printing_News_02_26_2015_2_26_2015&utm_medium=email&utm_term=0_861dc04374-e69c8e403e-226645849.

108. Tarun Tampi, "World's 1st 3D Printed and Battery Powered Rocket Engine," *3D Printing Industry News*, April 21, 2015, http://3dprintingindustry.com/2015/04/21/worlds-1st-3D printed-battery-powered-rocket-engine/?utm_source=3D+Printing+Industry+Update&utm_medium=email&utm_campaign=5b1097109d-RSS_EMAIL_CAMPAIGN&utm_term=0_695d5c73dc-5b1097109d-60484669.

109. Leading Edge Forum, 12.

110. Staff writer, "Bentley EXP 10 Speed 6 Conceptual Coupe Takes Advantage of 3D Metal Printing," *3ders.org*, March 4, 2015, http://www.3ders.org/articles/20150304-bentley-exp-10-speed-6-conceptual-coupe-takes-advantage-of-3d-metal-printing.html?utm_source=Daily+3D+Printing+News&utm_campaign=5c291d696f-Latest_3D_Printing_News_03_05_2015_3_4_2015&utm_medium=email&utm_term=0_861dc04374-5c291d696f-226645849.

111. Audrey Tan, "NTU Unveils Two Solar Eco Cars Including One Made with 3D printed Parts," *Straits Times* (Singapore), February 8, 2015,

http://www.straitstimes.com/singapore/ntu-unveils-two-solar-eco-cars-including-one-made-with-3d-printed-parts.

112. Spiros Tsantilas, "TE Connectivity 3D-Prints A Functioning Motorcycle," *Gizmag*, May 29, 2015, http://www.gizmag.com/te-3D printed-motorcycle/37729/.

113. Leading Edge Forum, 12–13.

114. Ibid.

115. Kyle Maxie, "Chinese Dr. Creates 3D Printed Skull Implant," *Engineering.com*, September 9, 2013, http://www.engineering.com/3DPrinting/3DPrintingArticles/ArticleID/6292/Chinese-Dr-Creates-3D printed-Skull-Implant.aspx.

116. Kashmira Gander, "3D Printed Pelvis Helps Man with Rare Bone Cancer Keep Walking," *Independent* (UK), February 10, 2014, http://www.independent.co.uk/news/uk/home-news/3D   printed-pelvis-helps-man-with-rare-bone-cancer-keep-walking-9119473.html.

117. Wohlers Report 2014, 19.

118. Eetu Kuneinen, "Medical Application: 3D Printing a New Nose," *3D Printing Industry News*, November 12, 2012, http://3dprintingindustry.com/2012/11/12/medical-application-3D printing-a-new-nose/.

119. Michael Molitch-Hou, "US Army's 3D Printed Skin Near Ready for Clinical Trials," *3D Printing Industry News*, July 21, 2014, http://3dprintingindustry.com/2014/07/21/us-armys-3D printed-skin-near-ready-clinical-trials/?utm_so.

120. Leading Edge Forum, 13.

121. Brian Heater, "Cornell Scientists 3D Print Ears with Help from Rat Tails and Cow Ears," *Engadget*, February 22, 2013, http://www.engadget.com/2013/02/22/3D printed-ear/; Kyle Maxie, "Artificial Human Ear Printed from Sheep Cells," *Engineering.com*, August 5, 2013, http://www.engineering.com/3DPrinting/3DPrintingArtic les/ArticleID/6116/Artificial-Human-Ear-Printed-from-Sheep-Cells. aspx.

122. Michael Molitch-Hou, "The 'Six Million Dollar' Ear," *3D printing Industry News,* May 6, 2013, http://3dprintingindustry. com/2013/05/06/the-six-million-dollar-ear/?utm_source=3 D+Printing+Industry+Update&utm_medium=email&utm_ campaign=cd0759105c-RSS_EMAIL_CAMPAIGN&utm_ term=0_695d5c73dc-cd0759105c-60484669.

123. Leading Edge Forum, 13; Rachel Park, "New Micro DSP 3D Printing Solution for the Hearing Aid Market," *3D Printing Industry News*, October 27, 2012, http://3dprintingindustry.com/2012/10/27/new-micro-dsp-3D printing-solution-for-the-hearing-aid-market/.

124. Ricardo Pirroni, "ClearCorrect Scales 3D Printed Digital Orthodontics Capacity by 30%," *3D Printing Industry News*, May 10, 2013, http://3dprintingindustry.com/2013/05/10/clearcorrect-scales-3D printed-digital-orthodontics-capacity-by-30/?utm_source=3D+ Printing+Industry+Update&utm_medium=email&utm_campaign= 15b09085d8-RSS_EMAIL_CAMPAIGN&utm_term=0_695d5c73dc-15b09085d8-60484669; staff writer, "Medical Success With 3D Printing," *3D Printing Insider*, http://3dprintinginsider.com/medical-success-with-3D printing_b8184; Wohlers Report 2014, 19, 240.

125. Staff writer, "Baby's Life Saved with Groundbreaking 3D Printed Device from University of Michigan That Restored His Breathing," Health System University of Michigan, May 22, 2013, http://www.uofmhealth.org/news/archive/201305/

baby%E2%80%99s-life-saved-groundbreaking-3D printed-device; Rob Stein, "Doctors Use 3D Printing to Help a Baby Breathe," *NPR*, March 17, 2014, http://www.npr.org/blogs/health/2014/03/17/289042381/doctors-use-3D printing-to-help-a-baby-breathe; David Sher, "Can Organs Be 3D Bioprinted? A Stem Cell Trachea Will Tell," *3D Printing Industry News*, February 6, 2014, http://3dprintingindustry.com/2014/02/06/can-organs-3d-bioprinted-stem-cell-trachea-will-tell/?utm_source=3D+Printing+Industry+Update&utm_medium=email&utm_campaign=66586a01ca-RSS_EMAIL_CAMPAIGN&utm_term=0_695d5c73dc-66586a01ca-60484669.

126. Michael Molitch-Hou, "Trachea 3D Printed with Ordinary MakerBot PLA," *3D Printing Industry News*, January 27, 2015, http://3dprintingindustry.com/2015/01/27/trachea-3d-printed-ordinary-makerbot-pla/.

127. David Sher, "Ordinary Replicator 2X Used to 3D Print Bone Cancer Treatments," *3D Printing Industry News*, February 3, 2015, http://3dprintingindustry.com/2015/02/03/amazing-3d-printing-app-uses-replicator-2x-cure-bone-infections-cancer/.

128. Michael Molitch-Hou, "Anatomically Accurate Aorta Cells 3D Printed at Sabancı University in Turkey," *3D Printing Industry News,* March 20, 2014, http://3dprintingindustry.com/2014/03/20/3d-printing-aorta-cells-turkey/?utm_source=3D+Printing+Industry+Update&utm_medium=email&utm_campaign=d340f2a8af-RSS_EMAIL_CAMPAIGN&utm_term=0_695d5c73dc-d340f2a8af-60484669

129. Krassenstein, "3D Printed Human Heart By 2023"; Liat Clark, "Bioengineer: The Heart Is One of the Easiest Organs to Bioprint, We'll Do It in a Decade," *Wired UK*, November 21, 2013, http://www.wired.co.uk/news/archive/2013-11/21/3D printed-whole-heart.

130. David Sher, "3D Printed Organ Evolution Continues with BioAssemblyBot," *3D Printing Industry News*, August 4, 2014, http://3dprintingindustry.com/2014/08/04/3D printed-organ-evolution-continues-bioassemblybot/?utm_source=3D+Printing+Industry+Update&utm_medium=email&utm_campaign=2460f66955-RSS_EMAIL_CAMPAIGN&utm_term=0_695d5c73dc-2460f66955-60484669.

131. Staff writer, "A Custom Artificial Heart," *Maker Faire*, 2013, http://makerfaire.com/makers/a-custom-artificial-heart/.

132. Todd Halterman, "3D Printing Used to Make Heart Problem Detector," *3D Printer World*, February 28, 2014, http://www.3dprinterworld.com/article/3D printing-used-make-heart-problem-detector.

133. Liat Clark, "Bioengineers 3D Print Tiny Functioning Human Liver," *Wired UK*, April 13, 2013, http://www.wired.co.uk/news/archive/2013-04/24/3D printed-liver; *Organovo*, www.organovo.com.

134. Eetu Kuneinen, "3D Printing a Vaccine?" *3D Printing Industry News*, November 20, 2012, http://3dprintingindustry.com/2012/11/20/3D printing-a-vaccine/; staff writer, "You Will Be Able to 3D Print Customised Medicines on Demand within a Decade," *3ders.org*, November 2, 2014, http://www.3ders.org/articles/20141102-you-will-be-able-to-3d-print-customised-medicines-on-demand-within-a-decade.html.

135. Brian Heater, "Inexpensive 3D Limbs Could Bring New Hope to Sudan's 50,000 Amputees," *Yahoo! Tech*, January 30, 2014, https://www.yahoo.com/tech/inexpensive-3d-limbs-could-bring-new-hope-to-sudans-75055744752.html; Scott Grunewald, "Making Mass-Produced 3D Printed Prosthetics a Reality in Uganda,"

3D Printing Industry News, January 21, 2014, https://www.
yahoo.com/tech/inexpensive-3d-limbs-could-bring-new-
hope-to-sudans-75055744752.html; http://3dprintingindustry.com/
2014/01/21/making-mass-produced-3D printed-prosthetics-reality-
uganda/?utm_source=3D+Printing+Industry+Update&utm_
medium=email&utm_campaign=8b8b072837-RSS_EMAIL_
CAMPAIGN&utm_term=0_695d5c73dc-8b8b072837-60484669.

136. Eddie Krassenstein, "Military May Soon Be Able to Copy
and 3D Print Exact Replicas of Bones and Limbs for Injured
Soldiers," *3D print.com*, February 15, 2015, http://3dprint.
com/44793/copy-and-3d-print-bones/?utm_source=Daily+3D+P
rinting+News&utm_campaign=fbd7b68c1e-Latest_3D_Printing_
News_02_17_2015_2_16_2015&utm_medium=email&utm_
term=0_861dc04374-fbd7b68c1e-226645849.

137. Staff writer, "3D Printed Lightweight Robotic Hand Wins 2012
R&D 100," *3ders.org*, August 9, 2012, http://www.3ders.org/
articles/20120809-3D printed-lightweight-robotic-hand-wins-2012-
RD-100.html.

138. Brooke Kaelin, "A Look at How 3D Printing Made Belgium's First Full-
Face Transplant Possible," *3D Printer World*, July 30, 2014, http://
www.3dprinterworld.com/article/look-how-3d-printing-made-
belgiums-first-full-face-transplant-possible; Alec, "Chinese Man
Who Lost Half of His Skull after Fall Will Have It Rebuilt with 3D Printed
Mesh," *3ders.org*, August 28, 2014, http://www.3dprinterworld.
com/article/look-how-3D printing-made-belgiums-first-full-face-
transplant-possible?utm_source=dlvr.it&utm_medium=twitter;
http://www.3ders.org/articles/20140828-chinese-man-who-lost-
half-of-his-skull-after-fall-will-have-it-rebuilt-with-3D printed-
titanium-mesh.html?utm_source=Inside+3D+Printing+Latest+
News&utm_campaign=d44daa61fc-Inside_3D_Printing_Daily_

News_8_29_2014_8_28_2014&utm_medium=email&utm_term=0_861dc04374-d44daa61fc-226645849; Paul Rogers, "How to Print a New Face," *Forbes*, March 13, 2014, http://www.forbes.com/sites/paulrodgers/2014/03/13/how-to-print-a-new-face/.

139. Sandra Helsel, "Michigan Tech Integrating Graphene and 3D Printed Scaffolds to Rebuild Nerve Tissue," *Inside 3D Printing*, May 14, 2015, http://inside3dprinting.com/michigan-tech-integrating-graphene-and-3D printed-scaffolds-to-rebuild-nerve-tissue/.

140. David Sher, "DeltaWASP 3D Printer Quadruples Prosthesis Production for Orthopedic Lab," *3D Printing Industry News*, February 4, 2015, http://3dprintingindustry.com/2015/02/04/deltawasp-3d-printer-helps-italian-orthopedic-lab-quadruple-production/?utm_source=3D+Printing+Industry+Update&utm_medium=email&utm_campaign=30e1dd966c-RSS_EMAIL_CAMPAIGN&utm_term=0_695d5c73dc-30e1dd966c-60484669.

141. Adrienne LaFrance, "To Help Solve Challenging Cardiac Problems, Doctors at Children's Press 'Print,'" *Washington Post*, May 13, 2013, http://www.washingtonpost.com/national/health-science/to-help-solve-challenging-cardiac-problems-doctors-at-childrens-press-print/2013/05/13/b2eee214-8d9b-11e2-9838-d62f083ba93f_story.html.

142. Remy Carreiro, "Doctors Use a 3D Printer to Help with Complicated Heart Surgery on a 4-Year-Old Girl," *Uproxx Tech*, January 19, 2015, http://uproxx.com/technology/2015/01/doctors-use-3d-printer-to-help-with-complicated-heart-surgery-on-4-year-old-girl/?utm_source=Daily+3D+Printing+News&utm_campaign=95e1872531-Latest_3D_Printing_News_01_21_2015_1_20_2015&utm_medium=email&utm_term=0_861dc04374-95e1872531-226645849.

143. Priyanka Dayal McCluskey, "3D Printer Helps Doctors Prep for Complex Surgeries," *Boston Globe*, January 18, 2015, http://www.bostonglobe.com/business/2015/01/18/with-printer-doctors-get-help-prepping-for-complex-surgeries/Wf4GVpGMHapbG6sWGYlEYP/story.html?p1=Article_InThisSection_Bottom&utm_source=Daily+3D+Printing+News&utm_campaign=e8ac90dd03-Latest_3D_Printing_News_01_26_2015_1_25_2015&utm_medium=email&utm_term=0_861dc04374-e8ac90dd03-226645849.

144. Michael Molitch-Hou, "Complex Separation of Conjoined Twins Successfully Planned with 3D Printing," *3D Printing Industry News*, February 27, 2015, http://3dprintingindustry.com/2015/02/27/complex-separation-of-conjoined-twins-successfully-planned-with-3D printing/?utm_source=3D+Printing+Industry+Update&utm_medium=email&utm_campaign=d107a31b65-RSS_EMAIL_CAMPAIGN&utm_term=0_695d5c73dc-d107a31b65-60484669.

145. Simon, "Chinese Doctors Use 3D Printed Replicas to Practice Separating Conjoined Twins," *3ders.org*, June 8, 2015, http://www.3ders.org//articles/20150608-chinese-doctors-use-3D printed-replicas-to-practice-separating-conjoined-twins.html.

146. Michael Dhar, "Surgeons Practice on Brains Made on 3D Printers," *HuffPost Healthy Living*, January 25, 2014, http://www.huffingtonpost.com/2013/11/20/surgeons-brains-3d-printers-practice_n_4309621.html.

147. Rachel Park, "Materialise Acquires OrthoView and Its Orthopedic Digital Pre-Operative Planning Software," *3D Printing Industry News*, October 21, 2014, http://3dprintingindustry.com/2014/10/21/materialise-acquires-orthoview-orthopedic-digital-pre-operative-planning-software/; Rachel Park, "3D Printed Surgical Guides

Make Their Malaysian Debut," *3D Printing Industry News*, June 20, 2013, http://3dprintingindustry.com/2013/06/20/3D printed-surgical-guides-make-their-malaysian-debut/.

148. Michael Molitch-Hou, "Breakthrough Tech from Materialise Converts 2D X-Rays into 3D Prints," *3D Printing Industry News*, September 22, 2014, http://3dprintingindustry.com/2014/09/22/breakthrough-tech-materialise-converts-2d-x-rays-3d-prints/?utm_source=3D+P rinting+Industry+Update&utm_medium=email&utm_campaign= 3e5a2583ab-RSS_EMAIL_CAMPAIGN&utm_term=0_695d5c73dc-3e5a2583ab-60484669n.

149. Michael Molitch-Hou, "Materialise Helps to Open 3D Printing Center in Beijing Hospital," *3D Printing Industry News*, June 24, 2015, http://3dprintingindustry.com/2015/06/24/materialise-opens-3D printing-center-in-beijing-hospital/?utm_source=3D+Printing+Ind ustry+Update&utm_medium=email&utm_campaign=bc6af9a60a-RSS_EMAIL_CAMPAIGN&utm_term=0_695d5c73dc-bc6af9a60a-60484669.

150. Mike Murphy, "See What You'll Look Like after Plastic Surgery with a 3D printed Bust of Your Head," *Quartz*, June 13, 2015, http://qz.com/427157/see-what-youll-look-like-after-plastic-surgery-with-a-3D printed-bust-of-your-head/.

151. Staff writer, "GE Oil and Gas Uses 3D Printing to Produce Control Valve Parts at Kariwa Plant," *Penn Energy*, February 26, 2015, http://www.pennenergy.com/articles/pennenergy/2015/02/ge-oil-and-gas-uses-3d-printing-to-produce-control-valve-parts-at-kariwa-plant.html?utm_source=Daily+3D+Printing+News&utm_campaign=cf2dee6313-Latest_3D_Printing_News_02_27_2015_2_27_2015&utm_medium=email&utm_term=0_861dc04374-cf2dee6313-226645849.

152. David Dodd, "Why Marketing Content Should Be More about Quarter-Inch Holes than Quarter-Inch Drills," *Business 2 Community*, April 17, 2012, http://www.business2community.com/content-marketing/why-marketing-content-should-be-more-about-quarter-inch-holes-than-quarter-inch-drills-0165309#!bLDrlH.

153. Cotteleer and Joyce, "3D Opportunity," 8.

154. Eliza Williams, "The Future of Car Design, According to Ford," *Creative Review*, April 17, 2015, http://www.creativereview.co.uk/cr-blog/2015/april/the-future-of-car-design-according-to-ford?utm_source=Daily+3D+Printing+News&utm_campaign=39af207ee3-Latest_3D_Printing_News_04_20_2015_4_19_2015&utm_medium=email&utm_term=0_861dc04374-39af207ee3-226645849.

155. Staff writer, "Personalizing New Daihatsu Copen Robe Roadster Design with Stratasys 3D Printing," *Stratasys Blog*, June 24, 2015, http://blog.stratasys.com/2015/06/24/daihatsu-copen-3D printing/?utm_source=Stratasys+Blog+EN&utm_campaign=d877672583-MailChimp&utm_medium=email&utm_term=0_7575e85682D877672583-19714869.

156. Michael Molitch-Hou, "Rinkak Provides Toyota with Mass 3D Printing for i-Road Project," *3D Printing Industry News*, July 6, 2015, http://3dprintingindustry.com/2015/07/06/rinkak-provides-toyota-with-mass-3D printing-for-i-road-project/?utm_source=3D+Printing+Industry+Update&utm_medium=email&utm_campaign=cf61aeec84-RSS_EMAIL_CAMPAIGN&utm_term=0_695d5c73dc-cf61aeec84-60484669.

157. David Sher, "On-the-Body Design Method for 3D Printed Wearables Created by TACTUM," *3D Printing Industry News*, June 26, 2015, http://3dprintingindustry.com/2015/06/26/madlabs-tactum-

visualizes-body-parametric-design-3D printing/?utm_source=3D+ Printing+Industry+Update&utm_medium=email&utm_ campaign=c3014826a1-RSS_EMAIL_CAMPAIGN&utm_ term=0_695d5c73dc-c3014826a1-60484669.

158. Todd Grimm, "The 3D Printing Conundrum," *TCT Magazine*, July 29, 2015, http://www.tctmagazine.com/tctblogs/grimmblog/the-3D printing-conundrum/.

159. Carolyn Conner Seepersad, "Challenges and Opportunities in Design and Additive Manufacturing," *3D Printing and Additive Manufacturing* 1, no. 1 (2014): 10.

160. BernatCuni,"Cunicode,"*Inside3DPrinting*,HongKong,August28,2014, http://bernatcuni.com/cunicode-design-for-creative-fabrication/.

161. Bob Vavra, "3D: Adding to Additive's Capabilities," *Plant Engineering*, February 17, 2015, http://www.plantengineering. com/single-article/3d-adding-to-additives-capabilities/3210f054 bbeefad0003da9ed21f28c1f.html?utm_source=Daily 3D Printing News&utm_campaign=10d3b6c594-Latest_3D_Printing_News_ 02_19_2015_2_19_2015&utm_medium=email&utm_term=0_ 861dc04374-10d3b6c594-226645849.

162. OwnFone, http://www.ownfone.com/.

163. Alec, "3D printed Braille Phone Manufacturers Ownfone Raise £786,000 In Investments," *3Ders.org*, December 30, 2014, http://www.3ders.org/articles/20141230-3D printed-braille-phone-manufacturers-ownfone-raise-in-investments.html?utm_source=I nside+3D+Printing+Latest+News&utm_campaign=45c860e562-Latest_3D_Printing_News_12_31_2014_12_31_2014&utm_ medium=email&utm_term=0_861dc04374-45c860e562-226645849.

164. Hod Lipson and Melba Kurman, *Fabricated: The New World of 3D Printing* (Indianapolis, IN: John Wiley & Sons, 2013), 18–20.

165. Chris Anderson, *The New Industrial Revolution* (New York: Crown Business, 2012), 98.

166. Cotteleer and Joyce, "3D Opportunity," 15.

167. Hannah Rose Mendoza, "Ultrasonic 3D Printing Allows for Electronics to be Embedded in Metal via Sound," *3DPrint.com*, August 17, 2014, http://3dprint.com/12075/ultrasonic-3d-printing-uam/

168. *Local Motors*, https://localmotors.com/about/; Noah Joseph, "Local Motors Builds XC2V Flypmode Prototype for DARPA," *Autoblog*, July 27, 2011; Ari, "Congratulations to DARPA XC2V Participants & Winners!" *LM: Life*, March 15, 20011, http://www. autoblog.com/2011/06/27/local-motors-builds-xc2v-flypmode-prototype-for-darpa/; http://lmlife.local-motors.com/2011/03/ congratulations-to-darpa-xc2v.html#!/2011/03/congratulations-to-darpa-xc2v.html; Rebecca Boyle, "How the First Crowdsourced Military Vehicle Can Remake the Future of Defense Manufacturing," *Popular Science*, June 30, 2011; staff writer, "President Obama Recognizes Local Motors, DARPA and American Manufacturing," *SEMA News* 14, no. 26 (June 30, 2011), http://www.popsci.com/ cars/article/2011-06/how-first-crowdsourced-military-car-can-remake-future-defense-manufacturing; http://www.sema.org/ sema-enews/2011/26/president-obama-recognizes-local-motors-darpa-and-american-manufacturing-in-speec.

169. *Creative Commons*, http://creativecommons.org/about.

170. Adrian Bowyer, "3D Printing and Humanity's First Imperfect Replicator," *3D Printing and Additive Manufacturing* 1, no. 1 (2014): 5.

171. IBM Report, 7.

172. Ibid.

173. David Sher, "Low Poly Pokemon Project Challenges the Future of IP and 3D Printing," *3D Printing Industry News*, September 24, 2014, http://3dprintingindustry.com/2014/09/24/low-poly-pokemon-project-challenges-future-ip-3D printing/.

174. Staff writer, "Digital Natives by Matthew Plummer Fernandez," *DeZeen Magazine*, October 12, 2012, http://www.dezeen.com/2012/10/12/digital-natives-by-matthew-plummer-fernandez/.

175. Staff writer, "Creating Mash Ups with 3D Printing," *3D Printing Industry News*, May 11, 2014, http://3dprintingindustry.com/2013/05/11/creating-mash-ups-with-3D   printing/?utm_source=3D+Printing+Industry+Update&utm_medium=email&utm_campaign=efaa27a0b4-RSS_EMAIL_CAMPAIGN&utm_term=0_695d5c73dc-efaa27a0b4-60484669.

176. Leading Edge Forum, 8.

177. Briar Thompson, "Reaching into the White Powder: A Policy Brief on 3D Printing and Pacific Security," Pacific Security Scholars Policy Brief Series, 9, http://fas.org/wp-content/uploads/2014/03/Thompson-3D printing.pdf.

178. James Morgan, "Amaze Project Aims to Take 3D Printing 'into Metal Age,'" *BBC News Science and Environment*, October 13, 2013, http://www.bbc.com/news/science-environment-24528306.

179. *Organovo*, www.organovo.com; *N3D Biosciences*, http://www.n3dbio.com/; *Cyfuse Biomedical K. K.*, http://www.cyfusebio.com;

Bio3D Technologies, http://bio-3d.com/about-us.html; *OxSyBio*, http://www.isis-innovation.com/spinout/OxSyBio.html; *3Dynamic Systems*, http://www.bioprintingsystems.com/about.html; Nancy Fumero, "Regenovo is China's Organovo," *3D Printing Industry News*, January 17, 2014, http://3dprintingindustry.com/2014/01/17/regenovo-chinas-organovo/?utm_source=3D+Printing+Industry+Update&utm_medium=email&utm_campaign=ffdd1be1ed-RSS_EMAIL_CAMPAIGN&utm_term=0_695d5c73dc-ffdd1be1ed-60484669.

180. Scott Grunewald, "3D Bioprinted Vascular Network Brings Us Closer to Push Button Organ Printing," *3D Printing Industry News*, July 3, 2014, http://3dprintingindustry.com/2014/07/03/bioprinted-vascular-network-brings-us-closer-push-button-organ-printing/?utm_source=3D+Printing+Industry+Update&utm_medium=email&utm_campaign=e3db0db805-RSS_EMAIL_CAMPAIGN&utm_term=0_695d5c73dc-e3db0db805-60484669; David Sher, "Harvard Scientists Inch Closer to Getting 3D Printed Organs' Blood Flowing," *3D Printing Industry News*, February 25, 2014, http://3dprintingindustry.com/2014/02/25/harvard-3D printed-organs-blood-flowing/?utm_source=3D+Printing+Industry+Update&utm_medium=email&utm_campaign=91f70e8d4a-RSS_EMAIL_CAMPAIGN&utm_term=0_695d5c73dc-91f70e8d4a-60484669; Shane Taylor, "Bioprinting Vascular Systems," *3D printing Industry News*, November 8, 2013, http://3dprintingindustry.com/2013/11/08/bioprinting-vascular-systems/?utm_source=3D+Printing+Industry+Update&utm_medium=email&utm_campaign=21095237c5-RSS_EMAIL_CAMPAIGN&utm_term=0_695d5c73dc-21095237c5-60484669; Kyle Maxey, "Blood Vessel Bio-Printing to Enter Clinical Trials," *Engineering.com*, January 9, 2014, http://www.engineering.com/3DPrinting/3DPrintingArticles/ArticleID/6932/Blood-Vessel-Bio-Printing-to-Enter-Clinical-Trials.aspx; staff writer, "Scientists Use 3D Printing to Make

Artificial Blood Vessels," *Phys.org*, May 31, 2014, http://phys.org/news/2014-05-scientists-3d-artificial-blood-vessels.html.

181. Shane Taylor, "President Obama Visits TechShop and Praises Multifunctional 3D Printer," *3D Printing Industry News*, June 24, 2014, http://3dprintingindustry.com/2014/06/24/3d-printer-obama-techshop-zego/?utm_source=3D+Printing+Industry+Update&utm_medium=email&utm_campaign=5500958631-RSS_EMAIL_CAMPAIGN&utm_term=0_695d5c73dc-5500958631-60484669.

182. "Maker Culture," *Wikipedia*, http://en.wikipedia.org/wiki/Maker_culture.

183. Mark Hatch, *The Maker Movement Manifesto* (New York: McGraw-Hill Education, 2014), 11–31.

184. Anderson, *The New Industrial Revolution*, 13.

185. Leading Edge Forum, 2.

186. Scott Crump, "Scott Crump, Chairman/CIO, Stratasys @ TCT Show + Personalize 2013," YouTube, October 28, 2013, http://www.youtube.com/watch?v=OyJ4plgW1BM; staff writer, "Inventor of 3D Printing Scott Crump: 'My Dreams Started in a Garage,'" *On 3D Printing*, September 17, 2013, http://on3dprinting.com/tag/scott-crump/.

187. Bre Pettis, "Maker Nation," *Popular Mechanics*, June 2015, 64.

188. *Popular Mechanics*, June 2014, 72.

189. Amy Syracuse, "Market Focus: Amateur Woodworkers," *Target Marketing*, April 2006, http://www.targetmarketingmag.com/article/market-focus-amateur-woodworkers-32900/1; "Woodworkers," *Occupational Outlook Handbook*, January 8, 2014, http://www.bls.gov/ooh/production/woodworkers.htm.

190. Myron Levin, "Saws Cut Off 4,000 Fingers a Year: This Gadget Could Fix That," *Mother Jones*, May 16, 2013, http://www.motherjones.com/politics/2013/05/table-saw-sawstop-safety-finger-cut; "Best Table Saw Review," *Side-By-SideReviews.com*, http://sidebysidereviews.com/table-saw-review/.

191. *FabFoundation*, http://www.fabfoundation.org/about-us/; Michelle Matisons, "World's Largest 3D Printing Fab Lab Opens in Haifa, Israel at MadaTech National Museum," *3DPrint.com*, January 13, 2015, http://3dprint.com/36673/largest-fab-lab-opens-in-haifa/?utm_source=Daily+3D+Printing+News&utm_campaign=f144462ef1-Latest_3D_Printing_News_01_15_2015_1_15_2015&utm_medium=email&utm_term=0_861dc04374-f144462ef1-226645849.

192. FabCafe, http://fabcafe.com/intro.

193. Wohlers Report 2014, 24.

194. Staff writer, "Startup Cities: The Best New Places to Start a Business in America," *Popular Mechanics*, February 2015, 62–72.

195. "Hackerspace," *Wikipedia*, http://en.wikipedia.org/wiki/Hackerspace.

196. "Men's Sheds," *Wikipedia*, http://en.wikipedia.org/wiki/Men%27s_Sheds.

197. "Techshop," *Wikipedia,* http://techshop.ws/.

198. Staff, "Startup Cities," 64.

199. Pettis, "Maker Nation," 64.

200. Staff writer, "3D Printing Patents Expiring in 2014 Will See Market Erupt," *Designboom,* August 5, 2013, http://www.designboom.com/technology/3D printing-patents-expiring-in-2014-will-see-market-erupt/; Melba Kurman and Hod Lipson, "Why Patents Won't Kill 3D printing Innovation," *Livescience,* July 29, 2013, http://www.livescience.com/38494-3D printing-and-patent-protection.html.

201. "Fab@Home," *Wikipedia*, http://en.wikipedia.org/wiki/Fab@Home.

202. Wohlers Report 2014, 99.

203. "MakerBot Industries," *Wikipedia,* http://en.wikipedia.org/wiki/MakerBot_Industries.

204. "Wright Brothers," *Wikipedia,* http://en.wikipedia.org/wiki/Wright_brothers.

205. Cotteleer and Joyce, "3D Opportunity," 6–7.

206. Shanie Phillips, "USPS 3D Printing Revenue Not So Significant, Says Brookings," *Inside 3DP*, July 23, 2014, http://www.inside3dp.com/usps-3D printing-revenue-significant-says-brookings/.

207. Lee Ewing, "Breaking the Mold: UAS Modeling and Simulation Expands into 3D Part Printing," *Unmanned Systems*, 30.

208. Antonio Regalado, "You Must Make the New Machines," *MIT Technology Review,* January 4, 2013, http://www.technologyreview.com/news/509281/you-must-make-the-new-machines/.

209. Kevin Zeese and Margaret Flowers, "Output vs. Employment: America's Disappearing Jobs," *Global Research*, February 28, 2013, http://www.globalresearch.ca/ouput-vs-employment-americas-disappearing-jobs/5324614.

210. Lisa Harrington, "Is U.S. Manufacturing Coming Back?," *Inbound Logistics*, August 2011, http://www.inboundlogistics.com/cms/article/is-us-manufacturing-coming-back/.

211. McKinsey Report, 113.

212. Thomas Campbell, Christopher Williams, Olga Ivanova, and Banning Garrett, "Could 3D Printing Change the World?" *Atlantic Council Strategic Foresight Report*, October 2011, 7, http://www.atlanticcouncil.org/images/files/publication_pdfs/403/101711_ACUS_3DPrinting.PDF.

213. Sally Kohn, "The 3D Revolution Will Blow You Away," *CNN*, April 30, 2014, http://www.cnn.com/2014/04/30/opinion/kohn-3d-printers/index.html?hpt=hp_t4.

214. Staff writer, "3D Printing Market in Emerging Economies Is Expected to Reach $4.5 Billion by 2020—Allied Market Research," *PR Newswire*, September 17, 2014, http://www.prnewswire.co.uk/news-releases/3D printing-market-in-emerging-economies-is-expected-to-reach-45-billion-by-2020---allied-market-research-275450361.html.

215. Lipson and Kurman, *Fabricated*, 35; Melba Kurman, "Carrots, Not Sticks: Rethinking Enforcement of Intellectual Property Rights for 3D

printed Manufacturing," *3D Printing and Additive Manufacturing* 1, no. 1 (2014): 238–39.

216. Campbell et al., "Could 3D Printing Change the World?," 1.

217. IBM Report, 10.

218. Andrew Sissons and Spencer Thompson, "Three Dimensional Policy: Why Britain Needs a Policy Framework for 3D Printing," *Big Innovation Center*, October 2012, 6, 8, 11, 17, 19, 27, http:// www.biginnovationcentre.com/Assets/Docs/Reports/3D%20 printing%20paper_FINAL_15%20Oct.pdf.

219. Campbell et al., "Could 3D Printing Change the World?," 7.

220. Lipson and Kurman, *Fabricated*, 35.

221. Wohlers Report 2014, 172.

222. "Technical White Paper: HP Multi Jet Fusion Technology," 1.

223. Barack Obama, "Remarks by the President in the State of the Union Address," The White House Office of the Press Secretary, February 12, 2013, http://www.whitehouse.gov/the-press-office/2013/02/12/ remarks-president-state-union-address.

224. Staff writer, "Obama Name-Checks 3D Printing, Calls For 15 'Innovation Hubs,'" *Fast Company*, February 13, 2013, http://www. fastcodesign.com/1671864/obama-name-checks-3D printing- calls-for-15-innovation-hubs; "About America Makes," https:// americamakes.us/about/overview.

225. Michael Molitch-Hou, "Youngstown State University Opens 3D Printing Center as US Manufacturing Hubs Take Root," *3D Printing*

Industry News, February 7, 2014, http://3dprintingindustry. com/2014/02/07/youngstown-state-university-opens-3D printing-center-us-manufacturing-hubs-take-root/?utm_sourc e=3D+Printing+Industry+Update&utm_medium=email&utm_ campaign=a7dca2accb-RSS_EMAIL_CAMPAIGN&utm_ term=0_695d5c73dc-a7dca2accb-60484669.

226. Walter Wessel, "The 'Maker City Initiative'—Bringing Optimism to the Future of Youngstown, OH," *3D Printing News*, August 16, 2014, http://www.real3dprinter.com/the-maker-city-initiative- bringing-optimism-to-the-future-of-youngstown-oh/.

227. "Digital Manufacturing and Design Innovation Institute," *Advanced Manufacturing Portal*, http://manufacturing.gov/ dmdii.html; Michael Molitch-Hou, "President Obama Announces Two New Advanced Manufacturing Hubs," *3D Printing Industry News*, March 3, 2014, http://3dprintingindustry.com/2014/03/03/ president-obama-advanced-manufacturing-hubs/?utm_sourc e=3D+Printing+Industry+Update&utm_medium=email&utm_ campaign=82a039bcc1-RSS_EMAIL_CAMPAIGN&utm_ term=0_695d5c73dc-82a039bcc1-60484669.

228. "Next Generation Power Electronics National Manufacturing Innovation Institute," *Advanced Manufacturing Portal*, http:// manufacturing.gov/doe-led_institutes.html.

229. Staff writer, "Obama Name-Checks 3-D Printing, Calls For 15 'Innovation Hubs'," *Fast Company*; February 13, 2013; http:// www.fastcodesign.com/1671864/obama-name-checks-3-d- printing-calls-for-15-innovation-hubs.

230. IBM Report, 12.

231. Ibid., 102.

232. Lipson and Kurman, *Fabricated*, 35; Kurman, "Carrots, Not Sticks," 50, citing www.census.gov/econ/susb.

233. Staff writer, "The Stats," *Money*, March 2015, 24.

234. McKinsey Report, 111.

235. Ibid., 105.

236. IBM Report, 8.

237. Ibid., 9.

238. Nancy Weil, "The Quotable Bill Gates: In His Own Words," *Computerworld*, June 23, 2008, http://www.computerworld.com/article/2534366/it-management/the-quotable-bill-gates--in-his-own-words.html.

239. Nick Bilton, "Disruptions: On the Fast Track to Routine 3D Printing," *New York Times Bits*, February 17, 2013, http://bits.blogs.nytimes.com/2013/02/17/disruptions-3D printing-is-on-the-fast-track/?_php=true&_type=blogs&_r=0.

240. Staff writer, "Inside 3D Printing Conference Brings Reality to the Hype," *3D Printer*, April 23, 2013, http://www.3dprinter.net/inside-3D printing-conference-brings-reality-to-the-hype.

241. Thompson, "Reaching into the White Powder," 5.

242. Obama, "Remarks by the President."

243. Smith, "You Must Make the New Machines."

244. Robert Appleton, "Additive Manufacturing Overview for the United States Marine Corps," *RW Appleton & Co. Inc.*, June 14, 2014, 26.

245. "Historical Components of the Dow Jones Industrial Average," *Wikipedia*, http://en.wikipedia.org/wiki/Historical_components_of_ the_Dow_Jones_Industrial_Average.

246. "Databases, Tables and Calculators by Subject: Seasonally Adjusted Unemployment Rate," *Bureau of Labor Statistics*, http://data.bls. gov/timeseries/LNS14000000.

247. "Table A-4. Employment Status of the Civilian Population 25 Years and over by Educational Attainment," *Bureau of Labor Statistics*, http:// www.bls.gov/news.release/empsit.t04.htm; "Survey Output," *Bureau of Labor Statistics*, http://data.bls.gov/pdq/SurveyOutputServlet.

248. Thompson, "Reaching into the White Powder," 6, 13.

249. IBM Report, 4.

250. Ibid., 9.

251. Staff writer, "3D Printing Could Revolutionize War and Foreign Policy," *Space Daily*, January 5, 2015, http://www.spacedaily.com/ reports/How_3D_printing_could_revolutionise_war_and_foreign_ policy_999.html

252. Kurman, "Carrots, Not Sticks," 47.

253. Ibid.

254. James Lefebvre, "This 3D Printed Toyota Engine Really Revs," *3D Printing Industry News*, February 8, 2015, http://3dprintingindustry.com/2015/02/08/3Dprinted-toyota-engine-really-revs/?utm_source=3D+Printing+Industry+Update&utm_medium=email&utm_campaign=4c06699c63-RSS_EMAIL_CAMPAIGN&utm_term=0_695d5c73dc-4c06699c63-60484669.

255. "Warp Drive," *Wikipedia*, http://en.wikipedia.org/wiki/Warp_drive.

256. M. Brandt, "Additive Manufacturing: The Next Industrial Revolution," presented at Inside 3D Printing, Melbourne, Australia, July 10, 2014.

257. Rachel Park, "Remanufacturing with Optomec's LENS 3D Print Engine," *3D Printing Industry News*, July 17, 2014, http://3dprintingindustry.com/2014/07/17/remanufacturing-optomecs-lens-3d-print-engine/?utm_source=3D+Printing+Industry+Update&utm_medium=email&utm_campaign=21cb757eb0-RSS_EMAIL_CAMPAIGN&utm_term=0_695d5c73dc-21cb757eb0-60484669.

258. Eric Johnson, "Additive Manufacturing: Enabling Design and Manufacturing Today," presentation at Innoplast Solutions: 3D Printing the Future, Las Vegas, Nevada, February 18, 2015.

259. IBM Report, 11.

260. Kurman, "Carrots, Not Sticks," 47–48.

261. Melba Kurman and Hod Lipson, "The Truth about 3D-Printing Piracy," *Popular Mechanics*, June 2014, 73.

262. Wohlers Report 2014, 171.

263. Robert Bugge, "Additive Manufacturing ('AM') and US Government Contracting," *3DPrintingStocks.com*, August 17, 2014, https://3dprintingstocks.com/am/.

264. Marcus Weisgerber, "The Defense Industry Is Expanding the Use of 3D Printing," *National Journal*, September 30, 2014, http://www.nationaljournal.com/defense/the-defense-industry-is-expanding-the-use-of-3D printing-20140930.

265. Staff writer, "3D Printing Could Revolutionize War."

266. Appleton, "Additive Manufacturing Overview for the United States Marine Corps," 25.

267. Michael Molitch-Hou, "Product Liability Law in the World of 3D Printing," *3D Printing Industry News*, November 14, 2013, http://3dprintingindustry.com/2013/11/14/product-liability-law-world-3D printing/?utm_source=3D+Printing+Industry+Update&utm_medium=email&utm_campaign=b806a14bd9-RSS_EMAIL_CAMPAIGN&utm_term=0_695d5c73dc-b806a14bd9-60484669.

268. Leading Edge Forum, 23.

269. Wohlers Report 2014, 206.

270. Leading Edge Forum, 21.

271. Ibid., 18.

272. Daniel L. Cohen, "Fostering Mainstream Adoption of Industrial 3D Printing: Understanding the Benefits and Promoting Organizational Readiness," *3D Printing and Additive Manufacturing* 1, no. 2 (2014): 65.

273. Bugge, "Additive Manufacturing ('AM') and US Government Contracting."

274. IBM Report, 10.

275. Staff writer, "3D Printer Value Samsung Electronics Not Hurrying in 3D Printer Business," *Business Korea*, October 7, 2014, http://www.businesskorea.co.kr/article/6659/3d-printer-value-samsung-electronics-not-hurrying-3d-printer-business.

276. Michael Molitch-Hou, "Samsung Innovation Team to Explore 3D Printing, Robotics, and UAVs," *3D Printing Industry News*, February 9, 2015, http://3dprintingindustry.com/2015/02/09/samsung-innovation-team-explore-3d-printing-robotics-uavs/.

277. Scott Grunewald, "Roccat's Modular MMO Mouse with Customizable 3D Printed Buttons," *3D printing Industry News*, August 14, 2014, http://3dprintingindustry.com/2014/08/14/roccats-modular-mmo-mouse-customizable-3D printed-buttons/?utm_source=3D+Printing+Industry+Update&utm_medium=email&utm_campaign=e523fb70aa-RSS_EMAIL_CAMPAIGN&utm_term=0_695d5c73dc-e523fb70aa-60484669.

278. Wohlers Report 2014, 240.

279. Alex Chausovsky, "The Impact of 3D Printing on Aerospace and Defence," 3D Printing: Defence and Aerospace, K2B International, Nanyang Executive Center, Nanyang Technological University, Singapore, October 2, 2014.

280. IBM Report, 10.

281. Ibid., 3.

282. Daniel Cohen, Katy George, and Colin Shaw, "Are You Ready for 3D Printing?" McKinsey, February 2015, http://www.mckinsey.com/insights/manufacturing/are_you_ready_for_3D_printing.

283. McKinsey Report, 110–11.

284. Hod Lipson, "Is Additive Manufacturing a Real Revolution?" *3D Printing and Additive Manufacturing* 1, no. 2, 61, June 2014.

285. Ivan Pope, "The Coming Ecosystem of 3D Printing: Part 1," *3D Printing Industry News*, June 19, 2014, http://3dprintingindustry.com/2014/06/19/coming-ecosystem-3D printing/?utm_source=3D+Printing+Industry+Update&utm_medium=email&utm_campaign=65f8f6fa50-RSS_EMAIL_CAMPAIGN&utm_term=0_695d5c73dc-65f8f6fa50-60484669.

286. Ivan Pope, "The Coming Ecosystem of 3D Printing: Part 4," *3D Printing Industry News*, July 7, 2014, http://3dprintingindustry.com/2014/07/07/coming-ecosystem-3D printing-part-4/?utm_source=3D+Printing+Industry+Update&utm_medium=email&utm_campaign=f3a0c0ef21-RSS_EMAIL_CAMPAIGN&utm_term=0_695d5c73dc-f3a0c0ef21-60484669; Michael Molitch-Hou, "3D Hubs Adds 10,000th 3D Printer to Network," *3D Printing Industry News*, January 8, 2015, http://3dprintingindustry.com/2015/01/08/3d-hubs-adds-10000th-3d-printer-network/?utm_source=3D+Printing+Industry+Update&utm_medium=email&utm_campaign=b3c6bd6de4-RSS_EMAIL_CAMPAIGN&utm_term=0_695d5c73dc-b3c6bd6de4-60484669.

287. Ingrid Lunden, "Tony Hsieh, Vegas Tech Fund Put $10M Into Factorli, a Factory for US Hardware Startups," *Techcrunch*, May 21, 2014, http://techcrunch.com/2014/05/21/tony-hsieh-vegas-tech-fund-put-10m-into-factorli-a-factory-for-us-hardware-startups/.

288. Ivan Pope, "The Coming Ecosystem of 3D Printing: Part 2," *3D Printing Industry News*, June 25, 2014, http://3dprintingindustry. com/2014/06/25/coming-ecosystem-3D printing-part-2/?utm_ source=3D+Printing+Industry+Update&utm_medium= email&utm_campaign=e39ac8253d-RSS_EMAIL_CAMPAIGN& utm_term=0_695d5c73dc-e39ac8253d-60484669.

289. Michael Molitch-Hou, "Yobi3D is Google for 3D Printable Content," *3D Printing Industry News*, August 9, 2014, http://3dprintingindustry.com/2014/08/09/yobi3d-google-3d-printable-content/?utm_source=3D+Printing+Industry+Update& utm_medium=email&utm_campaign=fb2957a0cb-RSS_EMAIL_ CAMPAIGN&utm_term=0_695d5c73dc-fb2957a0cb-60484669.

290. Michael Molitch-Hou, "Amazon Sets Out to Conquer Entire 3D Printing Industry with New Patent Application," *3D Printing Industry News*, February 25, 2015, http://3dprintingindustry.com/2015/02/25/ amazon-sets-out-to-conquer-entire-3D printing-industry-with-new-patent-application/?utm_source=3D+Printing+Industry+Update& utm_medium=email&utm_campaign=b7d38790b2-RSS_EMAIL_ CAMPAIGN&utm_term=0_695d5c73dc-b7d38790b2-60484669.

291. Scott Grunewald, "Leading Precision Parts Manufacturer Adopts 3D Printing to Stay Competitive," *3D Printing Industry News*, July 28, 2014, http://3dprintingindustry.com/2014/07/28/ leading-precision-parts-manufacturer-adopts-3D printing-stay-competitive/?utm_source=3D+Printing+Industry+Update&u tm_medium=email&utm_campaign=1bd45ab2bc-RSS_EMAIL_ CAMPAIGN&utm_term=0_695d5c73dc-1bd45ab2bc-60484669.

292. Cohen, "Fostering Mainstream Adoption of Industrial 3D Printing," 66.

293. *3DPrinterOS*, July 8, 2015, http://www.3dprinteros.com/network-surpasses-2000-printers-2x-as-fast-as-3d-hubs/.

294. Eetu Kuneinen, "U.S. Army Deploying Mobile FabLabs," *3D Printing Industry News*, March 6, 2013, http://3dprintingindustry.com/2013/03/06/u-s-army-deploying-mobile-fablabs/.

295. David Sher, "US Army Planning 3D Printed Soldier Garments for Augmented Mobility and Protection," *3D Printing Industry News*, August 7, 2014, http://3dprintingindustry.com/2014/08/07/us-army-planning-3D printed-soldier-garments-augmented-mobility-protection/?utm_source=3D+Printing+Industry+Update&utm_medium=email&utm_campaign=cf2922a220-RSS_EMAIL_CAMPAIGN&utm_term=0_695d5c73dc-cf2922a220-60484669.

296. Scott Grunewald, "The U.S. Army Wants You!...to 3D Print Them Weapons," *3D Printing Industry News*, June 5, 2014, http://3dprintingindustry.com/2014/06/05/u-s-army-wants-3d-print-weapons/?utm_source=3D+Printing+Industry+Update&utm_medium=email&utm_campaign=ab57df841f-RSS_EMAIL_CAMPAIGN&utm_term=0_695d5c73dc-ab57df841f-60484669.

297. Juho Vesanto, "Research at US ARL: Using 3D Printing to Produce Replaceable and Blast-Proof Vehicle Parts," *3D Printing Industry News*, September 25, 2013, http://3dprintingindustry.com/2013/09/25/research-us-arl-using-3D printing-produce-replaceable-blast-proof-vehicle-parts/?utm_source=3D+Printing+Industry+Update&utm_medium=email&utm_campaign=f97cb6a2a5-RSS_EMAIL_CAMPAIGN&utm_term=0_695d5c73dc-f97cb6a2a5-60484669.

298. Eric Pfeiffer, "Navy Could Soon Use 3D Printers to Manufacture Drones And Weapons," *Yahoo! News*, May 28, 2013, http://

news.yahoo.com/blogs/sideshow/navy-could-soon-3d-printers-manufacture-drones-weapons-183412096.html.

299. Matthew Cox, "REF's 3D Printer Spits out Fix for M249 SAW," *Kit Up!*, October 16, 2013, http://kitup.military.com/2013/10/ref-lab-builds-bipod-m249.html.

300. Bryant Jordan, "Navy Sees 3D Printing aboard Ships in Future," *Military.com*, April 8, 2014, http://www.military.com/daily-news/2014/04/08/navy-sees-3D printing-aboard-ships-in-future.html?comp=700001075741&rank=1; Evan Chavez, "Not on the Poop Deck: US Navy to Give 3D Printing Its Sea Legs," *3D Printing Industry News*, April 18, 2014, http://3dprintingindustry.com/2014/04/18/3D printing-us-navy/; Sydney Freedberg Jr., "Navy Warship Is Taking 3D Printer to Sea: Don't Expect a Revolution," *Breaking Defense*, April 22, 2014, http://breakingdefense.com/2014/04/navy-carrier-is-taking-3d-printer-to-sea-dont-expect-a-revolution/.

301. David Sher, "The US Army Is Seriously Considering 3D Printing Food on the Front Lines," *3D Printing Industry News*, August 7, 2014, http://3dprintingindustry.com/2014/08/07/us-army-seriously-considering-3D printing-food-front-lines/?utm_sourc e=3D+Printing+Industry+Update&utm_medium=email&utm_campaign=cf2922a220-RSS_EMAIL_CAMPAIGN&utm_term=0_695d5c73dc-cf2922a220-60484669.

302. Sandra Helsel, "U.S. Army to 3D Print Skulls to Study the Effects of Shockwaves," *Inside 3D Printing*, August 6, 2014, http://www.inside3dprinting.com/arl-to-3d-print-skulls-to-study-the-effects-of-shockwaves/?utm_medium=newsletter&utm_content=more&utm_source=inside3dprintingnews.

303. Scott Grunewald, "The US Army Is Using Advanced 3D Modeling and 3D Printing Technologies to Study Brain Injuries," *3D Printing Industry News*, August 11, 2014, http://3dprintingindustry.com/2014/08/11/3d-modelling-3D printing-us-army-brain-injury/?utm_source=3D+Printing+Industry+Update&utm_medium=email&utm_campaign=3ff2d4b00c-RSS_EMAIL_CAMPAIGN&utm_term=0_695d5c73dc-3ff2d4b00c-60484669.

304. Cotteleer and Joyce, "3D Opportunity," 14, n. 22.

305. Michael Molitch-Hou, "US Army's 3D Printed Skin Near Ready for Clinical Trials," *3D Printing Industry News*; July 21, 2014, http://3dprintingindustry.com/2014/07/21/us-armys-3d-printed-skin-near-ready-clinical-trials/?utm_so.

306. Melba Kurman, "Intellectual Property in the Age of 3D Printed Manufacturing," US Congressional Briefing, August 5, 2014, Washington, DC; reprinted as Melba Kurman, "How to Build a 3D Printing Economy: Intellectual Property, Industry Standards and Consumer Safety," International Trademark Association 3D Printing/Additive Manufacturing: Cutting-Edge IP and Business Implications Course Materials, New York, March 10–11, 2015, p. 3 (INTA Course Materials).

307. "About Sols," *Sols*, http://www.sols.com/sols/about.

308. Michael Molitch-Hou, "SOLS Custom 3D Printed Insoles Introduced to over 43K Physical Therapists, " *3D Printing Industry News*, February 3, 2015, http://3dprintingindustry.com/2015/02/03/sols-custom-3D printed-insoles-introduced-43k-physical-therapists/?utm_source=3D+Printing+Industry+Update&utm_medium=email&utm_campaign=30e1dd966c-RSS_EMAIL_CAMPAIGN&utm_term=0_695d5c73dc-30e1dd966c-60484669.

309. Joseph Scott, "Ten Profiles of 3D Printer Enabled Innovators," *Inside 3D Printing Hong Kong*, August 26, 2014; *Artisan Instruments*, http://www.artisanorgans.com/; *BeastGrip*, http://www.beastgrip.com/; *MrSpeakers*, https://mrspeakers.com/mrspeakers-mad-dog-headphones/; *Lucky Bug Lures*, http://www.luckybuglures.com/lb_product_series/zombie-maxx/.

310. Rachel Park, "Going Large on 3D Printed Aerospace Parts," *3D Printing Industry News*; January 24, 2013; http://3dprintingindustry.com/2013/01/24/going-large-on-3d-printed-aerospace-parts/.

311. Juho Vesanto, "3D Printed Aston Martin DB5 Replicas," *3D Printing Industry News*; November 16, 2012; http://3dprintingindustry.com/2012/11/16/3d-printed-aston-martin-in-james-bond-skyfall/.

312. Michael Molitch-Hou, "Come See the Amazing, the Extraordinary, the Stupefying 3D Printed Car!" *3D Printing Industry News*, September 14, 2014, http://3dprintingindustry.com/2014/09/14/come-see-amazing-extraordinary-stupefying-3D printed-car/?utm_source=3D+Printing+Industry+Update&utm_medium=email&utm_campaign=dbd70f586e-RSS_EMAIL_CAMPAIGN&utm_term=0_695d5c73dc-dbd70f586e-60484669; "The Printable Car," *Popular Mechanics*, November 2014, 89.

313. "High Speed Sintering," *Loughborough University*, http://www.lboro.ac.uk/microsites/enterprise/e2hs/technology/high-speed-sintering.html.

314. David Sher, "3D Systems' 3D Printing Is Taking on Injection Molding," *3D Printing Industry News*, June 13, 2014, http://3dprintingindustry.com/2014/06/13/3d-systems-3D printing-taking-injection-molding/?utm_source=3D+Printing+Industry+Update&utm_medium=email&utm_campaign=c374fd2cea-RSS_EMAIL_CAMPAIGN&utm_term=0_695d5c73dc-c374fd2cea-60484669.

315. Staff writer, "Google's New Smartphone Will Be 3D Printed by 3D Systems," *On 3D Printing*, November 23, 2013, http://on3dprinting.com/2013/11/23/google-smartphone-project-ara-3d-printed-3d-systems/; Shane Taylor, "Google Enters 3D Printing Arena," *3D Printing Industry News*, November 28, 2013, http://3dprintingindustry.com/2013/11/28/google-enters-3d-printing-arena/?utm_source=3D+Printing+Industry+Update&utm_medium=email&utm_campaign=9681fc3441-RSS_EMAIL_CAMPAIGN&utm_term=0_695d5c73dc-9681fc3441-60484669; "High-volume, customized manufacturing becomes a reality," *3D Systems*, June 16, 2014, http://www.3dsystems.com/ru/node/6708; Staff writer, "3D Systems releases first details of high-speed 3D printing assembly line for Google's Project Ara," *3ders.org*, June 17, 2014, http://www.3ders.org/articles/20140617-3d-systems-high-speed-3d-printing-assembly-line-google-project-ara.html.

316. Gary Anderson, "The Future of 3D Printing With Terry Wohlers," *Engineering.com*, September 9, 2013, http://www.engineering.com/3DPrinting/3DPrintingArticles/ArticleID/6294/The-Future-of-3D-Printing-With-Terry-Wohlers.aspx.

317. "3D Printing Is Merged with Printed Electronics," *Optomec*, March 23, 2012, http://www.optomec.com/site/latest_news/news95.

318. Shane Taylor, "Potential Cost, Eco and Functional Benefits of 3D Printing Mobile Device Antennae," *3D Printing Industry News*, June 4, 2013, http://3dprintingindustry.com/2013/06/04/potential-cost-eco-functional-benefits-of-3D printing-mobile-device-antennae/?utm_source=3D+Printing+Industry+Update&utm_medium=email&utm_campaign=e7de0ec21e-RSS_EMAIL_CAMPAIGN&utm_term=0_695d5c73dc-e7de0ec21e-60484669.

319. Juho Vesanto, "Disney's Research On 3D Printing Technology," *3D Printing Industry News*, October 9, 2012, http://3dprintingindustry. com/2012/10/09/disneys-research-on-3Dprinting-technology/;http:// www.tctmagazine.com/additive-manufacturing/disney-3d-prints-convention-breaking-loudspeakers/.

320. *OwnFone*, http://www.ownfone.com/; David Sher, "3D Printable OwnFone Unleashes Kickstarter with Massive Line-Up and Home Printable Phone," *3D Printing Industry News*, February 9, 2015, http://3dprintingindustry.com/2015/02/09/ownfone-launches-huge-expansion-run-home-3d-printable-mobile-phone/?utm_so urce=3D+Printing+Industry+Update&utm_medium=email&utm_ campaign=1199e6513d-RSS_EMAIL_CAMPAIGN&utm_ term=0_695d5c73dc-1199e6513d-60484669.

321. Staff writer, "US Researchers Develop 3D Printed Tiny Lithium Batteries," *3ders.org*, June 19, 2013, http://www.3ders.org/ articles/20130619-us-researchers-develop-3D printed-tiny-lithium-batteries.html; "Orders of Magnitude (Length)," *Wikipedia*, http:// en.wikipedia.org/wiki/Orders_of_magnitude_(length).

322. Arjun Bharadwaj, "The Possibilities of Nanoscale Additive Manufacturing," *3D Printing Industry News*, November 20, 2013, http:// 3dprintingindustry.com/2013/11/20/possibilities-nanoscale-additive-manufacturing/?utm_source=3D+Printing+Industry+Update&u tm_medium=email&utm_campaign=7a89b101a3-RSS_EMAIL_ CAMPAIGN&utm_term=0_695d5c73dc-7a89b101a3-60484669.

323. David Savastano, "Northeastern University's NanoOPS System Makes Inroads into Nanoscale Electronics Manufacturing," *Printed Electronics Now*, May 21, 2014, http://www.printedelectronicsnow. com/articles/2014/05/northeastern-universitys-nanoops-system-makes-inro.

324. Leading Edge Forum, 24; Joshua Johnson, "Will Hybrid Additive/ Subtractive Fabrication Devices Prove to be the Key to Unlocking an Even More Successful Manufacturing Future?" *3D Printing Industry News*, November 20, 2012, http://3dprintingindustry. com/2012/11/20/hybrid-additivesubtractive-fabrication-devices-and-manufacturing-future/; Todd Grimm, "Matsuura Releases Hybrid Machine," *Engineering.com*, February 29, 2012, http://www. engineering.com/3DPrinting/3DPrintingArticles/ArticleID/4255/ Matsuura-Releases-Hybrid-Machine.aspx.

325. Scott Grunewald, "The 3D Printing VDK6000 Robotic Work Center Can Do Just about Everything, Including Making the Kitchen Sink," *3D Printing Industry News*, July 30, 2014, http://3dprintingindustry. com/2014/07/30/3D printing-vdk6000-robotic-work-center/; "VDK 6000 Robotic Cell for Metal 3D Printing and Metal Part Refurbishing," *Flexible Robotic Environment*, http://www. fresystems.com/product-vdk6000.cfm.

326. Michael Molitch-Hou, "CEO Jennifer Lewis on the Future of Electronics 3D Printing & Voxel8's Huge $12M Funding," *3D Printing Industry News*, July 24, 2015, http://3dprintingindustry. com/2015/07/24/voxel8-ceo-jennifer-lewis-on-how-12m-in-funding-will-fuel-the-future-of-electronics-3d-printing/?utm_sou rce=3D+Printing+Industry+Update&utm_medium=email&utm_ campaign=293d6d5a74-RSS_EMAIL_CAMPAIGN&utm_ term=0_695d5c73dc-293d6d5a74-60484669.

327. Sandra Helsel, "Analysis: Demand for 3D Printing Skills Soars," *Inside 3D Printing*, September 12, 2014, http://inside3dprinting. com/analysis-demand-for-3D printing-skills-soars/?utm_source= Inside%203D%20Printing%20Latest%20News&utm_ campaign=268be65f09-Inside_3D_Printing_Daily_

News_09_12_2014_9_11_2014&utm_medium=email&utm_
term=0_861dc04374-268be65f09-226645849.

328. Wohlers Report 2015, 134; staff writer, "3D Printing Predictions
for 2013," *3ders.org*, December 30, 2012; http://www.3ders.
org/articles/20121229-3D   printing-predictions-for-2013.html;
Max Raskin and Llan Kolet, "Personal 3D Printer Sales Jump
35,000% Since 2007," *Bloomberg*, October 24, 2012, http://www.
bloomberg.com/news/2012-10-24/personal-3D-printer-sales-
jump-35-000-since-2007.html.

329. Michael Molitch-Hou, "Gartner: 3D Printers to Reach 2.3 Million
Shipments Totaling $13.4 Billion Worldwide by 2018," *3D Printing
Industry News*, October 27, 2014, http://3dprintingindustry.
com/2014/10/27/2-million-3dp-shipments-by-2018/?utm_sour
ce=3D+Printing+Industry+Update&utm_medium=email&utm_
campaign=dcc84ed912-RSS_EMAIL_CAMPAIGN&utm_
term=0_695d5c73dc-dcc84ed912-60484669.

330. *Pirate Bay*, http://thepiratebay.sx/browse; Christopher Solomon,
"This Man Will Save You from the Evils of the Internet," *Popular
Mechanics*, February 2015, 87, 96; Jose Pagliery, "The Deep Web
You Don't Know About," *CNN Money*, March 10, 2014, http://
money.cnn.com/2014/03/10/technology/deep-web/index.html.

331. Michael Weinberg, "What's the Deal with Copyright and 3D
Printing?" *Public Knowledge*, January 2013, 3, https://www.
publicknowledge.org/files/What's%20the%20Deal%20with%20
Copyright_%20Final%20version2.pdf.

332. "Last Chance to Register for Our 3D Printing Webinar on July 15th,"
Smartech Markets, July 14, 2014, http://smartechpublishing.com/

news/last-chance-to-register-for-our-3D printing-webinar-on-july-15th-register-h.

333. Shane Taylor, "Mink: The MakeUp 3D Printer," *3D Printing Industry News*, May 7, 2014, http://3dprintingindustry.com/2014/05/07/mink-makeup-3d-printer/?utm_source=3D+Printing+Industry+Update &utm_medium=email&utm_campaign=a163a4c026-RSS_EMAIL_ CAMPAIGN&utm_term=0_695d5c73dc-a163a4c026-60484669; Scott Hudson and Eric Brockmeyer, "Printing Teddy Bears: A Technique for 3D Printing of Soft Interactive Objects," *Disney Research*, April 26, 2014, http://www.disneyresearch.com/project/ printed-teddy-bears/; David Sher, "Today's 3D Printeers Will Be Tomorrow's Engineers," *3D Printing Industry News*, June 16, 2014, http://3dprintingindustry.com/2014/06/16/todays-3d-printeers-will-tomorrows-engineers/?utm_source=3D+Printing+Industry +Update&utm_medium=email&utm_campaign=b578b02066-RSS_EMAIL_CAMPAIGN&utm_term=0_695d5c73dc-b578b02066-60484669.

334. *SexShop3D*, http://sexshop3d.com/; Scott Grunewald, "You Can Now Buy 3D Printable Sex Toys," *3D Printing Industry News*, August 13, 2014, http://3dprintingindustry.com/2014/08/13/can-now-buy-3d-printable-sex-toys/?utm_source=3D+Printing+Industry+Updat e&utm_medium=email&utm_campaign=8a56956e9f-RSS_EMAIL_ CAMPAIGN&utm_term=0_695d5c73dc-8a56956e9f-60484669.

335. Iain Thomson, "Study Finds Open-Source Home 3D Printer Could Save $2,000 a Year," *The Register*, August 2, 2013, http:// www.theregister.co.uk/2013/08/02/study_finds_opensource_ home_3d_printer_could_save_2000_a_year/; B. T. Wittbrodt, A. G. Glover, J. Laureto, G. C. Anzalone, D. Oppliger, J. L. Irwin, and J. M. Pearce, "Life-Cycle Economic Analysis of Distributed Manufacturing with Open-Source 3D Printers," *Academia. edu*, June 2, 2013, http://www.academia.edu/4067796/

Life-Cycle_Economic_Analysis_of_Distributed_Manufacturing_
with_Open-Source_3D_Printers.

336. Gary Anderson, "The Future of 3D Printing with Terry Wohlers,"
Engineering.com, September 9, 2013, http://www.engineering.
com/3DPrinting/3DPrintingArticles/ArticleID/6294/The-Future-of-
3D-Printing-With-Terry-Wohlers.aspx.

337. Scott Kirsner, "A 3D Printer in Every Home?," *BostonGlobe.com*,
October 20, 2013, http://www.bostonglobe.com/business/
2013/10/19/printer-every-home/ttvYYbjw6zHxb0YrScn6mJ/story.
html; Dave Johnson, "3D Printing: Don't Believe the Hype,"
CBSNews.com, June 21, 2013, http://www.cbsnews.com/8301-
505143_162-57590222/; Lipson and Kurman, *Fabricated*, 40.

338. Dr. Jon Harrop, "The Fastest Growing Sectors in 3D Printing for
2015," *IDTechEx*, February 5, 2015, http://www.idtechex.com/
research/articles/the-fastest-growing-sectors-in-3D printing-for-2015-
00007399.asp?donotredirect=true.

339. Scott Dunham, "Asia's Mixed Signals on 3D Printing," *3D
Printing Industry News*, July 5, 2013, http://3dprintingindustry.
com/2013/07/05/asias-mixed-signals-on-3D printing/; Lance
Whitney, "iPhone 6 Demand Challenges Apple Supplier Foxconn,"
CNET Magazine, September 17, 2014, http://www.cnet.com/news/
iphone-6-demand-challenges-apple-supplier-foxconn/.

340. Staff writer, "3D Printer Value Samsung Electronics Not Hurrying
in 3D Printer Business," *Business Korea*, October 7, 2014, http://
www.businesskorea.co.kr/article/6659/3d-printer-value-samsung-
electronics-not-hurrying-3d-printer-business.

341. "Ken Olsen," *Wikipedia*, http://en.wikipedia.org/wiki/Ken_Olsen;
Strohmeyer, "The 7 Worst Tech Predictions."

342. "It'll Never Work," https://www.lhup.edu/~dsimanek/neverwrk. htm; "Things People Said: Bad Predictions," *Rinkworks*, http:// www.rinkworks.com/said/predictions.shtml; "Lord Kelvin," *Zapatopi*, December 14, 2008, http://zapatopi.net/kelvin/quotes/; Strohmeyer, "The 7 Worst Tech Predictions"; "Darryl F. Zanuck," *Wikipedia*, http://en.wikipedia.org/wiki/Darryl_F._Zanuck; Ashley Lutz, "20 Predictions from Smart People That Were Completely Wrong," *Business Insider*, May 2, 2012, http://www.businessinsider. com/false-predictons-2012-5?op=1; "Worst Predictions," *Human Science*, http://humanscience.wikia.com/wiki/Worst_Predictions.

343. Jelmer Luimstra, "Disney: '3D Printer in Every Home within a Decade,'" *3D Printing.com*, October 31, 2013, http://3dprinting. com/news/disney-3d-printer-every-home-within-decade/.

344. Wohlers Report 2014, 99.

345. Shane Taylor, "HP 3DP?," *3D Printing Industry News*, October 24, 2013, http://3dprintingindustry.com/2013/10/24/hp-3dp/.

346. Kurman, "Intellectual Property in the Age of 3D," 2.

347. Shane Taylor, "Home Metal 3D Printer: The Mini Metal Maker," *3D Printing Industry News*, November 18, 2013, http://3dprintingindustry.com/2013/11/18/home-metal-3d-printer-mini-metal-maker/?utm_source=3D+Printing+Industry+Update &utm_medium=email&utm_campaign=8fc8bf58de-RSS_EMAIL_ CAMPAIGN&utm_term=0_695d5c73dc-8fc8bf58de-60484669.

348. Marcia Goodrich, "Scientists Build a Low-Cost, Open-Source 3D Metal Printer," *Michigan Tech News*, December 19, 2013, http:// www.mtu.edu/news/stories/2013/november/scientists-build-low-cost-open-source-3d-metal-printer.html.

349. Kyle Maxey, "Liquid Metal 3D Printing," *Engineering.com*, July 11, 2013, http://www.engineering.com/3DPrinting/3DPrintingArticles/ArticleID/5988/Liquid-Metal-3D-Printing.aspx.

350. Soulskill, "New 3D Printer Can Print with Carbon Fiber," *Slashdot*, January 28, 2014, http://classic.slashdot.org/story/14/01/28/2351239; "MarkForged," www.markforged.com.

351. Scott Grunewald, "Five Color, Five Material 3D Printer RoVa3D Fully Funds on Kickstarter," *3D Printing Industry News*, July 2, 2014, http://3dprintingindustry.com/2014/07/02/five-color-five-material-3d-printer-rova3d-fully-funds-kickstarter/?utm_source=3D+Printing+Industry+Update&utm_medium=email&utm_campaign=6bcb50d3eb-RSS_EMAIL_CAMPAIGN&utm_term=0_695d5c73dc-6bcb50d3eb-604846695.

352. "Argentum," *Cartesian Co.*, http://www.cartesianco.com/product/the-argentum/.

353. "Fabtotum," *Indiegogo*, https://www.indiegogo.com/projects/fabtotum-personal-fabricator.

354. McKinsey Report, see graphics in opening pages.

355. Gary Anderson, "The Voxeljet (VJET) IPO Primer: The Company with a Little 'v' Could Make a Big Splash," *3DPrintingStocks.com*, October 1, 2013, http://3dprintingstocks.com/voxeljet-ipo-primer/; Rachel Park, "Unsurprisingly, Wohlers Report 2013 Reveals Continued Growth in 3D Printing," *3D Printing Industry News*, May 24, 2013, http://3dprintingindustry.com/2013/05/24/unsurprisingly-wohlers-report-2013-reveals-continued-growth-in-3D printing/; Wohlers Report 2015, 120.

356. Gershenfeld, "How to Make Almost Anything," 51–52.

357. "Bill Gates," *Brainy Quote*, http://www.brainyquote.com/quotes/quotes/b/billgates404193.html.

358. Molitch-Hou, "Consumer 3D Printing More than 5 Years Away"; "Gartner's Hype Cycle Special Report for 2014," *Gartner*, August 14, 2014, https://www.gartner.com/doc/2816917.

359. McKinsey Report, 110.

360. IBM Report, 5.

361. Ibid., 4.

362. Daniel L. Cohen; "Fostering Mainstream Adoption of Industrial 3D Printing: Understanding the Benefits and Promoting Organizational Readiness;" *3D Printing and Additive Manufacturing;* Vol. 1, No. 2, 2014, p. 66.

363. IBM Report, 11.

364. Staff writer, "Google's New Smartphone Will Be 3D Printed by 3D Systems," *On 3D Printing*, November 23, 2013, http://on3dprinting.com/2013/11/23/google-smartphone-project-ara-3d-printed-3d-systems/.

365. Nick Statt, "Transformers, Meet 3D printing: Hasbro and 3D Systems Team Up," *Cnet*, February 14, 2014, http://www.cnet.com/news/transformers-meet-3D printing-hasbro-and-3d-systems-team-up/.

366. Rachel Park, "3D Printing Big Brands On-Demand, Under License via Shapeways," *3D Printing Industry News*, July 21, 22014,

http://3dprintingindustry.com/2014/07/21/3D printing-big-brands-demand-license-via-shapeways/?utm_source=3D+Printing+Industry+Update&utm_medium=email&utm_campaign=c0500effde-RSS_EMAIL_CAMPAIGN&utm_term=0_695d5c73dc-c0500effde-60484669; Michael Molitch-Hou, "Almost All of Your, Our, My Little Ponies 3D Printable Thru Shapeways," *3D Printing Industry News*, October 18, 2014, http://3dprintingindustry.com/2014/10/18/almost-little-ponies-3d-printable-thru-shapeways/?utm_source=3D+Printing+Industry+Update&utm_medium=email&utm_campaign=63bc59c616-RSS_EMAIL_CAMPAIGN&utm_term=0_695d5c73dc-63bc59c616-60484669.

367. "Hasbro to Start Selling 3D printed Transformers," *Chameleon Toys for You*, August 18, 2014, http://toptoys2012.com/hasbro-to-start-selling-3D printed-transformers-scrabble-and-monopoly/; Scott Grunewald, "Shapeways & Hasbro Let Fans Sell Fan-Made Transformers and My Little Pony Products on SuperFanArt," *3D Printing Industry News*, August 28, 2014, http://3dprintingindustry.com/2014/08/28/shapeways-hasbro-let-fans-sell-fan-made-transformers-little-pony-products-superfanart/?utm_source=3D+Printing+Industry+Update&utm_medium=email&utm_campaign=4a0960bf1b-RSS_EMAIL_CAMPAIGN&utm_term=0_695d5c73dc-4a0960bf1b-60484669.

368. Scott Grunewald, "Yes, You Can 3D Print a Copy of Your Phallus," *3D Printing Industry News*, August 18, 2014, http://3dprintingindustry.com/2014/08/18/yes-can-3d-print-copy-phallus/?utm_source=3D+Printing+Industry+Update&utm_medium=email&utm_campaign=0bba049398-RSS_EMAIL_CAMPAIGN&utm_term=0_695d5c73dc-0bba049398-60484669.

369. *SexShop3D*, http://sexshop3d.com/; Scott Grunewald, "You Can Now Buy 3D Printable Sex Toys," *3D Printing Industry News*, August

13, 2014, http://3dprintingindustry.com/2014/08/13/can-now-buy-3d-printable-sex-toys/?utm_source=3D+Printing+Industry+Updat e&utm_medium=email&utm_campaign=8a56956e9f-RSS_EMAIL_CAMPAIGN&utm_term=0_695d5c73dc-8a56956e9f-60484669; Scott Grunewald, "New "Dildo Generator" Lets You Design your Own 3D Printed Sex Toys, *3D Printing Industry News*, June 13, 2014, http://3dprintingindustry.com/2014/06/13/new-dildo-generator-lets-design-3d-printed-sex-toys/?utm_source=3D+Printing+Indu stry+Update&utm_medium=email&utm_campaign=c374fd2cea-RSS_EMAIL_CAMPAIGN&utm_term=0_695d5c73dc-c374fd2cea-60484669.

370. "3D Me," *3D Systems Cubify.com*, http://cubify.com/en/Store/DDDme.

371. Steve Miller, "Star Wars—D-Tech Me Experience Returns to Star Wars Weekends at Disney's Hollywood Studios Starting May 17, 2013," *Disney Parks Blog*, May 6, 2013, http://disneyparks.disney.go.com/blog/2013/05/star-wars-d-tech-me-experience-returns-to-star-wars-weekends-at-disneys-hollywood-studios-starting-may-17-2013/; "3D Print Your Little Princess on to a Disney Princess," *3D Printer*, August 28, 2012, http://www.3dprinter.net/disney-d-tech-me-princess.

372. *Petfig*, http://petfig-en.3dwave.net/.

373. *OwnFone*, http://www.ownfone.com/.

374. Anderson, *The New Industrial Revolution*, 72.

375. Michael Molitch-Hou, "The Future of Footwear: 3D Printed Shoes that React to Your Movements," *3D Printing Industry News*,

February 16, 2015, http://3dprintingindustry.com/2015/02/16/future-footwear-3D printed-shoes-react-movements/.

376. "Topology Optimization," *Wikipedia*, http://en.wikipedia.org/wiki/Topology_optimization.

377. Staff writer, "Construction Steelwork Makes Its 3D Printing Premiere," *Engineering.com*, June 6, 2014, http://www.engineering.com/3DPrinting/3DPrintingArticles/ArticleID/7720/Construction-Steelwork-Makes-its-3D   printing-Premiere.aspx; Sandra Helsel, "Arup Uses 3D Printing to Create Tensegrity-Inspired Structural Bridge Parts," *Inside 3D Printing*, August 13, 2014, http://inside3dprinting.com/arup-uses-3D printing-to-create-tensegrity-inspired-structural-bridge-parts/.

378. Michael Molitch-Hou, "Airbus 3D Printed Components to Launch on Next UK Satellite," *3D Printing Industry News*, March 19, 2015, http://3dprintingindustry.com/2015/03/19/airbus-3D   printed-components-to-launch-on-next-uk-satellite/?utm_source=3D+Printing+Industry+Update&utm_medium=email&utm_campaign=3825d4b91c-RSS_EMAIL_CAMPAIGN&utm_term=0_695d5c73dc-3825d4b91c-60484669.

379. McKinsey Report, 108.

380. Staff writer, "3D Printed Customized Joint Replacement—Mayo Clinic," *3D Printing Industry News*, April 21, 2013, http://3dprintingindustry.com/2013/04/21/3D printed-customized-joint-replacement-mayo-clinic/?utm_source=3D+Printing+Industry+Update&utm_medium=email&utm_campaign=596e1d60bb-RSS_EMAIL_CAMPAIGN; Wohlers Report 2014, 19.

381. Rachel Park, "Researching Breast Implant Improvements Using 3DP," *3D Printing Industry News*, April 26, 2013, http://3dprintingindustry.com/2013/04/26/researching-breast-implant-improvements-using-3dp/.

382. Tiago Cordeiro, "As impressoras 3D que importam (3D Printers That Matter)," *Galileu (Galileo Magazine)*, August 23, 2014, http://revistagalileu.globo.com/Revista/noticia/2014/08/impressoras-3d-que-importam.html.

383. Ibid.

384. Tyler Koslow, "Starers Beware! This 3D Printed Garment Knows When You're Looking at It," *3D Printing Industry News*, October 5, 2015, http://3dprintingindustry.com/2015/10/05/starers-beware-this-3d-printed-garment-knows-when-youre-looking-at-it/?utm_source=3D+Printing+Industry+Update&utm_medium=email&utm_campaign=b1bbb1fc77-RSS_EMAIL_CAMPAIGN&utm_term=0_695d5c73dc-b1bbb1fc77-60484669.

385. Wohlers Report 2014, 209.

386. Sandrine Ceustemont, "3D printed Bionic Ants Team Up to Get the Job Done," *New Scientist Tech*, March 26, 2015, http://www.newscientist.com/article/dn27248-3dprinted-bionic-ants-team-up-to-get-the-job-done.html?utm_source=Daily+3D+Printing+News&utm_campaign=31782305dc-Latest_3D_Printing_News_04_02_2015_4_2_2015&utm_medium=email&utm_term=0_861dc04374-31782305dc-226645849#.VSBN9p3D_rf; Sandra Helsel, "3D printed Artificial Ants Designed for Work in Factories of the Future," *Inside 3D Printing*, April 2, 2015, http://inside3dprinting.com/3D printed-artificial-ants-designed-for-work-in-factories-of-the-future/.

387. Sandra Helsel, "Roboticists Create Swarm of 3D printed Fish-Like Robots," *Inside 3D Printing*, June 8, 2015, *http://inside3dprinting. com/roboticists-create-swarm-of-3D printed-fish-like-robots-that-swarm/*; "Collective Cognitive Robots," *Artificial Life Laboratory, Graz, Austria, http://zool33.uni-graz.at/artlife/cocoro.*

388. Tyler Koslow, "3D Printed Micro-Fish to Explore the Oceans of Our Bodies," *3D Printing Industry News*, August 31, 2015, http://3dprintingindustry.com/2015/08/31/3d-printed-micro-fish-to-explore-the-oceans-of-our-bodies/?utm_source=3 D+Printing+Industry+Update&utm_medium=email&utm_ campaign=a215f7c7a5-RSS_EMAIL_CAMPAIGN&utm_ term=0_695d5c73dc-a215f7c7a5-60484669.

389. Cotteleer and Joyce, "3D Opportunity," 15.

390. Seepersad, "Challenges and Opportunities," 10.

391. Steven Ashley, "Flying on Flexible Wings," *Scientific American*, Nov. 2003, 84, 86.

392. Michael Molitch-Hou, "The Cavity Skateboard: Printed in One Single Piece," *3D Printing Industry News*, December 20, 2013, http://3dprintingindustry.com/2013/12/20/cavity-skateboard-printed-one-single-piece/?utm_source=3D+Printing+Industry+ Update&utm_medium=email&utm_campaign=0aff416389-RSS_EMAIL_CAMPAIGN&utm_term=0_695d5c73dc-0aff416389-60484669; David Sher, "Futuristic Tennis Racket 3D Printed by CRP to Jumpstart Italian Creativity," *3D Printing Industry News*, November 17, 2014, http://3dprintingindustry.com/2014/11/17/tennis-racket-3D printed-crp/?utm_source=3D+Printing+Industry+Update&u tm_medium=email&utm_campaign=20b8bd2289-RSS_EMAIL_ CAMPAIGN&utm_term=0_695d5c73dc-20b8bd2289-60484669.

393. David Sher, "Pensar Development's 3D Printed DNA Shoe Will Make You Think about the Possibilities," *3D Printing Industry News*, September 30, 2014, http://3dprintingindustry.com/2014/09/30/pensar-developments-3D printed-dna-shoe-will-make-think-possibilities/?utm_source=3D+Printing+Industry+Update&utm_medium=email&utm_campaign=ecb4b2e78b-RSS_EMAIL_CAMPAIGN&utm_term=0_695d5c73dc-ecb4b2e78b-60484669.

394. Evan Chavez, "Stunning 3D Printed Speakers from Akemake Reflect the Nature That Inspired Designs," *3D Printing Industry News*, July 3, 2014, http://3dprintingindustry.com/2014/07/03/stunning-3D printed-speakers-akemake-reflect-nature-inspired-designs/?utm_source=3D+Printing+Industry+Update&utm_medium=email&utm_campaign=e3db0db805-RSS_EMAIL_CAMPAIGN&utm_term=0_695d5c73dc-e3db0db805-60484669.

395. David Sher, "Biomimicry Inspired Soft Seat Makes Comfortable Seating More Natural," *3D Printing Industry News*, August 13, 2014, http://3dprintingindustry.com/2014/08/13/biomimicry-inspired-soft-seat-makes-comfortable-seating-natural/?utm_source=3D+Printing+Industry+Update&utm_medium=email&utm_campaign=8a56956e9f-RSS_EMAIL_CAMPAIGN&utm_term=0_695d5c73dc-8a56956e9f-60484669; "Biomimicry: 3D Printed Soft Seat," *Lilian van Daal*, http://lilianvandaal.com/?portfolio=3D printed-softseating.

396. "Biomimetics," *Wikipedia*, http://en.wikipedia.org/wiki/Biomimetics.

397. Fatima Qasim, "Technology Imitates Nature: the Brave New World of 3D Printing," *World Trademark Review* 54 (April/May 2015): 48.

398. Patrick Benjamin, "On 3D Printing Chairs: Plato vs. Cthulhu," *3D Printing Industry News*, February 25, 2014, http://3dprintingindustry.

com/2014/02/25/3D printing-chairs-plato-vs-cthulhu/?utm_sou rce=3D+Printing+Industry+Update&utm_medium=email&utm_ campaign=91f70e8d4a-RSS_EMAIL_CAMPAIGN&utm_ term=0_695d5c73dc-91f70e8d4a-60484669; *Maximoriera.com*, http://www.maximoriera.com/.

399. Andrew Wheeler, "MONAD's 3D Printed Electric Violin: Terrifyingly Cool," *3D Printing Industry News*, April 7, 2015, http://3dprintingindustry.com/2015/04/07/monads-3D printed-electric-violin-terrifyingly-cool/?utm_source=3D+Printing+Indust ry+Update&utm_medium=email&utm_campaign=489ab97152-RSS_EMAIL_CAMPAIGN&utm_term=0_695d5c73dc-489ab97152-60484669.

400. Staff writer, "Futuristic EDAG Genesis 3D Printed Car World Premiere at 2014 Geneva Motor Show," *3Ders.org*, March 4, 2014, http://www.3ders.org/articles/20140304-futuristic-edag-genesis-3D printed-car-world-premiere-at-2014-geneva-motor-show.html.

401. Tina Casey, "New 'WaterBone' Lightweight Vehicle Design Could Increase EV Battery Range," *Clean Technica*, April 27, 2015, https:// cleantechnica.com/2015/04/27/new-waterbone-lightweight-vehicle-design-increase-ev-battery-range/?utm_source=Daily+ 3D+Printing+News&utm_campaign=b866e39153-Latest_3D_ Printing_News_04_28_2015_4_27_2015&utm_medium=email&utm_ term=0_861dc04374-b866e39153-226645849.

402. "Fact Sheet: 3D Printed Faucets from DXV by American Standard," *Webwire*, June 5, 2015, http://www.webwire.com/ViewPressRel. asp?aId=198107.

403. "Bionic Handling Assistant—Flexible and Compliant Movement," *Festo*, http://www.festo.com/cms/en_corp/9655.htm.

404. Evan Ackerman, "Festo Launches SmartBird Robotic Seagull," *IEEE Spectrum*, March 24, 2011, http://spectrum.ieee.org/automaton/robotics/industrial-robots/festo-launches-incredibly-lifelike-smartbird.

405. Alec, "3D Printed 'Robobird,' A Robotic Bird of Prey That Will Keep Airports and Farms Bird-Free," *3ders.org*, September 8, 2014, http://www.3ders.org/articles/20140908-3D printed-robird-a-robotic-bird-of-prey-that-will-keep-airports-and-farms-bird-free.html?utm_source=Inside+3D+Printing+Latest+News&utm_campaign=f5f6f090c6-Inside_3D_Printing_Daily_News_09_10_2014_9_9_2014&utm_medium=email&utm_term=0_861dc04374-f5f6f090c6-226645849.

406. Staff writer, "Self-Repairing Trainers 3D printed from Biological Cells by Shamees Aden," *Dezeen Magazine*, December 11, 2013, http://www.dezeen.com/2013/12/11/3D printed-trainers-synthetic-biology-protocells-shamees-aden-wearable-futures/.

407. Staff writer, "World's First 3D Printed Photosynthetic Wearable Embedded with Living Matter Unveiled at TED2015," *TCT Magazine*, May 13, 2015, http://www.tctmagazine.com/prsnlz/worlds-first-3D printed-photosynthetic-wearable-ted-2015/.

408. Joshua A. Kirsch, "Biomemetics," *Popular Mechanics*, July/August 2014, 22.

409. Thomas A. Campbell, Skylar Tibbits, and Banning Garrett, "The Programmable World," *Scientific American*, November 2014, 62.

410. Staff writer, "BAE Systems Debuts Futuristic 3D Printed Aircraft Concepts," *Engineering.com*, July 7, 2014, http://www.engineering.

com/3DPrinting/3DPrintingArticles/ArticleID/7964/BAE-Systems-Debuts-Futuristic-3D printed-Aircraft-Concepts.aspx.

411. Jonny Rowntree, "What Does The Future Hold For 3D Printing & 4D Printing?," *3DPrint.com,* August 31, 2014, http://3dprint.com/13472/3d-printing-future/; Thomas A. Campbell, Skylar Tibbits, Banning Garrett, "The Programmable World," *Scientific American,* November 2014, p. 62; Sarah Zhang, "Scientists 3D Printed Self-Assembling Wood and Carbon Fiber," *Gizmodo,* October 14, 2014, http://gizmodo.com/scientists-3d-printed-self-assembling-wood-and-carbon-f-1646263682?utm_source=Inside+3D+Printing+Latest+News&utm_campaign=dfc8793cb5-Latest_3D_Printing_News_10_17_2014&utm_medium=email&utm_term=0_861dc04374-dfc8793cb5-226645849.

412. Bauke Stelma, "Adding the Fourth Dimension to 3D Printing," *Extreme Tech,* May 14, 2015, http://www.extremetech.com/extreme/206368-adding-the-fourth-dimension-to-3D printing?utm_source=Daily+3D+Printing+News&utm_campaign=eb35791fce-Latest_3D_Printing_News_05_27_2015_5_27_2015&utm_medium=email&utm_term=0_861dc04374-eb35791fce-226645849.

413. "Entering a New Dimension: 4D Printing," *University of Pittsburgh*, September 30, 2013, http://www.news.pitt.edu/news/entering-new-dimension-4d-printing.

414. Rachel Park, "Are You Ready for This...4D Printing Is on the Way," *3D Printing Industry News,* February 27, 2013, http://3dprintingindustry.com/2013/02/27/are-you-ready-for-this-4d-printing-is-on-the-way/; Tuan Nguyen, "The Next Big Thing: 4D Printing," *The Bulletin,* February 28, 2013, http://www.smartplanet.com/blog/bulletin/the-next-big-thing-4d-printing/13898; Skylar Tibbitts, "The Emergence of 4D Printing," TED talk, February 2013, http://

www.ted.com/talks/skylar_tibbits_the_emergence_of_4d_printing. html?utm_source=newsletter_daily&utm_campaign=daily&utm_ medium=email&utm_content=image__2013-04-04; Ben Rooney, "If You Think 3D Printing Is Disruptive, Wait for 4D," *Wall Street Journal Tech Europe*, July 30, 2013, http://blogs.wsj.com/tech-europe/2013/07/30/if-you-think-3D printing-is-disruptive-wait-for-4d/; "4D Printing Project, *Stratasys*, "http://www.stratasys.com/industries/education/4d-printing-project; Donna Taylor, "Move Over 3D Printing: Self-Assembling 4D-Printed Materials Are on the Way; *Gizmag*," June 3, 2013, http://www.gizmag.com/4d-printing-self-assembly/27734/; Shane Taylor, "Funding to Explore & Develop 4D Printing Materials," *3D Printing Industry News*, October 8, 2013; http://3dprintingindustry.com/2013/10/08/funding-explore-develop-4d-printed-materials/?utm_source=3D+Printing+Indus try+Update&utm_medium=email&utm_campaign=a7fc82d720-RSS_EMAIL_CAMPAIGN&utm_term=0_695d5c73dc-a7fc82d720-60484669; Eujin Pei, "4D Printing: A Paradigm Shift in Additive Manufacture," *3D Printing Industry News*, July 4, 2014, http://3dprintingindustry.com/2014/07/04/4d-printing-paradigm-shift-additive-manufacture/?utm_source=3D+Printing+Industr y+Update&utm_medium=email&utm_campaign=365d43f7e8-RSS_EMAIL_CAMPAIGN&utm_term=0_695d5c73dc-365d43f7e8-60484669.

415. Sarah Rich, "Aircraft Design Inspired by Nature and Enabled by Tech," *Smithsonian.com*, August 16, 2012, http://www.smithsonianmag.com/arts-culture/aircraft-design-inspired-by-nature-and-enabled-by-tech-25222971/?no-ist.

416. Cohen, "Fostering Mainstream Adoption of Industrial 3D Printing," 65.

417. "The Future by Airbus," *Airbus*, 2011, 18, http://www.airbus.com/presscentre/corporate-information/key-documents/?eID=dam_frontend_push&docID=16457.

418. Sarah Griffiths, "Flights of Fancy! Designer Paints Concept Airplanes Inspired by Dinosaurs, Dolphins and Even Chickens—But Could They Ever Fly?," *DailyMail.com*, April 16, 2014, http://www.dailymail.co.uk/sciencetech/article-2605934/Flights-fancy-Designer-paints-concept-airplanes-inspired-dinosaurs-dolphins-chickens-sky.html.

419. Steve Hargreaves, "Counterfeit Goods Becoming More Dangerous," *CNN Money*, September 27, 2012, http://money.cnn.com/2012/09/27/news/economy/counterfeit-goods/.

420. Jayne O'Donnell, "Counterfeit Products Are a Growing, and Dangerous, Problem," *USA Today, June 6, 2012,* http://usatoday30.usatoday.com/money/perfi/columnist/odonnell/story/2012-06-01/confident-consumer-jayne-odonnell/55406774/1.

421. Staff writer, "NASA Identifies Counterfeiting as One of Greatest Challenges," *PCB Design 007*, November 6, 2012, http://www.pcbdesign007.com/pages/zone.cgi?a=87719&artpg=1.

422. Connor M. McNulty, Neyla Arnas, and Thomas A. Campbell, "Toward the Printed World: Additive Manufacturing and Implications for National Security," *Defense Horizons National Defense University*, September 2012, 10.

423. John Cheek, "3D Printing: IP Challenges Ahead," IPO webinar, March 25, 2013, http://www.ipo.org/index.php/2013/03/3D printing-ip-challenges-ahead/.

424. *Applied DNA Sciences*, http://www.adnas.com/.

425. "Accessible Text from GAO Report No. GAO-10-389," US Government Accountability Office, April 29, 2010, http://www.gao.gov/assets/310/302318.html.

426. "Defense Logistics Agency Requires DNA Marking to Combat Counterfeit Parts," *Defense Logistics Agency PR Newswire*, October 31, 2012, http://www.prnewswire.com/news-releases/defense-logistics-agency-requires-dna-marking-to-combat-counterfeit-parts-176623411.html.

427. Clara Guibourg, "DNA New 'Protection' against Copper Thieves," *The Local*, June 3, 2012, http://www.adnas.com/sites/default/files/sweden-copper-june-2012.pdf; "CustoMerQ Botanical DNA Ink to Protect Sekiaji and Sekisaba Fish in Japan," *Applied DNA Sciences via Yahoo! Finance*, February 14, 2014, http://finance.yahoo.com/news/customerq-botanical-dna-ink-protect-133000203.html; "Applied DNA Sciences Partners With UK Metropolitan Police Service to Combat Crime in London," *Applied DNA Sciences via Yahoo! Finance*, December 21, 2012, http://finance.yahoo.com/news/applied-dna-sciences-partners-uk-133000103.html.

428. "The SigNature DNA Difference: The Premier Anticounterfeiting and Law Enforcement Solution," *Applied DNA Science*, http://www.adnas.com/products/the-signature-dna-difference.

429. Ibid.

430. "Quantum Dot," *Wikipedia*, http://en.wikipedia.org/wiki/Quantum_dot.

431. Michael Molitch-Hou, "Quantum Dots to Hinder 3D Printed Counterfeits," *3D Printing Industry News*, July 1, 2014, http://3dprintingindustry.com/2014/07/01/quantum-dots-hinder-3D printed-counterfeits/?utm_source=3D+Printing+Industry+Update&utm_medium=email&utm_campaign=6a78ebc918-RSS_EMAIL_CAMPAIGN&utm_term=0_695d5c73dc-6a78ebc918-60484669.

432. Deven R. Desai and Gerard Magliocca, "Patents, Meet Napster: 3D Printing and the Digitalization of Things," 102 Geo. L.J. 1691, October 9, 2013, 42–45, http://papers.ssrn.com/sol3/papers.cfm?abstract_id=2338067.

433. Kurman, "Carrots, Not Sticks," 49.

434. Rachel Park, "Cody Wilson Unveils the 'Fully' 3D Printed Gun to Andy Greenberg at *Forbes*," *3D Printing Industry News*, May 4, 2013, http://3dprintingindustry.com/2013/05/04/cody-wilson-unveils-the-fully-3D printed-gun-to-andy-greenberg-at-forbes/?utm_source=3D+Printing+Industry+Update&utm_medium=email&utm_campaign=4c09d6471c-RSS_EMAIL_CAMPAIGN&utm_term=0_695d5c73dc-4c09d6471c-60484669.

435. Andy Greenberg, "3D Printed Gun's Blueprints Downloaded 100,000 Times in Two Days (with Some Help from Kim Dotcom)," *Forbes*, May 8, 2013, http://www.forbes.com/sites/andygreenberg/2013/05/08/3D printed-guns-blueprints-downloaded-100000-times-in-two-days-with-some-help-from-kim-dotcom/.

436. David Sher, "Them Crazy (Japanese) Cowboys Have Gone and Done It Again," *3D Printing Industry News*, February 19, 2014, http://3dprintingindustry.com/2014/02/19/crazy-japanese-

cowboys-gone-done/?utm_source=3D+Printing+Industry+Update &utm_medium=email&utm_campaign=b38eee45d8-RSS_EMAIL_ CAMPAIGN&utm_term=0_695d5c73dc-b38eee45d8-60484669.

437. Michael Molitch-Hou, "Japanese 3D Printed Gun Maker Sentenced to Two Years," *3D Printing Industry News*, October 20, 2014, http://3dprintingindustry.com/2014/10/20/japanese-3D printed-gun-maker-sentenced-two-years/.

438. Michael Molitch-Hou, "AR-15 with 3D Printed Lower Receiver Seized in Oregon," *3D Printing Industry News*, June 29, 2015, http://3dprintingindustry.com/2015/06/29/ar-15-with-3D printed-lower-receiver-seized-in-oregon/?utm_source=3D+Printing+Ind ustry+Update&utm_medium=email&utm_campaign=f00f9af6fe-RSS_EMAIL_CAMPAIGN&utm_term=0_695d5c73dc-f00f9af6fe-60484669.

439. Section 922(p)(1) of Title 18 of the United States Code (2006) makes it illegal to make or possess any gun that is undetectable by an airport metal detector or that is not visible to an airport x-ray machine; Nora Engstrom, "3D Printing and Product Liability: Identifying the Obstacles," *University of Pennsylvania Law Review* 162, no. 36 (n.d.), n. 7 2013, http://papers.ssrn.com/sol3/papers. cfm?abstract_id=2347757.

440. "World's First 3D Printed Metal Gun Manufactured by Solid Concepts," *Solid Concepts*, https://www.solidconcepts.com/news-releases/ worlds-first-3D printed-metal-gun-manufactured-solid-concepts/.

441. Alyssa Parkinson, "1911 3D Printed Guns Will Sell to Lucky 100," *Solid Concepts Blog*, December 19, 2013, https://blog.solidconcepts. com/industry-highlights/1911-3D printed-guns-will-sell-lucky-100/.

442. Michael Molitch-Hou, "AR-15 with 3D Printed Lower Receiver Seized in Oregon," *3D Printing Industry News,* June 29, 2015, http://3dprintingindustry.com/2015/06/29/ar-15-with-3d-printed-lower-receiver-seized-in-oregon/?utm_source=3D+Printing+Ind ustry+Update&utm_medium=email&utm_campaign=f00f9af6fe-RSS_EMAIL_CAMPAIGN&utm_term=0_695d5c73dc-f00f9af6fe-60484669.

443. Alyssa Parkinson, "1911 3D Printed Guns Will Sell to Lucky 100," *Solid Concepts Blog,* December 19, 2013, https://blog.solidconcepts.com/industry-highlights/1911-3d-printed-guns-will-sell-lucky-100/.

444. David Sher, "3D Printed Guns Take First Victim: Internet Freedom in Australia," *3D Printing Industry News*, May 26, 2014, http://3dprintingindustry.com/2014/05/26/3D printed-guns-take-first-victim-internet-freedom-australia/?utm_source =3D+Printing+Industry+Update&utm_medium=email&utm_ campaign=b61ffc12e6-RSS_EMAIL_CAMPAIGN&utm_ term=0_695d5c73dc-b61ffc12e6-60484669; Alec, "'Ghost Gun' Bill SB 808 on 3D Printed Guns Passed in California, Now Heads to Governor," *3ders.org*, September 1, 2014, http://www.3ders.org/articles/20140901-ghost-gun-bill-sb-808-on-3D printed-guns-passed-in-california-now-heads-to-governor.html.

445. Zack Epstein, "3D Printing Used To Make First Real Handheld Railgun, Which Fires Plasma Projectiles at 560 mph," *Yahoo! Tech*, October 19, 2015, https://www.yahoo.com/tech/s/3d-printing-used-first-real-handheld-railgun-fires-134325053.html.

446. Nick Leghorn, "Hands on With America's First 3D-Printed Metal Silencer," *TheTruthAboutGuns.com*, April 6, 2015, http://www.thetruthaboutguns.com/2015/04/foghorn/hands-on-worlds-first-3d-printed-metal-silencer/.

447. Staff writer, "Man Uses 3D-Printed Gun to Kill His Wife in 'Elementary,'" *3ders.org*, January 11, 2014, http://www.3ders.org/articles/20140111-man-uses-3D printed-gun-to-kill-his-wife-in-elementary.html.

448. Martin Evans, "'3D Printed Gun' Discovered by Police," *Telegraph* (London), October 25, 2013, http://www.telegraph.co.uk/news/uknews/crime/10403432/3D printed-gun-discovered-by-police.html.

449. Michael Molitch-Hou, "Aussie Police Raid Home Stocked with Cannabis, Rifle, and 3D Printed Weaponry," *3D Printing Industry News*, February 10, 2015, http://3dprintingindustry.com/2015/02/10/aussie-police-raid-home-stocked-cannabis-rifle-3D printed-weaponry/?utm_source=3D+Printing+Industry+Update&utm_medium=email&utm_campaign=243ab29f7f-RSS_EMAIL_CAMPAIGN&utm_term=0_695d5c73dc-243ab29f7f-60484669.

450. Lipson and Kurman, *Fabricated*, 220.

451. Staff writer, "3D Printing Could Revolutionize War and Foreign Policy," *Space Daily,* January 5, 2015, http://www.spacedaily.com/reports/How_3D_printing_could_revolutionise_war_and_foreign_policy_999.html.

452. Staff writer, "Watch Out Police! 3D Printed Handcuffs Keys Have Arrived," *3D Printing Industry News*, July 19, 2012, http://3dprintingindustry.com/2012/07/19/watch-out-police-3D printed-handcuffs-keys-have-arrived/.

453. Gershenfeld, "How to Make Almost Anything," 53.

454. Michael Molitch-Hou, "3D Printed Skeleton Key Software to Open Any Pin Tumbler Lock," *3D Printing Industry News*,

August 28, 2014, http://3dprintingindustry.com/2014/08/28/3D printed-skeleton-key-software-open-pin-tumbler-lock/?utm_source=3D+Printing+Industry+Update&utm_medium=email&utm_campaign=4a0960bf1b-RSS_EMAIL_CAMPAIGN&utm_term=0_695d5c73dc-4a0960bf1b-60484669.

455.   Molteni, "Our 3D Printed Universe."

456.   Michael Molitch-Hou, "Jason vs. 3D Printing in RadioShack's New Ad Campaign," *3D Printing Industry News*, February 4, 2014, http://3dprintingindustry.com/2014/02/04/jason-vs-3D printing-radioshacks-new-ad-campaign/?utm_source=3D+Printing+Industry+Update&utm_medium=email&utm_campaign=d7c6f21f39-RSS_EMAIL_CAMPAIGN&utm_term=0_695d5c73dc-d7c6f21f39-60484669.

457.   Staff writer, "34-Year-Old French Man 3D Printed Fake Fronts for Cashpoints to Steal Thousands," *3ders.org*, August 23, 2014, http://www.3ders.org/articles/20140823-34-year-old-french-man-3D printed-fake-fronts-for-cashpoints-to-steal-thousands.html?utm_source=Inside+3D+Printing+Latest+News&utm_campaign=3db0fbec75-Inside_3D_Printing_Daily_News_8_25_2014_8_24_2014&utm_medium=email&utm_term=0_861dc04374-3db0fbec75-226645849.

458.   Ricardo Bilton, "Bad Guys Use 3D-Printed Bank Card Skimmers to Steal $100K," *Venture Beat VB*, August 18, 2013, http://venturebeat.com/2013/08/18/bad-guys-use-3D printed-credit-card-skimmers-to-steal-100k/.

459.   Staff writer, "3D Printer Confiscated in Organized Crime Raid," *Engineering.com*, October 6, 2014, http://www.engineering.com/3DPrinting/3DPrintingArticles/

ArticleID/8642/3D-Printer-Confiscated-in-Organized-Crime-Raid.
aspx.

460. Jelmer Luimstra, "Criminals Use 3D Printers to Mass-Produce Skimming
Devices," *3D Printing.com*, March 24, 2014, http://3dprinting.com/
news/criminals-use-3d-printers-mass-produce-skimming-devices/.

461. Lipson and Kurman, *Fabricated*, 220.

462. Michael Molitch-Hou, "Researchers Develop Method for 3D
Printing Chemotherapeutic Medicines on Desktop 3D Printer," *3D
Printing Industry News*, August 22, 2014, http://3dprintingindustry.
com/2014/08/22/researchers-develop-method-3D   printing-
chemotherapeutic-medicines-desktop-3d-printer/?utm_sourc
e=3D+Printing+Industry+Update&utm_medium=email&utm_
campaign=9696557936-RSS_EMAIL_CAMPAIGN&utm_term=0_
695d5c73dc-9696557936-60484669; Sebastian Pop, "3D Printed
Pills, the Next Step in Ingestible Medicine," *Softpedia*, August 18,
2014, http://news.softpedia.com/news/3D printed-Pills-The-Next-
Step-in-Medicine-Ingestible-Medicine-455397.shtml.

463. Chris Gayomali, "Can You 3D Print Drugs?" *The Week*, June 26, 2013,
http://theweek.com/article/index/246091/can-you-3d-print-drugs.

464. Thompson, "Reaching into the White Powder," 6.

465. Gayomali, "Can You 3D Print Drugs?"

466. Thompson, "Reaching into the White Powder," 6.

467. "Accessible Text from GAO Report No. GAO-10-389."

468. Lipson and Kurman, *Fabricated*, 239.

469. Scott Grunewald, "The FBI Wants to Use a Stratasys Objet24 to Study the 3D Printed Bombs of the Future," *3D Printing Industry News*, June 18, 2014, http://3dprintingindustry. com/2014/06/18/3D printed-bombs-fbi-stratasys-objet24/?utm_so urce=3D+Printing+Industry+Update&utm_medium=email&utm_ campaign=0ff3e14640-RSS_EMAIL_CAMPAIGN&utm_ term=0_695d5c73dc-0ff3e14640-60484669.

470. Stephanie Pappas, "3D-Printed Bacteria May Unlock Disease Secrets," *LiveScience*, October 7, 2013, http://www.livescience. com/40219-3D printed-bacteria.html; Jodi Connell, Eric Ritschdorff, Marvin Whiteley, and Jason Shear, "3D Printing of Microscopic Bacterial Communities," *Proceedings of the National Academy of Sciences* 110, no. 46 (May 23, 2013), http://www.pnas.org/ content/110/46/18380.abstract.

471. Lipson and Kurman, *Fabricated*, 3.

472. McNulty, Arnas, and Campbell, "Toward the Printed World," 3.

473. Staff writer, "3D Printing Could Revolutionize War and Foreign Policy," *Space Daily*, January 5, 2015, http://www.spacedaily.com/ reports/How_3D_printing_could_revolutionise_war_and_foreign_ policy_999.html

474. Kyle Maxey, "Hiding Contraband in Encrypted 3D Models," *Engineering.com*, November 7, 2013, http://www.engineering. com/3DPrinting/3DPrintingArticles/ArticleID/6599/Hiding-Contraband-in-Encrypted-3D-Models.aspx.

475. Daniel Castro, "Should Government Regulate Illicit Uses of 3D Printing?," *Information Technology & Innovation Foundation*,

May 2013, http://www.itif.org/publications/should-government-regulate-illicit-uses-3D printing.

476. Staff writer, "Baby's Life Saved with Groundbreaking 3D Printed Device from University of Michigan That Restored His Breathing," *Health System University of Michigan*, May 22, 2013, http://www.uofmhealth.org/news/archive/201305/baby%E2%80%99s-life-saved-groundbreaking-3D printed-device.

477. Andrew Wheeler, "MedShape Inc. Receives FDA Clearance for 3D Printed Titanium Medical Device," *3D Printing Industry News*, February 3, 2015, http://3dprintingindustry.com/2015/02/03/medshape-inc-receives-fda-clearance-3d-printed-titanium-medical-device/.

478. Kurman and Lipson, "The Truth about 3D-Printing Piracy," 73.

479. Weinberg, "What's the Deal with Copyright?"

480. "Gartner Reveals Top Predictions for IT Organizations and Users for 2014 and Beyond," *Gartner*, October 8, 2013, http://www.gartner.com/newsroom/id/2603215.

481. John Hornick, "Crowdsourcing Prior Art to Defeat 3D Printing Patent Applications," *3D Printing Industry News*, May 17, 2013, http://3dprintingindustry.com/2013/05/17/crowdsourcing-prior-art-to-defeat-3D printing-patent-applications/?utm_source=3D+Printing+Industry+Update&utm_medium=email&utm_campaign=4134896bc9-RSS_EMAIL_CAMPAIGN&utm_term=0_695d5c73dc-4134896bc9-60484669.

482. *Electronic Frontier Foundation*, https://www.eff.org/.

483. Kit Walsh, "Insider Insight—Fighting the 3D Printing Patent Applications," *3D Printing Industry News*, June 3, 2013, http://3dprintingindustry.com/2013/06/03/insider-insight-fighting-the-3D printing-patent-applications/?utm_source= 3D+Printing+Industry+Update&utm_medium=email&utm_ campaign=8a4b8575a8-RSS_EMAIL_CAMPAIGN&utm_ term=0_695d5c73dc-8a4b8575a8-60484669; Ari Honka, "EFF Fight for Open 3D Printing," *3D Printing Industry News*, March 26, 2013, http://3dprintingindustry.com/2013/03/26/eff-fight-for-open-3D printing/?utm_source=3D+Printing+Industry+Update& utm_medium=email&utm_campaign=8906d0e789-RSS_EMAIL_ CAMPAIGN.

484. Cory Doctorow, "Patent Lawyers: Help! The Evil Makers Won't Let Us Apply for Bullshit 3D Printing Patents!," *Boing Boing*, May 19, 2013, http://boingboing.net/2013/05/19/patent-lawyers-help-the-evil.html; "Comments," *3D Printing Industry News*, May 17, 2013, http://3dprintingindustry.com/2013/05/17/crowdsourcing-prior-art-to-defeat-3D printing-patent-applications/?utm_source=3D+ Printing+Industry+Update&utm_medium=email&utm_campaign= 4134896bc9-RSS_EMAIL_CAMPAIGN&utm_term=0_695d5c73dc-4134896bc9-60484669.

485. Comment on jpearce, "3D Printing Materials You Can't Patent," Thingiverse.com," May 2, 2013, XPLR Illuminate, https://xplr. com/products/illuminate/browser/?searchtags=UK+Intellectual+P roperty+Office+European+Patent+Office ; jpearce, "3-D Printing Materials You Can't Patent," Thingiverse.com, April 13, 2013, http://www.thingiverse.com/thing:73427.

486. Joshua M. Pearce, Department of Electrical and Computer Engineering, Mich Tech, http://www.mtu.edu/ece/department/ faculty/full-time/pearce/; Joshua Pearce, "The Case for Open

Source Appropriate Technology," *Environment: Development and Sustainability* 14 (2012): 425–431, http://papers.ssrn.com/sol3/papers.cfm?abstract_id=2043509.

487. US Constitution, Article I, Section 8, Clause 8.

488. John Hornick, "3D Printing and the Future (or Demise) of Intellectual Property," slide presentation available from the author, john.hornick@finnegan.com.

489. Jpearce, "3-D Printing Materials You Can't Patent," Thingiverse.com, April 13, 2013, http://www.thingiverse.com/thing:73427.

490. Rachel Park, "Championing 3D Printing Innovation and Freedom—EFF Leads a Challenge on Six 3D Printing Patent Applications," *3D Printing Industry News*, April 17, 2013, http://3dprintingindustry.com/2013/04/17/championing-3D printing-innovation-freedom-eff-leads-a-challenge-on-six-3D printing-patent-applications/?utm_source=3D+Printing+Industry+Update&utm_medium=email&utm_campaign=089035c6fc-RSS_EMAIL_CAMPAIGN; Hornick, "Crowdsourcing Prior Art."

491. *Sony Corp. v. Universal City Studios*, 464 U.S. 417 (1984) (the well-known "Betamax" case).

492. "Digital Audio Tape Recorders," collected articles, *Los Angeles Times*, http://articles.latimes.com/keyword/digital-audio-tape-recorders/recent/3.

493. Desai and Magliocca, "Patents, Meet Napster," 45.

494. Lipson and Kurman, *Fabricated*, 3.

495. Kurman, "Carrots, Not Sticks," 45, 47.

496. Ibid.

497. Michael Molitch-Hou, "The Bay Area Goes Maker Mad," *3D Printing Industry News*, May 17, 2013, http://3dprintingindustry.com/2013/05/17/the-bay-area-goes-maker-mad/.

498. Weinberg, "What's the Deal with Copyright?," 15–19; Haritha Dasari, "Assessing Copyright Protection and Infringement Issues Involved with 3D Printing and Scanning," *AIPLA Quarterly Journal* 41, no. 2 (Spring 2013): 289–303.

499. Desai and Magliocca, "Patents, Meet Napster," 40.

500. *In re Thorpe*, 777 F.2d 695 (Fed. Cir. 1985) ("[E]ven though product-by-process claims are limited by and defined by the process, determination of patentability is based on the product itself. The patentability of a product does not depend on its method of production. If the product in the product-by-process claim is the same as or obvious from a product of the prior art, the claim is unpatentable even though the prior product was made by a different process."), see also *Amgen Inc. v. F. Hoffman-La Roche Ltd.*, 580 F.3d 1340, 1370, n. 14 (Fed. Cir. 2009).

501. *Abbot Labs v. Sandoz, Inc.*, 566 F.3d 1282, 1292 (Fed. Cir. 2009).

502. Daniel Harris Brean, "Asserting Patents to Combat Infringement Via 3D Printing: It's No 'Use,'" *23 Fordham Intell. Prop. Media & Ent. L. J. 771*, April 17, 2013, http://iplj.net/blog/wp-content/uploads/2013/09/C01_Brean.pdf.

503. Davis Doherty, "Downloading Infringement: Patent Law as a Roadblock to the 3D Printing Revolution," *Harvard Journal of Law & Technology* 26, no. 1 (Fall 2012): 365.

504. Desai and Magliocca, "Patents, Meet Napster," 6, 46, 50 (suggesting personal use exemption and Digital Millennium Patent and Trademark Acts); Doherty, "Downloading Infringement," 365 (suggesting "innocent independent inventor" patent defense); Carlos J. Rosario, "3D Printing: Are We Prepared to Tackle the Inevitable Intellectual Property Challenges," *Westlaw Journal of Intellectual Property* 21, no. 7 (July 23, 2014): 3 (suggesting that "Congress must create a framework such that individuals are at least somewhat immune from the present IP laws").

505. Lucas Matheson, "The Future of 3D Printing: Smarter IP Strategies, Less Lawsuits," *3D Printing Industry News*, October 8, 2015, http://3dprintingindustry.com/2015/10/08/the-future-of-3d-printing-smarter-ip-strategies-less-lawsuits/?utm_sourc e=3D+Printing+Industry+Update&utm_medium=email&utm_campaign=4a3d0d5078-RSS_EMAIL_CAMPAIGN&utm_term=0_695d5c73dc-4a3d0d5078-60484669.

506. Kyle Maxey, "Hiding Contraband in Encrypted 3D Models," *Engineering.com*, November 7, 2013, http://www.engineering.com/3DPrinting/3DPrintingArticles/ArticleID/6599/Hiding-Contraband-in-Encrypted-3D-Models.aspx.

507. Staff writer, "3D Printing: Prepare Now for Data Onslaught," *Deloitte CIO Journal*, May 11, 2015, http://deloitte.wsj.com/cio/2015/05/11/3D printing-prepare-now-for-data-onslaught/?utm_source=Daily+3D+Printing+News&utm_campaign=01ad78513f-Latest_3D_Printing_News_05_13_2015_5_13_2015&utm_medium=email&utm_term=0_861dc04374-01ad78513f-226645849.

508. Lipson and Kurman, *Fabricated*, 229.

509. Leading Edge Forum, 22.

510. Lipson and Kurman, *Fabricated*, 229.

511. Kurman, "Carrots, Not Sticks," 49.

512. IBM Report, 12.

513. Desai and Magliocca, "Patents, Meet Napster," 58.

514. IBM Report, 12.

515. Thompson, "Reaching into the White Powder," 6.

516. Cohen, "Fostering Mainstream Adoption of Industrial 3D Printing," 64, n. 4.

517. Grunewald, "You Can Now Buy 3D Printable Sex Toys."

518. Engstrom, "3D Printing and Product Liability," 36–40.

519. Staff writer, "3D Printing and Product Liability: You May Not Be Protected under Current Liability Law," *3ders.org*, December 15, 2013, http://www.3ders.org/articles/20131215-3D printing-and-product-liability-you-may-not-be-protected-under-current-liability-law.html.

520. Roy Keidar, "Who Is to Blame for Faulty 3D Printed Products?" *Inside 3DP*, May 12, 2014, http://www.inside3dp.com/better-oversight-3D printed-products/.

521. Graeme Newman, "The New Age of Technology: 3D Printing," *Insurance Journal*, May 6, 2013, http://www.insurancejournal.com/magazines/features/2013/05/06/290460.htm.

522. Sam Barrett, "With 3D Printing Expected to Totally Transform Manufacturing, What Does It Mean for the Insurance Industry?," *Slipcase*, February 24, 2015, http://www.slipcase.com/magazine/378/with-3d-printing-expected-to-totally-transform-manufacturing-what-does-it-mean-for-the-insurance-industry.

523. "Insurance Implications of 3D Printing," *Zurich Insider*, August 2013, http://insider.zurich.co.uk/market-expertise/insurance-implications-of-3D printing/.

524. William Knowles, "Thorns of 3D Printing: Why This Emerging Technology Isn't Smelling So Sweet to Insurers," *Claims Management*, May 22, 2014, http://claims-management.theclm.org/home/article/Thorns-of-3D printing.

525. Newman, "The New Age of Technology: 3D Printing."

526. "3D Printing: Get Ready for the 3D Revolution," *Post*, February 11, 2014, http://www.postonline.co.uk/post/analysis/2326833/3D printing-get-ready-for-the-3d-revolution.

527. Melba Kurman, INTA Course Materials, 1.

528. *Steam Education*, http://www.steamedu.com/.

529. Gershenfeld, "How to Make Almost Anything," 57.

530. George Freedman, *The Next 100 Years* (New York: Anchor Books, 2010), 120–21, 127–35.

531. Michael Molitch-Hou, "3D Printing to Revolutionize STEM+ Education in Two to Three Years Says Report," *3D Printing Industry News*, October 23, 2013, http://3dprintingindustry.com/2013/10/23/3D printing-revolutionize-stem-education-two-three-years-says-report/?utm_source=3D+Printing+Industry+Update&utm_medium=email&utm_campaign=f168f7d2a4-RSS_EMAIL_CAMPAIGN&utm_term=0_695d5c73dc-f168f7d2a4-60484669.

532. Mark Trageser, "How 3D Printing Has Already Changed Toy Design, Is Currently Reinventing Everything, and the Amazing Future Ahead," presentation, Inside 3D Printing Conference and Trade Show, New York, April 4, 2014, http://kram-co.com/.

533. Michael Molitch-Hou, "BBC's Children's Programming to Focus on Tech, Including 3D Printing," *3D Printing Industry News*, September 4, 2014, http://3dprintingindustry.com/2014/09/04/bbcs-childrens-programming-focus-tech-including-3D printing/?utm_source=3D+Printing+Industry+Update&utm_medium=email&utm_campaign=a7a238cf52-RSS_EMAIL_CAMPAIGN&utm_term=0_695d5c73dc-a7a238cf52-60484669.

534. Shane Taylor, "3D Printing Education," *3D Printing Industry News*, July 20, 2013, http://3dprintingindustry.com/2013/07/20/3D printing-coming-to-usa-education/?utm_source=3D+Printing+Industry+Update&utm_medium=email&utm_campaign=0933ee8634-RSS_EMAIL_CAMPAIGN&utm_term=0_695d5c73dc-0933ee8634-60484669.

535. Noelle Swan, "The 'Maker Movement' Creates D.I.Y. Revolution," *Christian Science Monitor,* July 6, 2014, http://www.csmonitor.com/Innovation/2014/0706/The-maker-movement-creates-D.I.Y.-revolution.

536. Scott Grunewald, "SME and 3D Systems Team Up to Form Advisory Board for the M.Lab21 Education Initiative," *3D Printing Industry News*, September 1, 2014, http://3dprintingindustry.com/2014/09/01/sme-3d-systems-team-form-advisory-board-m-lab21-education-initiative/?utm_source=3D+Printing+Industry+Update&utm_medium=email&utm_campaign=eb2795b2a7-RSS_EMAIL_CAMPAIGN&utm_term=0_695d5c73dc-eb2795b2a7-60484669.

537. David Sher, "MakerBot Now Getting Serious About 3D Printing in Education," *3D Printing Industry News*, February 6, 2014, http://3dprintingindustry.com/2014/02/06/makerbot-now-getting-serious-3d-printing-education/?utm_source=3D+Printing+Industry+Update&utm_medium=email&utm_campaign=a7dca2accb-RSS_EMAIL_CAMPAIGN&utm_term=0_695d5c73dc-a7dca2accb-60484669.

538. "Autodesk Commits $250 Million in Software and Services to American Middle and High Schools," *Yahoo! Finance*, February 4, 2014, http://finance.yahoo.com/news/autodesk-commits-250-million-software-110000210.html.

539. Jelmer Luimstra, "Could Putting 3D Printers in Schools Lead to a New Steve Jobs?" *3DPrinting*.com, January 30, 2014, http://3dprinting.com/news/putting-3d-printers-schools-lead-new-steve-jobs/.

540. Scott Grunewald, "SeeMeCNC Looks to the Classroom with SeeMeEducate 3D Printing Curriculum," *3D Printing Industry News*, February 13, 2014, http://3dprintingindustry.com/2014/02/13/seemecnc-looks-classroom-seemeeducate-3Dprinting-curriculum/?utm_source=3D+Printing+Industry+Update&utm_medium=email&utm_campaign=9d6f98b257-RSS_EMAIL_CAMPAIGN&utm_term=0_695d5c73dc-9d6f98b257-60484669.

541. Michael Molitch-Hou, "Middle School Lab Devoted to Advanced Manufacturing Education," *3D Printing Industry News*, April 18, 2013, http://3dprintingindustry.com/2013/04/18/middle-school-lab-devoted-to-advanced-manufacturing-education/?utm_source=3D+Printing+Industry+Update&utm_medium=email&utm_campaign=ca7dc6b1f7-RSS_EMAIL_CAMPAIGN.

542. "Afinia 3D Printer-Enabled Innovators: Stories of Success, Vol. I," *Afinia 3D*, 14, http://www.afinia.com/wp-content/uploads/Afinia3D-eBook-Vol1.pdf.

543. "PA Cyber Engineering Students Build Own 3D Printers," *MarketWatch*, August 21, 2014, http://www.marketwatch.com/story/pa-cyber-engineering-students-build-own-3d-printers-2014-08-21?utm_source=Inside+3D+Printing+Latest+News&utm_campaign=a0014e8b90-Inside_3D_Printing_Daily_News_8_22_2014_8_21_2014&utm_medium=email&utm_term=0_861dc04374-a0014e8b90-226645849.

544. Nancy Fumero, "3D Printing Camp Preparing Future Workforce," *3D Printing Industry News*, January 24, 2014, http://3dprintingindustry.com/2014/01/24/3D printing-camp-preparing-future-workforce/?utm_source=3D+Printing+Industry+Update&utm_medium=email&utm_campaign=9b05e3c33a-RSS_EMAIL_CAMPAIGN&utm_term=0_695d5c73dc-9b05e3c33a-60484669.

545. Shane Taylor, "3D Printing Kids Camp in the US This Summer," *3D Printing Industry News*, July 2, 2014, http://3dprintingindustry.com/2014/07/02/3D printing-kids-camp-us-summer/?utm_source=3D+Printing+Industry+Update&utm_medium=email&utm_campaign=6bcb50d3eb-RSS_EMAIL_CAMPAIGN&utm_term=0_695d5c73dc-6bcb50d3eb-60484669.

546. T. J. McCue, "3D Printing Is Changing the Way We Think," *Harvard Business Review*, July 21, 2015, https://hbr.org/2015/07/3D printing-is-changing-the-way-we-think.

547. "MIT Professional Education Now Offers Additive Manufacturing: From 3D Printing to the Factory Floor Course," *Business Wire*, August 23, 2014, http://www.businesswire.com/news/home/20140423006241/en/MIT-Professional-Education-Offers-Additive-Manufacturing-3D#.U1kHAZK9KSO; Evan Chavez, "New York City College of Technology Continuing Studies Center Offers Fall Course on Fabrication and 3D Printing," *3D Printing Industry News*, September 24, 2013, http://3dprintingindustry.com/2013/09/24/new-york-city-college-technology-continuing-studies-center-offers-fall-course-fabrication-3D printing/?utm_source=3D+Printing+Industry+Update&utm_medium=email&utm_campaign=0abc151f5b-RSS_EMAIL_CAMPAIGN&utm_term=0_695d5c73dc-0abc151f5b-60484669.

548. Michael Molitch-Hou, "Florida Polytechnic University Opens Its Doors with RAD MakerBot Innovation Center," *3D Printing Industry News*, August 19, 2014, http://3dprintingindustry.com/2014/08/19/florida-polytechnic-university-opens-doors-rad-makerbot-innovation-center/?utm_source=3D+Printing+Industry+Update&utm_medium=email&utm_campaign=821c23164c-RSS_EMAIL_CAMPAIGN&utm_term=0_695d5c73dc-821c23164c-60484669.

549. Tom Novak, "New 3D Printer Lab Open To All Technology Students," *The Exponent*, February 10, 2014, http://www.purdueexponent.org/campus/article_7d70685a-18d4-52ed-a6f9-f69cc44a0d8d.html.

550. Wohlers Report 2014, 215–33.

551. Ricardo Pirroni, "Maker Machine: Bringing 3D Printing Tech to Aussie Schools," *3D Printing Industry News*, June 17, 2013, http://3dprintingindustry.com/2013/06/17/maker-machine-bringing-3D printing-tech-to-aussie-schools/?utm_source=3D+Printing+Industry+Update&utm_medium=email&utm_campaign=ad7c90036f-RSS_EMAIL_CAMPAIGN&utm_term=0_695d5c73dc-ad7c90036f-60484669.

552. Eetu Kuneinen, "Finnish Government Grants Funds for 3D Printing Trial in Schools," *3D Printing Industry News*, September 19, 2013, http://3dprintingindustry.com/2013/09/19/finnish-government-grants-funds-for-3D printing-trial-in-schools/?utm_source=3D+Printing+Industry+Update&utm_medium=email&utm_campaign=c953040e6f-RSS_EMAIL_CAMPAIGN&utm_term=0_695d5c73dc-c953040e6f-60484669.

553. Rachel Park, "Israel to Provide 3D Printers from Top to Bottom," *3D Printing Industry News*, August 14, 2013, http://3dprintingindustry.com/2013/08/14/israel-to-provide-3d-printers-from-top-to-bottom/?utm_source=3D+Printing+Industry+Update&utm_medium=email&utm_campaign=175729860f-RSS_EMAIL_CAMPAIGN&utm_term=0_695d5c73dc-175729860f-60484669.

554. Staff writer, "Japanese Government to Fund 3D Printing in Education," *3ders.org*, February 3, 2014, http://www.3ders.org/articles/20140203-japanese-government-to-fund-3D printing-in-education.html.

555. Shane Taylor, "Leaping into the 3D Printing-for-Education Race," *3D Printing Industry News*, September 5, 2014, http://3dprintingindustry.com/2014/09/05/leaping-3D printing-education-race/?utm_source=3D+Printing+Industry+Update&u

tm_medium=email&utm_campaign=e3c0cfa72b-RSS_EMAIL_ CAMPAIGN&utm_term=0_695d5c73dc-e3c0cfa72b-60484669.

556. Rachel Park, "New Zealand Incorporates 3D Printing into Curriculum," *3D Printing Industry News*, December 21, 2012, http://3dprintingindustry.com/2012/12/21/new-zealand-incorporates-3D printing-into-curriculum/.

557. Michael Molitch-Hou, "Singapore's Nanyang Technological University Constructs $30 Million AM Center," *3D Printing Industry News*, September 17, 2013, http://3dprintingindustry.com/2013/09/17/singapores-nanyang-technological-university-constructs-30-million-am-center/?utm_source=3D+Printing+Industry+Update& utm_medium=email&utm_campaign=8ff41201ed-RSS_EMAIL_ CAMPAIGN&utm_term=0_695d5c73dc-8ff41201ed-60484669.

558. Rachel Park, "New UK National Curriculum Specifies 3D Printing Is to 'Become Standard,'" *3D Printing Industry News*, July 13, 2013, http://3dprintingindustry.com/2013/07/10/new-uk-national-curriculum-specifies-3D printing-is-to-become-standard/?utm_so urce=3D+Printing+Industry+Update&utm_medium=email&utm_ campaign=f731bba372-RSS_EMAIL_CAMPAIGN&utm_ term=0_695d5c73dc-f731bba372-60484669.

559. Michael Molitch-Hou, "Renishaw Strives to Raise Young Engineers," *3D Printing Industry News*, February 20, 2014, http://3dprintingindustry.com/2014/02/20/renishaw-strives-raise-young-engineers/?utm_source=3D+Printing+Industry+Update &utm_medium=email&utm_campaign=1dc7ccffdf-RSS_EMAIL_ CAMPAIGN&utm_term=0_695d5c73dc-1dc7ccffdf-60484669.

560. Evan Chavez, "Ultimaker GB Launches 3D Printing Schools Initiative," *3D Printing Industry News*, January 28, 2014, http://

3dprintingindustry.com/2014/01/28/ultimaker-gb-launches-3D printing-schools-initiative/?utm_source=3D+Printing+Industry+Update&utm_medium=email&utm_campaign=03ca558081-RSS_EMAIL_CAMPAIGN&utm_term=0_695d5c73dc-03ca558081-60484669.

561. Juho Vesanto, "Tinkering With Technology—3D Printing Initiative For Primary Schools," *3D Printing Industry News*, November 5, 2012, http://3dprintingindustry.com/2012/11/05/tinkering-with-technology-3D printing-initiative-for-primary-schools/.

562. Shane Taylor, "3D Printing Coming to USA Education," *3D Printing Industry News*, July 20, 2013, http://3dprintingindustry.com/2013/07/20/3D printing-coming-to-usa-education/?utm_source=3D+Printing+Industry+Update&utm_medium=email&utm_campaign=0933ee8634-RSS_EMAIL_CAMPAIGN&utm_term=0_695d5c73dc-0933ee8634-60484669.

563. "NIH 3D Print Exchange," National Institutes of Health, http://3dprint.nih.gov/.

564. Scott Grunewald, "4th Graders Discover New Species of 3D Printed Insects in Their Classroom," *3D Printing Industry News*, May 12, 2014, http://3dprintingindustry.com/2014/05/12/3D printing-insects-4th-graders/?utm_source=3D+Printing+Industry+Update&utm_medium=email&utm_campaign=2f71f43630-RSS_EMAIL_CAMPAIGN&utm_term=0_695d5c73dc-2f71f43630-60484669.

565. Scott Grunewald, "8th Graders Use Autodesk to Design a Medical Device for a Disabled Man," *3D Printing Industry News*, September 1, 2014, http://3dprintingindustry.com/2014/09/01/8th-graders-use-autodesk-design-medical-device-disabled-man/?utm_source=3D+Printing+Industry+Update&utm_medium=

email&utm_campaign=eb2795b2a7-RSS_EMAIL_
CAMPAIGN&utm_term=0_695d5c73dc-eb2795b2a7-60484669.

566. Michael Molitch-Hou, "Chicago Magnet School to Launch $40,000 3D Printing Lab," *3D Printing Industry News*, February 21, 2014, http://3dprintingindustry.com/2014/02/21/chicago-magnet-school-launch-40000-3D printing-lab/?utm_source=3D+Printing+Industry+Update&utm_medium=email&utm_campaign=d1e21e8e32-RSS_EMAIL_CAMPAIGN&utm_term=0_695d5c73dc-d1e21e8e32-60484669.

567. Eetu Kuneinen, "3D Printing Personal Electronics in the Future with 'Carbomorph'?," *3D Printing Industry News*, December 20, 2012, http://3dprintingindustry.com/2012/12/20/3d-printing-personal-electronics-in-the-future-with-carbomorph/.

568. Pam Grout and Jeff Truesdell, "A Helping Hand for a Friend," *People*, March 10, 2014, http://www.people.com/people/archive/article/0,,20794591,00.html; Jeff Truesdell and Pam Grout, "Mason Wilde Gives Family Friend a Helping Hand—Literally," *People*, March 20, 2014, http://www.people.com/people/article/0,,20795392, 00.html; staff writer, "3D Printing Mechanical Hands—Robohand and MakerBot, "*3D Printing Industry News*, May 12, 2013, http://3dprintingindustry.com/2013/05/12/3D printing-mechanical-hands-robohand-and-makerbot/?utm_source=3D+Printing+Indu stry+Update&utm_medium=email&utm_campaign=efaa27a0b4-RSS_EMAIL_CAMPAIGN&utm_term=0_695d5c73dc-efaa27a0b4-60484669; Steve Henn and Cindy Carpien, "3D Printer Brings Dexterity to Children with No Fingers," NPR, June 18, 2013, http://www.npr.org/blogs/health/2013/06/18/191279201/3D-printer-brings-dexterity-to-children-with-no-fingers?utm_medium=Email&utm_campaign=20130624&utm_source=mostemailed.

569. Grout and Truesdell, "A Helping Hand"; Truesdell and Grout, "Mason Wilde Gives Family Friend a Helping Hand."

570. Juho Vesanto, "Self-taught Teenager's 3D Printed Robotic Hand," *3D Printing Industry News*, February 13, 2013, http://3dprintingindustry.com/2013/02/13/self-taught-teenagers-3D printed-robotic-hand/.

571. "The Boxtrolls," *Cubify*, http://cubify.com/store/boxtrolls?utm_source=newsletter&utm_medium=email&utm_campaign=weekof20140911.

572. Nancy Parker, "7 Educational Uses for 3D Printing," *Getting Smart*, November 14, 2012, http://gettingsmart.com/2012/11/7-educational-uses-for-3D printing/.

573. "Mathematics with 3D Printing," *Sketches of Topology*," http://sketchesoftopology.wordpress.com/2014/04/25/mathematics-with-3D printing/.

574. "Afinia 3D Printer-Enabled Innovators: Stories of Success, Vol. I," *Afinia 3D*, 13, http://www.afinia.com/wp-content/uploads/Afinia3D-eBook-Vol1.pdf.

575. Gershenfeld, "How to Make Almost Anything," 48, 57.

576. Ibid., 57.

577. *3D Systems Digital Dollhouse*, http://www.digitaldollhouse.com/; staff writer, "3D Systems Video Round Up of Product Announcements from CES," *3D Printing Industry News*, January 11, 2014, see especially minutes 34–36, http://3dprintingindustry.com/2014/01/11/3d-systems-video-round-product-announcements-ces/?utm_sourc

e=3D+Printing+Industry+Update&utm_medium=email&utm_
campaign=1e87d5efdc-RSS_EMAIL_CAMPAIGN&utm_
term=0_695d5c73dc-1e87d5efdc-60484669.

578. Michael Molitch-Hou, "17-Year-Old Entrepreneur Launches 3D
Printables Marketplace," *3D Printing Industry News*, August 6, 2014,
http://3dprintingindustry.com/2014/08/06/17-year-old-entrepreneur-
launches-3d-printables-marketplace/?utm_source=3D+Printing+Ind
ustry+Update&utm_medium=email&utm_campaign=671926b252-
RSS_EMAIL_CAMPAIGN&utm_term=0_695d5c73dc-
671926b252-60484669.

579. Wohlers Report 2014, 198.

580. "Mission Statement," *America Makes*, https://americamakes.us/
about/mission; "About America Makes," *America Makes*, https://
americamakes.us/about/overview.

581. Shane Taylor, "UK's £14.7m Investment in 3D Printing Industrial
Applications Announced," *3D Printing Industry News*, June 7, 2013,
http://3dprintingindustry.com/2013/06/07/uks-14-7m-investment-
in-3D printing-industrial-applications-announced/?utm_source=3D+
Printing+Industry+Update&utm_medium=email&utm_
campaign=3be16e2e82-RSS_EMAIL_CAMPAIGN&utm_
term=0_695d5c73dc-3be16e2e82-60484669; "Presentation by
Congressman Bill Foster," *3D Printing Politics*, Washington, DC,
September 17, 2014.

582. "United States Department of Energy National Laboratories,"
Wikipedia, http://en.wikipedia.org/wiki/United_States_Department_
of_Energy_national_laboratories.

583. Shane Taylor, "Which U.S. Agencies Are First to Open 3D Printables Sites?," *3D Printing Industry News*, August 9, 2014, http://3dprintingindustry.com/2014/08/09/u-s-agencies-first-open-3d-printables-sites/?utm_source=3D+Printing+Industry+Update &utm_medium=email&utm_campaign=fb2957a0cb-RSS_EMAIL_ CAMPAIGN&utm_term=0_695d5c73dc-fb2957a0cb-60484669; "3D Models—3D Printable," *NASA 3D Resources (Beta)*, http:// nasa3d.arc.nasa.gov/models/printable.

584. Michael Molitch-Hou, "3D Printing Has Fans on Capitol Hill with the Congressional Maker Caucus," *3D Printing Industry News*, February 28, 2014, http://3dprintingindustry.com/2014/02/28/3D printing-fans-capitol-hill-congressional-maker-caucus/?utm_sou rce=3D+Printing+Industry+Update&utm_medium=email&utm_ campaign=9716c99a64-RSS_EMAIL_CAMPAIGN&utm_ term=0_695d5c73dc-9716c99a64-60484669.

585. Ed Morris, statement made during U.S. Comptroller General Forum on Additive Manufacturing, Washington, DC, October 15–16, 2014.

586. Andrew Zaleski, "In Maryland, A Major Push to Become a 3D Printing Hub," *Fortune*, June 24, 2014, http://fortune.com/2014/06/24/ maryland-3D printing-hub/.

587. Sarah Helsel, "Network Launches to Develop 3D Additive Manufacturing in Canada," *Inside 3D Printing*, September 24, 2014, http://inside3dprinting.com/network-launches-to-develop-3d-additive-manufacturing-in-canada/?utm_source=Inside%203D%20 Printing%20Latest%20News&utm_campaign=4d2b01e2de-Inside_3D_Printing_Daily_News_9_24_2014_9_23_2014&utm_ medium=email&utm_term=0_861dc04374-4d2b01e2de-226645849.

588. Wohlers Report 2014, 211–12.

589. Sissons and Thompson, "Three Dimensional Policy," 11.

590. Eetu Kuneinen, "UK Government Investing in 3D Printing," *3D Printing Industry News*; October 24, 2012, http://3dprintingindustry. com/2012/10/24/uk-government-investing-in-3D printing/.

591. Shane Taylor, "UK's £14.7m Investment in 3D Printing Industrial Applications Announced," *3D Printing Industry News*, June 7, 2013, http://3dprintingindustry.com/2013/06/07/uks-14-7m-investment-in-3D   printing-industrial-applications-announced/?utm_source= 3D+Printing+Industry+Update&utm_medium=email&utm_ campaign=3be16e2e82-RSS_EMAIL_CAMPAIGN&utm_ term=0_695d5c73dc-3be16e2e82-60484669.

592. Rachel Park, "UK Government Cash Injection to Boost Manufacturing with a Dedicated 3D Printing Centre," *3D Printing Industry News*, January   16,   2014,   http://3dprintingindustry.com/2014/01/16/ government-cash-injection-boost-manufacturing-dedicated-3D printing-centre/?utm_source=3D+Printing+Industry+Update&u tm_medium=email&utm_campaign=ffdd1be1ed-RSS_EMAIL_ CAMPAIGN&utm_term=0_695d5c73dc-ffdd1be1ed-60484669.

593. Sissons and Thompson, "Three Dimensional Policy," 6, 8, 11, 19, 27.

594. Ibid., 3.

595. Ibid., 6.

596. Michael Molitch-Hou, "China to Open 10 3D Printing Innovation Centers," *3D Printing Industry News*, May 21, 2013, http:// 3dprintingindustry.com/2013/05/21/china-to-open-10-3D

printing-innovation-centers/?utm_source=3D+Printing+Industr y+Update&utm_medium=email&utm_campaign=8c7105ddbf-RSS_EMAIL_CAMPAIGN&utm_term=0_695d5c73dc-8c7105ddbf-60484669.

597.   Wohlers Report 2014, 141.

598.   Kyle Maxey, "Japan's Push for 3D Metal Printing," *Engineering.com*, August 20, 2013, http://www.engineering.com/3DPrinting/3DPrinti ngArticles/ArticleID/6197/Japans-Push-for-3D-Metal-Printing.aspx.

599.   Staff writer, "Research and Markets: Japanese 3D Printer Market Report 2014–2018," *Business Wire*, August 7, 2014, http://www. businesswire.com/news/home/20140807005302/en/Research-Markets-Japanese-3D-Printer-Market-Report#.U-Q7dUigSLw.

600.   Wohlers Report 2014, 147.

601.   Mark Lee and Park Hyeong, "South Korea Is Planning on Growth—With a 10 Year Roadmap," *3D Printing Industry News*, July 21, 2014, http://3dprintingindustry.com/2014/07/21/south-korea-planning-growth-10-year-roadmap/?utm_source=3 D+Printing+Industry+Update&utm_medium=email&utm_ campaign=c0500effde-RSS_EMAIL_CAMPAIGN&utm_ term=0_695d5c73dc-c0500effde-60484669; staff writer, "Korean Government Invests $2.3 million in 3D Printing Centers," *3ders.org*, April 23, 2014, http://www.3ders.org/articles/20140423-korean-government-invests-in-3D printing-centers.html.

602.   Campbell et al., "Could 3D Printing Change the World?," 5, http://www.atlanticcouncil.org/images/files/publication_pdfs/403/ 101711_ACUS_3DPrinting.PDF.

Index

Page numbers followed by *f* indicate illustrations

Rocket Lab, 31, 114
Rosario, Carlos, 195
RoVa3D, 126
Rutherford rocket engine, 31, 31*f*
Ryan, Tim, 225

Sabanci University, 16, 34
safety: authenticity and, 158, 160–161, 164–167; and legal issues, 180, 202–204
sales: of designs, 95–97; of printers, 116, 127
sales taxes, 176–177
Samsung, 99, 122
sanctions, 178
Sander, Peter, 28
satellite bracket, 138, 138*f*
scaffolding, 16
scale: current status of, 113; economies of, 76–78, 92–93
scanners, 45–46, 109
Schleimer, Saul, 219, 220*f*
Schouwenburg, Kegan, 111
Sciaky, 10
science education, 3D printers and, 215–217
Sculpteo, 107
Sears, 87–88
security: scanning and keying locks, 172; start-ups in, 107
Seepersad, Carolyn Conner, 42, 142
Segerman, Henry, 219, 219*f*–220*f*
self-assembly, 152–154
self-education, 221–225
service bureaus, 107–109
service economy, 73–74
SexShop3D, 121, 135
Shapeways, 94–95, 107, 135

About the Author

John Hornick is an IP counselor and litigator based in the Washington D.C. headquarters of the Finnegan IP law firm, one of the largest IP firms in the world. Based on his 30+ years of experience, he counsels clients on virtually every aspect of IP law, from licensing to litigation. He has litigated close to 100 IP cases in more than 30 U.S. federal courts in 18 states, five U.S. circuit courts of appeals, the U.S. Supreme Court, the U.S. International Trade Commission (ITC), and others. He has appeared before more than 100 judges, arbitrators, and mediators and has tried every type of IP case. He has successfully avoided litigation for clients in hundreds of other disputes.

John started the firm's 3D printing initiative and founded Finnegan's 3D Printing Working Group. John advises and educates clients about 3D printing and the IP issues of this rapidly developing and potentially disruptive technology, and how it may affect their businesses, both offensively and defensively. John closely follows the industry, frequently speaks and writes on 3D printing and its potential effects on IP law and the world, and has been recognized as a thought leader in this space. His articles have been published at www.3DPrintingIndustry.com, in the *Journal of 3D Printing & Additive Manufacturing*, for which he serves on the Editorial Board, and in *Wired Innovation*, and he writes a column for *3D Printing World*, published in English and Chinese. He was the only IP attorney selected by the National Academies to participate in the U.S.

Comptroller General Forum on Additive Manufacturing (which was the basis of a report to the U.S. Congress), and was invited by the National Association of Attorneys General to participate in its 3D printing initiative. John also serves on the Advisory Board of *Advanced Manufacturing Insight* and 3Discovered, and as a juror for the International Additive Manufacturing Award. He has been called "the industry's favorite lawyer" and is often quoted and interviewed on 3D printing. He holds a Certificate in Foundations of 3D Printing from Underwriters Laboratories Knowledge Solutions Training.

John lives in Washington, DC with his wife, Sarah Alexander, and their Siberian Huskies, Tundra and Everest.

John's 3D printing videos and articles can be found at:

Websites:
http://www.3DPrintingWillRockTheWorld.com
http://www.finnegan.com/johnhornick/

LinkedIn: https://www.linkedin.com/profile/preview?locale=en_US& trk=prof-0-sb-preview-primary-button,

Pinterest: https://www.pinterest.com/hornick0137/3d-printing-will-rock-the-world/.

Follow John's tweets at https://twitter.com/JHornick3D1Stop.

Made in the USA
Columbia, SC
28 December 2017